A Technology for
Test-Item Writing

THE EDUCATIONAL TECHNOLOGY SERIES

Edited by

Harold F. O'Neil, Jr.

U.S. Army Research Institute for
the Behavioral and Social Sciences
Alexandria, Virginia

Harold F. O'Neil, Jr. (Ed.) Learning Strategies

Harold F. O'Neil, Jr. (Ed.) Issues in Instructional Systems Development

Harold F. O'Neil, Jr. (Ed.) Procedures for Instructional Systems Development

Harold F. O'Neil, Jr. and Charles D. Spielberger (Eds.) Cognitive and Affective Learning Strategies

Jane Close Conoley (Ed.) Consultation in Schools: Theory, Research, Procedures

Harold F. O'Neil, Jr. (Ed.) Computer-Based Instruction: A State-of-the-Art Assessment

Gary D. Borich and Ron P. Jemelka. Programs and Systems: An Evaluation Perspective

Gale H. Roid and Thomas M. Haladyna. A Technology for Test-Item Writing

A Technology for
Test-Item Writing

GALE H. ROID
Western Psychological Services
Los Angeles, California

THOMAS M. HALADYNA
Teaching Research Division
Oregon State of Higher Education
Monmouth, Oregon

ACADEMIC PRESS **1982**
A Subsidiary of Harcourt Brace Jovanovich, Publishers
New York   London   Toronto   Sydney   San Francisco

ACADEMIC PRESS, INC.
111 Fifth Avenue, New York, New York 10003

United Kingdom Edition published by
ACADEMIC PRESS, INC. (LONDON) LTD.
24/28 Oval Road, London NW1 7DX

Library of Congress Cataloging in Publication Data

Roid, Gale H.
  A technology for test-item writing.

  (Educational technology series)
  Includes bibliographies and index.
  1. Criterion-referenced tests.
2. Examinations--Questions. I. Haladyna, Thomas M.
II. Title. III. Series.
LB3060.32.C74R64   371.2'71   81-20500
ISBN 0-12-593250-2   AACR2

PRINTED IN THE UNITED STATES OF AMERICA

82 83 84 85   9 8 7 6 5 4 3 2 1

Contents

II. PRACTICAL GUIDELINES FOR ITEM WRITING

III. ITEM-WRITING TECHNOLOGY: SIX PROMINENT METHODS

IV. REVIEW OF TEST ITEMS

V. SUMMARY AND FUTURE DIRECTIONS

Preface

Achievement testing has received much attention in the last 30 years, but less attention has been given to developments in the writing of test items, the basic building blocks of tests. Knowledge about item writing has largely been a collection of guidelines based on practical experience or conventional wisdom. Consequently, item writing has been seen as more an art than a science.

Early efforts of Wells Hively, John Bormuth, and Louis Guttman, among others, sought to change this state of affairs. Each of these investigators sought to define instructional content in terms of operational definitions or rules that could be used to produce test items of various formats. More important, each presented a theory of item writing and content specification that incorporated a wealth of ideas about learning and testing.

The steady progress that has occurred over the past decade in the technology of test-item writing has motivated the writing of this book. We feel that progress has been sufficient to report advances in test-item writing in a single volume that captures both the essence of traditional knowledge and these most recent advances.

Among those who may be most interested in this book are educational researchers, teachers, trainers, test developers, directors of evaluation or curriculum, instructional developers, and educational researchers who frequently use achievement tests in their investigations. Researchers have been heavily criticized for failing to provide detailed descriptions of the achievement tests they use in their research. Evidence for the content validity of these measures and for controlled item development is too often missing in research on learning. This book provides tools for the scientific development of test items as a means for developing better tests.

Anyone involved in the development of instruction may be searching for ways to sharpen his or her skills in item writing. Teachers have been looking for ways to make their tests match their classroom teaching. Professionals in military education have searched for and adopted a very strongly objective-based method in their training programs. Developers in public education, motivated by the competency-based movement, have turned to instructional programs with management-by-objectives. Training designers in industry have, for quite some time, developed programs that are highly structured and objective-based. All of these professionals can be aided by a technology of test-item writing.

The book is organized in five parts: Part I, Basic Concepts; Part II, Practical Guidelines for Item Writing; Part III, Item-Writing Technology: Six Prominent Methods; Part IV, Review of Test Items; Part V, Summary and Future Directions. The reader who is well versed in principles of measurement and of criterion-referenced (CR) testing, in particular, may be familiar with the contents of Parts I and II. Part III is intended to be read with few references to other sections.

Our hope is that this book will stimulate continuing research and concern for the improvement of achievement testing.

Acknowledgments

Portions of this work were supported by research contract number MDA 903-77-C-0189 from the Advanced Research Projects Agency of the Department of the Defense to the Teaching Research Division, Oregon State System of Higher Education. Also, grants from the National Institute of Education and the American Fund for Dental Health provided support for some of the authors' research related to this book. Harold F. O'Neil, Jr., of the Army Research Institute for the Behavioral and Social Sciences, Alexandria, Virginia, was instrumental, through his constant support of our research, in encouraging the writing of a book that would reflect progress in the technology of test-item writing.

Appreciation is expressed to the consultants and colleagues who have advised us or participated in our research. This group includes: John Bormuth, University of Chicago; Patrick Finn, University of New York at Buffalo; Gerald Lippey, Classroom Support Systems, San Jose, California; Harry Miller, Southern Illinois University at Carbondale; Jason Millman, Cornell University; Joan Shaughnessy of Teaching Research, Monmouth, Oregon; and Reed Williams, Southern Illinois University School of Medicine.

Pat-Anthony Federico of the Navy Personnel Research and Development Center, San Diego, California, helped in conceptualizing and planning the structure of a handbook that was a forerunner of this work.

The first author would like to express his gratitude to Western Psychological Services for its support of our continuing research in the midst of busy test-publishing activities. Also, he would like to thank George Geis of McGill University, Montreal, Canada and Casper F. Paulson, Jr. of Teaching Research, Monmouth, Oregon for giving him a deep appreciation for programmed instruction that subsequently led to an understanding of item-writing technology.

We are grateful to Penny Lane and Jeanne Deane who provided accurate and dependable typed drafts as well as editorial assistance. Finally, we thank our wives, Donna and Helen, and our children for their support and encouragement.

A Technology for
Test-Item Writing

I

BASIC CONCEPTS

The Need for a Technology of Item Writing

The development of achievement tests to measure student progress in instruction often begins with the writing of test questions, or *items*. Many textbooks on testing and measurement give descriptions of test theories, types of tests, principles of testing, and advice on test-item writing (e.g., Ebel, 1972; Gronlund, 1968; Thorndike & Hagen, 1969). Interestingly, the literature on test-item writing has usually taken the form of advice on how to write items. Along this line, Cronbach (1970) remarked: "The design and construction of achievement test items has been given almost no scholarly attention. The leading works of the generation—even the Lindquist *Educational Measurement* and the Bloom *Taxonomy*—are distillations of experience more than scholarly analyses [p. 509]."

Guttman (1969) put the problem in a slightly different perspective. He contended that there are many theories of test scores but no theories of content structure and specification. There are a number of theoretical approaches to the statistical analysis of test scores, the most prominent of which are classical test theory (Gulliksen, 1950; Lord, 1952; Lord & Novick, 1968; Nunnally, 1967), generalizability theory (Cronbach, Gleser, Nanda, & Rajaratnam, 1972), Bayesian methods (Novick & Jackson, 1974), and item-response theories (Lord & Novick, 1968; Wright & Stone, 1979). These theories offer test developers a number of different tools and procedures for analyzing the results of tests. But researchers have developed little formal methodology for describing and explicating content in terms of items and tests.

Within the past decade, there has been much progress toward a technology of item writing. This technology is based on several theories of content specification that are in various stages of development and refinement. In this book, several alternative theories and methods are presented and suggestions are made for future work in developing tools for defining the content of educational and training programs.

Purposes of This Book

Several forces have motivated the writing of this book. Foremost among these is the emergence of the idea that teaching and testing should be systematically related. A growing number of educational psychologists and others who study the process of classroom learning have realized that when content is clearly specified to students, when tests are carefully developed from these specifications, and when instruction is directly aimed at achieving these specifications, student learning is rapid and dramatically positive. In fact, systems that have these characteristics are beginning to achieve substantial gains in students' learning (Block, 1971; Kulik, Kulik, & Cohen, 1979, Robin, 1976; Walberg, 1980). A crucial element in these systems is the method of item development. It is the methods of item writing that specify the relationship between tests and the instruction. Tests based on systematic item development will be closely connected with the intent of instruction and will be more sensitive to instructional effects and more accurate in providing feedback to students.

A highly developed technology of item writing is not always present in applications of criterion-referenced testing where an individual's performance is compared to a standard rather than to the performance of other individuals. The most widely used methods of writing test questions, for both criterion-referenced and traditional norm-referenced tests, rely on the intuitive skills of the item writer (Bormuth, 1970, p. 10). Even when item writers are given learning objectives that describe what is to be learned in terms of expected student performance under specified conditions and standards, it has been shown in research by the authors (Roid & Haladyna, 1978) that two writers will not generate the same items or items of similar quality. A technology of item writing is emerging that can remedy these deficiencies in conventional methods by providing:

1. Item-writing methods based on a logical and precisely defined relationship between the instruction given and the test items written.
2. Item-writing methods defined by a set of operations open to public

inspection rather than defined by the private, intuitive standards of the item writer.

3. Item-writing methods that are specific and public so that they can be easily replicated by many test developers, and not just the original item writer.

Item-writing methods of the kind described will produce tests that are more scientific, thereby contributing to the advancement of instructional research, educational evaluation, and the use of test data in the formation of public policy.

A third purpose of this book is to document the great increase in research and development on test-item writing in recent years. No single source has yet recorded this progress. Thus, there is a need to report developments in item writing in an integrative manner to capture the essence of various approaches to item writing and to indicate the range and feasibility of each approach in education and training.

A fourth purpose of this work is to describe recent and important processes for reviewing and evaluating test items once they have been developed. Any item-development procedure will produce a large number of items, but there is a need for logical and empirical review of both procedures and items.

In logical item review, items or procedures for generating items must be studied by content experts who identify flaws and judge the consistency between teaching and tests. In empirical item review, field testing provides data for determining whether items are free from flaws such as ambiguities, miskeyings or other discrepancies. The goal of item review is not to select items but rather to remove flaws from them. Also, when instruction is effective, gains are made by students that should be reflected in the statistical characteristics of the items. Thus, paralleling the development of item-writing technology, is the evolution of a science of item review that promises to further assist test developers in their creation of better achievement tests.

A fifth aim of this book is to respond to the need, in many educational programs, for the creation of large numbers of test items. Virtually all instructional systems require large numbers of test items, so that parallel forms can be used for pretests, posttests, retests, and quizzes. Multiple test forms allow students to complete instructional units on a flexible schedule with immediate feedback. Multiple forms also discourage the memorization of answers or cheating. In addition, instructional systems need items that cover all aspects of a curriculum so that overall summative judgments can be made about the effectiveness of a program. Furthermore, such assessments can lead to diagnostic judgments regarding strengths and weaknesses in an instructional program. And, finally, research on instruction frequently requires multiple test forms. Researchers must generate large numbers of items that carefully and completely represent the achievement intended by an instructional program.

The item-writing methods described and illustrated in subsequent chapters provide bases for creating large numbers of items that address each of three areas: (*a*) instructional achievement tests, (*b*) program assessments, and (*c*) research.

A sixth purpose of this book is to provide item-writing methods that are open to public inspection. A test can be precisely described if the manner in which test items have been created in relation to the instructional system can be specified. This will be important particularly where pass–fail decisions on the basis of tests can make a significant impact on students' lives or training future. Also, if two instructional systems are being compared, it is important to know whether the tests used to assess them were created in a similar way. The methods to be described in this book can allow for a more rigorous form of research on learning and the effectiveness of instructional systems because the precise nature of test instruments can be defined by the instructor.

Anderson (1972) wrote a very pointed criticism of educational research studies, focusing on their failure to define and describe the process of test-item writing. He found that 50% of the studies he surveyed did not provide even minimal item definition, a deficiency that inhibits the reproducibility of the research. Anderson called for operational definitions of the relationship between test items and instructional treatments used in *all* educational research studies.

If this book communicates one major idea, it will have accomplished its goal. Simply stated, that central idea is that tools for writing and reviewing test items are now available and can help the test developer improve the quality of achievement tests substantially. Any technology is aimed at increasing the productivity of a process by providing tools or procedures for reducing manual operations. Item-writing technology is a collection of separate methods that can be used by the test developer to produce more items of high quality than could be written without these methods. Just as any business can be more productive with new tools, test development can become more effective and efficient with new test-item writing tools.

Emergence of an Item-Writing Technology

The technology of test-item writing had its beginnings in the work of Bormuth (1970), Guttman (1969), and Hively and his colleagues (Hively, Patterson, & Page, 1968). Hively *et al.* (1968) developed sets of test questions for use in a curriculum development project in mathematics and science. They created a device they termed an *item form* from which test items would be created. Each item form contained wording, variable elements, and rules for replacing variable elements. Using item forms, researchers were able to create curriculum-specific test items. Once an item form and all of its replacement variables had been specified, literally hundreds of items could be generated without the need for writing each question.

During the 1960s and 1970s, the steady growth of computer-assisted instruction systems made possible the creation of test-item banks and the development of programs for generating the actual wording or elements in test questions. Hence, a computerized technology of test-item writing exists. One example of computer-generated test-item writing is the work of Vickers (1973), who created items for FORTRAN programming.

Other developments include Bormuth's theory of achievement testing based on a linguistic analysis of prose materials (Bormuth, 1970); adaptions of behavioral objectives to include specific item-writing guidelines (Baker, 1974; Popham, 1975); Guttman's facet theory as applied to achievement testing (Berk, 1979; Engel & Martuza, 1976; Guttman, 1969); an approach to higher level thinking posited by Miller, Williams, and Haladyna (1978) that leads to objectifiable test items; Tiemann and Markle's interesting work with measuring concepts (Tiemann & Markle, 1978); and the refinement by Millman (1980) of computer-based item generation.

A New Approach to Testing

Paralleling the development of item-writing methods during the 1960s and 1970s was the criterion-referenced test movement. Glaser (1963) was the first to use the term *criterion-referenced* (CR) to designate a type of test that was designed to measure the stated outcomes of instruction. CR tests were to provide descriptions of student achievement relative to a standard defined by the intent of instruction. According to Hambleton, Swaminathan, Algina, and Coulson (1978), since the time Glaser wrote, the literature has accumulated over 600 references to criterion-referenced testing, ranging from theoretical treatises to practical, how-to accounts.

The effective criterion-referenced test is built from test items that logically reflect the intent of instruction. Such a test must be composed of items that tap all important aspects of the instructional domain on which the tests are based. Further, the quality of test items should be uniformly high. Therefore, the item-writing techniques and item-review procedures described in this book are a direct extension of the criterion-referenced testing movement.

There has been considerable discussion and debate in the educational-measurement literature on the definition of criterion-referenced testing and on methods of establishing CR validity and reliability. These discussions are reviewed in greater depth in Chapter 2, but one important perspective should be mentioned here. In a classic paper on the meaning of educational measurements, Messick (1975) makes several important points. First, he believes that construct

validity should be the basis for interpreting test scores. Second, construct validation procedures are well known (Cronbach & Meehl, 1955) but seldom used in
educational testing. Third, a construct-validity approach to test-item generation
is in contrast to a behavioral approach, in which the sum of items directly
represents the trait under study. Messick (1975) says that "construct validity, by
linking test behavior to a more general attribute, process, or trait, provides not
only an evidential basis for interpreting the processes underlying test scores but
also a rational basis for inferring testable implications from the broader network
of the construct's meaning [p. 961]."

From the perspective reflected in Messick's comments, it becomes clear that
the methods for generating test items may be used in either of two contexts:
operational definition or construct validity. The former leads to test scores that
are interpreted solely on the basis of what the items broadly represent. That is,
there is common agreement that the item and the trait are matched. The latter is
based on the underlying meaning of test items as posited by a theory of the
relations between a test and other variables in the real world (a nomological
network). Fortunately, either approach to measurement can employ the item-
writing procedures described in the present book.

Overview

The first objective of this book is to present a conceptual framework for
examining criterion-referenced achievement testing. The main part of the book is
devoted to the topic of actually constructing achievement test items. In this book,
test items are seen as used to measure achievement that is the target of instruction
(rather than the result of learning). The scope of cognitive behaviors covered by
these item-writing techniques ranges from factual learning to higher level thinking and skills. The purpose is to give the reader a background for the study of the
technology as well as the actual steps in writing high-quality test items for
criterion-referenced tests.

PART I: BASIC CONCEPTS

The present chapter has described how the need for a technology of test-item
writing linked to criterion-referenced testing has emerged over the last two dec-
ades. It has outlined the goals of this book and has briefly sketched the ways in
which a technology of test-item writing can solve common problems in achievement testing.

Chapter 2 is devoted to a discussion of the fundamental concepts in the
implementation of criterion-referenced achievement tests. A backdrop for the
emergence of criterion-referenced testing is the rapid advancement of the

instructional-systems approach that is receiving increased attention in education and training. Chapter 2 characterizes systematic instruction and describes its antecedents. Then, criterion-referenced testing is discussed in terms of its meaning and its application to problems within educational measurement and systematic instruction.

PART II: PRACTICAL GUIDELINES FOR ITEM WRITING

Chapter 3 provides some preliminary concepts important to the reading of the chapters dealing with item-writing methods. First, knowledge and skills are described and differentiated. Then, types of instructional intent are identified as they relate to item-writing techniques.

Chapters 4 and 5 examine some of the conventional wisdom of item writing, based on the practical experience of test developers. These chapters form a background for the chapters on item-writing technology. Any application of item-writing methods must include the commonsense evaluation of common flaws in item construction; Chapters 4 and 5 provide guidelines for such an evaluation. Chapter 4 focuses on test items for assessing knowledge including most of the familiar item formats, such as multiple choice. Chapter 5 provides recommendations for designing the rating scales, checklists, and observations used in the assessment of cognitive skills. As will be seen, the technology of item writing, presented in Chapters 6 to 11, has been applied more widely to tests of knowledge and higher level thinking than to tests of skills. Reference tables at the end of Chapter 5 indicate the type of test format and item-writing method best suited for different kinds of instructional intent.

PART III: ITEM-WRITING TECHNOLOGY: SIX PROMINENT METHODS

Chapters 6 to 11 contain accounts of the rationale and procedures for each of several prominent item-writing methods that currently form the core of a technology of item writing. Chapter 6 deals with the theory of John Bormuth (1970), who has proposed a linguistic basis for transforming prose material into test questions. Research on extensions of Bormuth's work by the authors of this book is also presented. Chapter 7 contains an account of the technology of item forms. Hively's earliest work (Hively, Patterson, & Page, 1968) is traced to the present, and suggestions are offered for future directions in research and development of item forms. Chapter 8 deals with a promising new entrant in the methodology of item writing—facet-design theory, which was originally applied to attitude measurement. Guttman (1969) initially presented a reconception of facet theory in the area of achievement testing. Chapter 8 reports recent progress and discusses the strengths and limitations of the mapping-sentence method of facet-design theory. Chapter 9 is devoted to the promising work of Tiemann and Markle (1978) in measuring concepts. These researchers' approach is highly useful when an instructional program contains concepts learned through examples. Chapter 10 deals with an approach to higher level thinking that offers more than simple procedures for item writing (Miller, Williams, & Haladyna, 1978). This approach includes a typology by means of which objectives and test items can be classified into four distinct categories of higher level thinking. Directions for future research are also suggested. Chapter 11 reviews a method for classifying items and assessing their adequacy in measuring their associated objectives. The method, called the Instructional Quality Inventory (Ellis, Wulfeck, Richards, Wood, & Merrill, 1978), is widely used in military training in the United States.

PART IV: REVIEW OF TEST ITEMS

Two types of item review are seen as critical steps in the development of criterion-referenced tests. Chapter 12 contains an account of logical item review. This procedure insures the consistency between items and objectives that is so desirable in criterion-referenced testing. Chapter 13 deals with empirical item review, based on the field testing of items. There are a number of new approaches to item review, and a theoretical rationale is presented for certain recommended indexes of item adequacy.

PART V: SUMMARY AND FUTURE RESEARCH

Chapter 14 concludes the book, summarizing the rationale for the technology of item writing. Chapter 14 also describes the frontiers of development in item writing and the new directions that can be anticipated in the future of test construction. Promising new areas of research are described, and recommendations for future investigations are presented.

References

Anderson, R. C. How to construct achievement tests to assess comprehension. *Review of Educational Research*, 1972, *42*, 145–170.

Baker, E. L. Beyond objectives: Domain-referenced tests for evaluation and instructional improvement. *Educational Technology*, 1974, *14* (6), 10–16.

Berk, R. A. *Some guidelines for determining the length of objective-based criterion-referenced tests.* Paper presented at the annual meeting of the National Council on Measurement in Education, San Francisco, April 1979.

Block, J. H. (Ed.). *Mastery learning: Theory and practice.* New York: Holt, 1971.

Bormuth, J. R. *On the theory of achievement test items.* Chicago, Illinois: Univ. of Chicago Press, 1970.

Cronbach, L. J. Review of *On the theory of achievement test items* by J. R. Bormuth. *Psychometrika,* 1970, *35,* 509–511.

Cronbach, L. J., Gleser, G. C., Nanda, H., & Rajaratnam, N. *The dependability of behavioral measurements.* New York: Wiley, 1972.

Cronbach, L. J., & Meehl, P. E. Construct validity in psychological tests. *Psychological Bulletin,* 1955, *52,* 281–302.

Ebel, R. *Essentials of educational measurement.* Englewood Cliffs, New Jersey: Prentice-Hall, 1972.

Ellis, J. A., Wulfeck, II, W. H., Richards, R. E., Wood, N. D., & Merrill, M. D. *The instructional quality inventory: I. Introduction and Overview* (NPRDC Special Report 79-3). San Diego, California: Navy Personnel Research and Development Center, 1978.

Engel, J. D., & Martuza, V. R. *A systematic approach to the construction of domain-referenced multiple-choice test items.* Paper presented at the meetings of the American Psychological Association, Washington, D.C., September 1976.

Glaser, R. Instructional technology and the measurement of learning outcomes: Some questions. *American Psychologist,* 1963, *18,* 519–521.

Gronlund, N. E. *Constructing achievement tests.* Englewood Cliffs, New Jersey: Prentice-Hall, 1968.

Gulliksen, H. *Theory of mental tests.* New York: Wiley, 1950.

Guttman, L. Integration of test design and analysis. In *Proceedings of the 1969 invitational conference on testing problems.* Princeton, New Jersey: Educational Testing Service, 1969.

Hambleton, R. K., Swaminathan, H., Algina, J., & Coulson, D. B. Criterion-referenced testing and measurement: A review of technical issues and developments. *Review of Educational Research,* 1978, *48,* 1–47.

Hively, W., Patterson, H. L., & Page, S. A "universe-defined" system of arithmetic achievement tests. *Journal of Educational Measurement,* 1968, *5,* 275–290.

Kulik, J. A., Kulik, C., & Cohen, P. A. A meta-analysis of outcome studies of Keller's personalized system of instruction. *American Psychologist,* 1979, *34*(4), 307–318.

Lord, F. *A theory of test scores* (Psychometric Monograph No. 7). Chicago, Illinois: Univ. of Chicago Press, 1952.

Lord, F. M., & Novick, M. R. *Statistical theories of mental test scores.* Reading, Massachusetts: Addison-Wesley, 1968.

Messick, S. The standard problem: The meaning and values in measurement and evaluation. *American Psychologist,* 1975, *30,* 955–966.

Miller, H. G., Williams, R. G., & Haladyna, T. M. *Beyond facts: Objective ways to measure thinking.* Englewood Cliffs, New Jersey: Educational Technology, 1978.

Millman, J. Computer-based item generation. In R. A. Berk (Ed.), *Criterion-referenced measurement.* Baltimore, Maryland: Johns Hopkins University Press, 1980.

Novick, M. R., & Jackson, P. H. *Statistical methods for educational and psychological research.* New York: McGraw-Hill, 1974.

Nunnally, J. *Psychometric theory.* New York: McGraw-Hill, 1967.

Popham, W. J. *Educational evaluation.* Englewood Cliffs, New Jersey: Prentice-Hall, 1975.

Robin, A. Behavioral instruction in the college classroom. *Review of Educational Research,* 1976, *46,* 313–354.

Roid, G. H., & Haladyna, T. M. A comparison of objective-based and modified-Bormuth item writing techniques. *Educational and Psychological Measurement,* 1978, *35,* 19–28.

Thorndike, R. L., & Hagen, E. *Measurement and evaluation in psychology and education.* New York: Wiley, 1969.

Tiemann, P. W., & Markle, S. M. *Analyzing instructional content: A guide to instruction and evaluation*. Champaign, Illinois: Stipes Publishing, 1978.

Vickers, F. D. Creative test generators. *Educational Technology,* 1973, *13*(3), 43–44.

Walberg, H. J. A psychological theory of educational productivity. In F. H. Farley and N. Gordon (Eds.), *Perspectives on educational psychology*. Chicago: National Society for the Study of Education, 1980, and Berkeley, California: McCutchan, 1980.

Wright, B. D., & Stone, M. H. *Best test design*. Chicago, Illinois: Mesa Press, 1979.

2

A Context for the Technology of Test-Item Writing

A number of developments in education have brought about important changes in the theory and practice of both instruction and achievement testing. The common element in these developments is the recognition that there should be an explicit relationship between the instructional objectives, the instruction, and tests (Shoemaker, 1975). Rapidly accumulating research from diverse sources shows that when instruction is systematic in nature and tests are planned to represent the intents of instruction logically, there are substantial increases in amount learned, duration of learning, and incidental learning, as well as many positive effects on students' attitudes (Block, 1971; Bloom, 1976; Hartley & Davies, 1976; Kulik, Kulik, & Cohen, 1979; Robin, 1976; Walberg, 1980).

Any form of systematic instruction has three common elements: (*a*) statements describing the intent of instruction, (*b*) instruction that is designed to help the student achieve the intended outcomes of instruction, and (*c*) criterion-referenced (CR) tests that are explicitly related to both intent of instruction and instruction itself. As Figure 2.1 suggests, the three elements are viewed as unique enterprises, but there is substantial interdependence among the three.

The technology of test-item writing is viewed as an important part of the development of criterion-referenced tests which, in turn, are essential elements of systematic instruction, evaluation of instruction, and research on learning.

Therefore, the purpose of this chapter is to provide a context for the

Figure 2.1. Three aspects of systematic instruction.

technology of test-item writing. In the first two major sections, systematic instruction is characterized in terms of theories of learning. It is in this context that
the technology has its greatest applicability. Next, the most prominent examples
of systematic instruction are introduced and described. Finally, criterion-
referenced tests are defined, and some concepts basic to this approach to testing
are discussed.

Systematic Instruction

There are at least two broad types of theories dealing with learning. One is
represented by reinforcement theory, and the experimental analysis of behavior.
The other includes cognitive theories, which view learning from several perspectives such as those of developmental and information processing. A complete
discourse on these alternative views of learning will not be attempted here.
However, it is important to recognize that either approach is compatible with
systematic forms of instruction, although the behavioral approach is clearly most
directly related to many of the implemented examples of systematic instruction.
    In terms of a behavioral approach to learning, systematic forms of instruc-

tion involve at least four factors: (*a*) definition of the target behavior, including task analysis; (*b*) cues and instructional stimuli; (*c*) eliciting student responses of progressive approximation to the target behavior; and (*d*) contingencies of reinforcement to strengthen and maintain the desired behavior (Keller, 1968; Skinner, 1968, pp. 19–21). The considerable richness of behavioral learning theory cannot be fully described here, but the theory's intricacies are reflected in the applied work of Johnston (1975) and Sherman (1974), as well as in the theoretical work of Bandura (1969), Premack (1965), and others.

Alternatively, explanations for school learning can be derived from information processing theory (Neisser, 1967), hierarchical theory (Ausubel, 1968), or theories that emphasize categories of learning (Gagné, 1977), among many others. Each theory employs psychological constructs to describe the learning process, and each requires us to make inferences on the basis of observable behaviors of learners, about the influence of these constructs on other constructs. These are general theories of learning. These attempts to construct models of school learning may fall short of what theories actually are, but they provide ample descriptions of how learning occurs in classrooms. These two models provide part of the context for the technology of test-item writing.

Models of School Learning

Two attempts to explain school learning are Bloom's model of school learning (Bloom, 1976) and Spady's model of *competency-based education* (1977). Each source represents an attempt to describe a formal model for school learning that embodies familiar constructs in learning:aptitude, quality of instruction, time, and student characteristics. Each model is reviewed here to provide a theoretical context for systematic instruction.

BLOOM'S MODEL OF SCHOOL LEARNING

In Bloom's explanation of school learning, *achievement,* defined as that which is measured by a criterion-referenced test is a function of (*a*) cognitive entry characteristics, (*b*) affective entry characteristics, and (*c*) the quality of instruction.

To portray this explanation, as Bloom does, a linear model is posited as follows:

$$Y = F[X_1, X_2, X_3]$$

where Y is achievement as measured by a criterion-referenced text, X_1 is a set of cognitive entry characteristics, X_2 is a set of affective entry characteristics such as attitudes and personality, and X_3 is the quality of instruction.

Bloom's analysis of these three constructs, which he submits are causally related to learning, accounts for nearly all the variance when corrected for the unreliability of measurements. Specifically, cognitive entry characteristics account for up to 50% of the variance, affective entry characteristics 25%, and quality of instruction 25%. Although these percentages' sum is 100%, there is some overlap when we combine them in a linear model. Bloom hypothesized that when the three conditions are present, they account for nearly 90% of all variance. Walberg (1980) in an analysis of determinants of learning reports similar findings.

Two assumptions of the model are critical to its understanding. The first is that the family history, home environment, and other background influences on the learner are causally related to the rate and amount of learning. That is, both cognitive and affective entry characteristics work uniquely and together to form the basis for student capability. The substance of this capability can be summarized in two constructs: aptitude for learning and motivation. Of course, other constructs have been hypothesized to work, to a lesser extent, to influence capability.

The second assumption is that these cognitive and affective entry characteristics are modifiable. That is, we know that student aptitude for learning is a strong determinant of the rate and amount of learning but that student aptitude can be modified by providing a quality of instruction that insures steady progress through sequential units of instruction. Bloom argues—and presents data to support his belief—that aptitude for learning actually increases as the student learns to learn. The relationship among Bloom's constructs are shown symbolically in Figure 2.2.

Bloom's analysis of learning in the classroom reveals that we can expect a normal distribution of test scores to represent the amount of learning that has occurred in the classroom but that this pattern of learning can be changed by improving the quality of instruction. Thus, the theory posits that when quality of instruction is improved, both cognitive and affective entry characteristics are improved and that ultimately, as a result of their modified learning history,

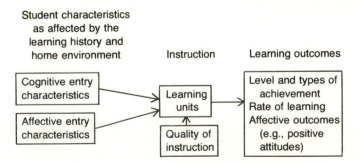

Figure 2.2 Influence of entry characteristics and quality of instruction on learning outcomes.

students who originally might have been predicted to be low achievers will achieve satisfactorily. Clearly, test development is central to Bloom's schema, because achievement must be assessed for learning units and outcomes.

COMPETENCY-BASED EDUCATION

Spady (1977) has used the term *competency-based education* (CBE) to describe a model of school learning that is slightly broader than Bloom's but far less formalized. *Competency* refers to a broad array of knowledge and skills that transcends what we perceive as normal schooling. For example, a competency may include all the knowledge and skills needed in a particular life role, such as that of political citizen, consumer, or family member.

The CBE model implies that units of instruction are not set by strict time limits (quarters, semesters), and grading has no role in a CBE system. Student performance is evaluated as either satisfactory or not. In spirit, CBE is very similar to mastery learning. In practice, CBE implementations in public schools and colleges may not resemble rigorous mastery-learning methods, although most states have some form of competency testing. Clearly, to implement CBE requires creative test development and item writing. Creating tests and items that reflect elements of life roles can be challenging indeed.

An important characteristic of CBE is that it distinguishes between the typical goals of education and competencies. Goals usually pertain to what students must achieve within the confines of school; competencies reflect continuing, posteducation life goals.

CBE has six critical elements. These elements, described here briefly, are of interest both because they are valid parts of an instructional model and because they are both similar to and different from Bloom's analysis of school learning.

Outcomes

The typical set of knowledge and skills that a school curriculum is designed to help the student acquire may form the background for the learning of life-role competencies. Thus, in some respects, competencies may be viewed as behaviors that involve higher level thinking. The hope of CBE is that competencies can be clearly described in terms of objectives, and can be directly represented in instruction. Research indicates that providing objectives to students is a promising device for enhancing learning (Melton, 1978; Duchastel & Merrill, 1973; Hartley & Davies, 1976).

Time

One of the most critical factors of this model, and seemingly of all others, is time for student learning. Rosenshine and Berliner (1978) refer to this as *en-*

gaged time; Bloom (1974) calls it *elapsed time,* which he defines as, "the amount of time spent from the beginning of a learning unit until the completion of the unit at the criterion level of mastery [p. 684]." If standards of performance are held constant, then time to learn is variable. Thus, many students will spend more time in learning. Any instruction that extends the time for learning will benefit by increased learning for its students (Bloom, 1976; Rosenshine & Berliner, 1978).

Instruction

All forms of systematic instruction require that instruction be closely integrated with goals or objectives as well as with testing. In CBE, the focus of instruction is on the intended outcomes that often transcend the confines of "normal" schooling. In other words, to achieve high levels of performance for students with respect to specific competencies, instruction must be based on aspects of the "real" world.

Measurement

As noted previously, measurement is a vital aspect of the total teaching-learning process. In CBE, the attempt is to reduce the punitive nature of tests. Instead, they provide either diagnosis or reinforcement for sufficient achievement. When a student does not perform up to a standard, the test result is used to identify weak areas for remedial instruction. As Spady (1977) pointed out, the technology of measurement is in its infancy, and there is much to learn about efficient means of competency-based measurement. Critics such as Burton (1978) and Glass (1978) have been severe in their condemnation of the use of standards in judging performance. As Haladyna (1976) has pointed out, standard setting is not an aspect of measurement but a use of the results of measurement to judge the adequacy of performance. Therefore, the question of where to set standards is more a judgment than a measurement problem.

Certification

CBE involves recognizing student performance by issuing certificates of achievement at various stages in students' education. Certificates may be one of several criteria for graduation. There are a good number of problems in certification. However, it is clear that tests are to be used to ascertain the degree to which each student is progressing in the achievement of well-stated life goals, that some formal document is to be drafted that recognizes the achievement of each learner, and that this document is to become part of the school record leading to graduation.

Program Adaptability

This sixth and final element of CBE permits the instructional program to be revised continually as a function of data gathered in the evaluation of the program. Such a model for program change is a mandatory part of program evaluation and review in the state of Oregon (Oregon Department of Education, 1974).

SUMMARY

To provide a framework for the subsequent discussion of examples of systematic instruction, criterion-referenced testing, and the technology of item writing, we have reviewed two approaches to school learning that are becoming popular at all levels of education. The two are very similar but also different in a number of ways. Bloom's model for school learning is an analysis of the major constructs that account for many cognitive and affective outcomes of instruction. He provides a description of major factors in learning—the cognitive and affective characteristics of students and the quality of instruction. Bloom's model could be expanded to include specific methods for instruction and testing that could comprise a type of systematic instruction, although he does not explicitly do this. Also, the research base for this model is very young, and many persons are currently working on research and summarizing research using new means of research reviews such as meta-analysis (Glass, 1976).

While Bloom's model for school learning will require further research, it is specific enough to be testable and implemented in classroom studies of learning. Spady's model has been described in more global terms than Bloom's. However, CBE has rapidly gained a strong foothold in public education at the secondary level where many states have implemented some form of CBE with respect to graduation requirements. The work that remains is to continue the conceptual and technical developments of the model, and its associated test design, item development, standard setting, reliability, and validity. Thus, the criticisms of CBE by Glass (1978) and Burton (1978) seem timely and well aimed, considering the infancy of the model. Nonetheless, it appears that the concept of CBE will prevail for many years to come, as both CBE and Bloom's model for school learning have attracted widespread attention.

Forms of Systematic Instruction

From theories of learning, one must move to actual operating examples in order to see the richness of applications of those models to a technology of item writing. This section is devoted to the examination of six forms of systematic instruction that are currently being implemented at various educational levels throughout the United States. These forms all vary widely in terms of methods for specifying instructional intent, providing instruction, and testing. These forms also vary widely in their stages of development, impact in American education, underlying theoretical rationale, research bases, and specificity of methods by which the form is implemented. These forms include mastery learning (Bloom, 1968), Individually Perscribed Instruction, or IPI (Hambleton, 1974), Individually Guided Education, or IGE (Klausmeier, 1977a), Program for Learning in Accordance with Needs, or PLAN (Flanagan, 1969, 1971), Instructional Systems Development, or ISD (O'Neil, 1979) and the Personalized System of Instruction, or PSI (Keller, 1968; Robin, 1976). Among this varied collection mastery learning is the least formal and more a statement of what could be done in the classroom. With few modifications, mastery learning can be widely implemented in most public schools. The next three systems, IPI, IGE, and PLAN, are very highly structured and based on long and careful development with reasonably sufficient data bases and research. ISD is a general systems model, approved for military training applications. The ISD has recently been supplemented by a method of quality assurance that includes one of the emerging technologies of test-item writing, the Instructional Quality Inventory, described in Chapter 11. Finally, the PSI approach is very popular in college-level instruction, and has a growing research base (e.g., Johnston, 1975). PSI is based on Keller's (1968) behavioral approach to instruction and testing.

MASTERY LEARNING

Although Bloom's model for school learning (Bloom, 1976) is useful in describing how students learn, it is his mastery learning paradigm that has been implemented as an instructional strategy in experimental studies (Block, 1971).

Mastery learning is the ideal instructional system from the standpoint of Bloom's analysis of school learning. In his general model, Bloom hypothesized that learning is a function of the student's entry characteristics and the quality of instruction. Further, Bloom stated that elapsed time is a major determinant of the amount of learning that occurs. The mastery learning instructional strategy provides for a corrective cycle for students who perform below standard. Elapsed time is increased for low-achieving students, and they are retested. Thus, mastery learning forces many potentially low-achieving students to stay on task and continue to learn, whereas in traditional instruction a lower level of achievement might be accepted because the same time requirement holds for each student.

The mastery approach is less formal than other forms of systematic instruction, as there is no one curriculum or set of learning modules that are called *mastery learning*. In fact, the mastery learning strategy can be applied to instruction at virtually any level or curriculum area. There are four basic aspects of mastery learning:

1. Learning is organized into units of instruction that are usually linearly or sequentially related and are also represented by objectives.
2. Students are presented with these objectives, and these become guides for both instruction and testing.
3. Instruction is delivered in any number of ways, and no suggestion is made to use any particular type of instruction. However, the quality of the instruction is critical, and there is much to be learned about appropriate instruction as a function of cognitive learning styles, aptitude, and affective characteristics.
4. Two types of tests are given: formative or summative. The formative test is diagnostic and gives students a sense of the adequacy of their progress in the unit. Thus, the formative test provides feedback to the learner to guide future studies. The test that is used to assign students either to subsequent units or to remedial instruction is the summative test, which is more comprehensive in scope than the formative test. The consequences of the summative test are that each student is either retained for remedial instruction or promoted to subsequent units of instruction.

In summary, mastery learning is less differentiated than other forms of systematic instruction, yet it allows the instructor more freedom in developing instructional methods, tests, and content on which instruction is based. Mastery learning is more like what is currently termed *conventional* instruction, the important exceptions being the unit-mastery notion and the use of tests to provide diagnostic and summative information.

The technology of test-item writing will become increasingly important to developers of mastery-learning courses, as they are faced with designing multiple, parallel test forms. Assessing the student's mastery of a unit and the progress of the student in the domain of achievement represented by the units requires some considerable attention to the precision of the relationship between test items and the instructional materials.

INDIVIDUALLY PRESCRIBED INSTRUCTION (IPI)

The Learning and Development Center at the University of Pittsburgh has for some time implemented a form of systematic instruction (Glaser, 1968). In his review, Hambleton (1974) found that over 250 schools had used IPI instructional materials in the areas of math reading, science, handwriting, and spelling. IPI functions in the following way. At the beginning of the school year, a placement test is used to locate the student's progress relevant to the curriculum. Materials are selected to fit the student's "learning style," and short tests are administered to determine if progress in learning has been adequate. Thus, students proceed in linear fashion through units of instruction, tests being used to guide remedial instruction as well as to evaluate overall progress. Overall progress is governed by progress relevant to each skill described as part of instruction. That is, students are not sent to a new unit until all skills are mastered in the previous unit. Reviewing three models, Hambleton (1974) reports that IPI is the most thoroughly developed and comprehensive in scope with a core of research studies emanating from the developers in Pittsburgh.

The tests used in IPI math are an excellent example of the use of the technology of item writing as described in Chapter 7 for quantitative items.

INDIVIDUALLY GUIDED EDUCATION (IGE)

This form of systematic instruction began in the 1960s guided primarily by Klausmeier and his colleagues (Klausmeier, 1976, 1977a, 1977b; Klausmeier, Morrow, & Walter, 1968; Klausmeier, Rossmiller, & Saily, 1977). The process leading to IGE was based on an analysis of conditions that were believed to exist in the public schools at that time. Some of these conditions were: (*a*) children worked in group-paced instruction, (*b*) norm-referenced tests were used to measure achievement, and (*c*) there was little time for teachers to plan instruction.

IGE was planned to overcome these conditions, which are generally viewed as unfavorable to productive learning. The new conditions in over 3000 IGE schools in the United States include:

1. Instructional programming
2. Criterion-referenced student evaluation
3. Compatible curriculum materials
4. A home–school community program
5. Statewide apparatus to facilitate IGE schools
6. A research base that refines IGE
7. An administrative structure that supports the above

Naturally, a host of studies and reports on IGE, such as those of Klausmeier and his colleagues, describe its organization as well as its effects.

The development and implementation of IGE is quite impressive, and among forms of systematic instruction, IGE appears to be one of the best researched, best developed, and most widely implemented. The technology of test-item writing to be described in Chapters 6 through 11 has considerable potential for the criterion-referenced evaluations that are an important element of IGE.

PROGRAM FOR LEARNING IN ACCORDANCE WITH NEEDS (PLAN)

Organized in the 1960s, PLAN is a major, computer-supported, individualized program of instruction that was developed by the American Institutes of

Research (Flanagan, 1971). Hambleton (1974) reports that over 105 schools actively participate in PLAN in the areas of language arts, social studies, mathematics, and science.

PLAN consists of over 1100 modules of instruction, each module taking a student about 2 weeks to complete. Each module contains five objectives and several units of instruction that represent different instructional approaches. Each student is given an instructional unit based on previous performance and information collected from a variety of sources. Each student is given a program of study that contains recommended modules and units along with a recommended sequence of modules. Student progress is carefully monitored through testing after each module and an overall achievement test. Post instruction module tests lead to several decisions: pass, hold for brief review, hold for substantial review, or restudy the module. The overall PLAN achievement test measures global progress. The module tests and the overall test must involve attention to the issues of specifying the relationship between the test items and the content of modules, as discussed in Chapter 1.

As Hambleton (1974) points out, PLAN is one of the most ambitious projects of its kind, but unfortunately it does not possess an adequate research base or adequate documentation of the validity of the tests used as part of the assessment system. In fact, there are two versions of PLAN, the original, conceived at the American Institutes of Research, and the commerical version currently marketed by Westinghouse Learning Corporation. The former is more comprehensive; the latter is more practical and economical.

INSTRUCTIONAL SYSTEMS DEVELOPMENT (ISD)

A model for instructional systems development has been approved for adoption throughout the United States military and is referred to as the ISD model (Branson, 1979; Logan, 1979; TRADOC, 1975). The model is based on a survey of other models and of the literature on instructional development. Developed by Branson (1979) and colleagues at the Center for Educational Technology at Florida State University under contract with the Army Combat Arms Training Board, the ISD model defines five phases or sequential sets of activities: analysis, design, development, implementation, and control. An overview of the model is shown in Figure 2.3. In the analysis phase, job and task analyses are carried out, job performance measures are constructed, and existing courses are analyzed. In the design phase, learning objectives are developed, along with CR tests designed to measure the objectives; entry behavior is described; and sequencing is determined. In the development phase, learning activities are specified, existing materials are reviewed, and instruction is developed and validated. In the implementation phase, the instructional management plan and instruction itself are begun. Finally in the control phase, the student' learning in the course and on the job is evaluated and the system is revised where needed.

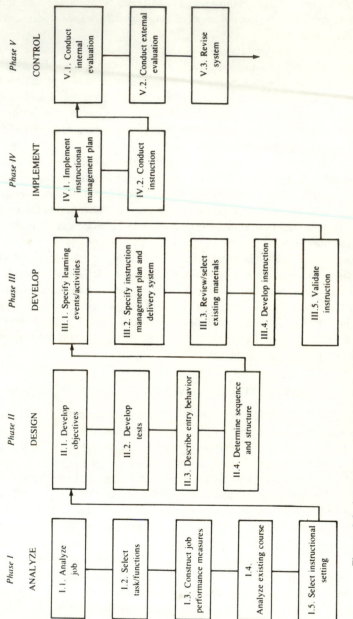

Figure 2.3. Interservice procedures for instructional system development model. (From O'Neil, 1979.)

24

The references describing the ISD model (Logan, 1979; TRADOC, 1975) clearly specify that CR tests are an integral part of the system. The development of tests is seen as a matter of writing items to match each of the objectives. This aspect of the ISD model is of particular interest, because the technology of test-item writing is intended to illuminate and, perhaps, go beyond the method of writing items from statements of objectives. Some of the methods of item writing to be described can be seen as involving elaboration of objectives so that they very specifically describe how test items will be derived from them. Thus, it is hoped that various item-writing technologies will provide more detail to the design phase, as described in the ISD model.

Since the ISD model (TRADOC, 1975) is approved for all military training development, it will be interesting to track the evaluations of the effectiveness of the model or courses developed from it. One reference on this topic would be Branson (1979), who discusses some of the successes and resistances to the model in the Navy and Army training schools.

PERSONALIZED SYSTEM OF INSTRUCTION (PSI): BEHAVIOR INSTRUCTION (THE KELLER PLAN)

Just as IGE is used extensively in public schools, behavioral instruction is well implemented in college and university education. Keller (1968), in his classic paper, espoused a method of instruction that was based on reinforcement theory but was also in keeping with the fundamental Bloom model for mastery learning. The main features of Keller's approach are very clearly similar to those of systems already discussed, particularly those of mastery learning:

1. Students progress at their own pace.
2. Students must successfully complete one unit of instruction before trying another.
3. Instruction is self-administered, and lectures and demonstrations are mostly for motivational purposes.
4. Most information is transmitted in writing.
5. Proctors are used extensively to provide tutorial instruction.

Research on PSI is impressive, and this system is used extensively in higher education with varying degrees of success. Robin's (1976) review of research indicates that of 39 studies that contrasted behavioral instruction with more conventional methods, 30 were in favor of behavioral instruction, 6 showed no differences, and only 1 favored traditional instruction. The two unaccounted studies had multiple comparisons with partially supportive results. Robin further reported that retention and attitudes were better in PSI groups than in traditionally taught classes. Kulik, Kulik, and Cohen (1979) also report meteoric success for this approach to instruction.

Although some forms of PSI use oral exams administered by proctors, others use written tests that would seem to be a natural application for the techniques of item writing, such as concept-testing (Chapter 9), higher level thinking (Chapter 10), and others.

In summary, this form of systematic instruction, although it has some limitations—described by Robin (1976)—exemplifies the mastery-learning model in many ways and has the added advantage of being an instructional system that has been carefully developed with guiding principles of instruction and that has a strong supportive research base.

SUMMARY

The six forms of systematic instruction we have discussed reveal the strong role that tests play both in providing guidance to the learner and in yielding information regarding the effectiveness of the instructional program. Although standardized tests have served capably in a number of ways, the kinds of tests that are curriculum specific and useful in reflecting how student behavior is modified as a result of instruction are not standardized in the traditional sense. Instead, we are dealing with the criterion-referenced test. The next section of the chapter deals with the kinds of interpretations that can be made from all tests and presents a description of the criterion-referenced test, including the steps one ideally follows in the development of such a test. In examining the definition and fundamental nature of the CR test, the reader will see the role that well-defined item-writing methods can and should play in test development.

Criterion-Referenced Testing

THE ROLE OF TESTING IN SYSTEMATIC FORMS
OF INSTRUCTION

As noted in the preceding section, systematic instruction requires close monitoring of student progress. As we know, tests can be used for various purposes. Traditionally, tests have been used to (a) motivate students into studying, (b) assign grades, (c) evaluate instructional programs, (d) evaluate teaching effectiveness, (e) group students for instruction, or (f) select students for special programs or assignments. In systematic instruction, tests take on different purposes. First and foremost, tests are used to certify that student achievement has been satisfactory. The judgment rendered is ''pass'' or ''needs more instruction.'' Second, tests can be used during instruction to see if crucial concepts have been mastered or objectives achieved during the course of instruction. Some models require tests at the onset of instruction. These pretests perform a useful function in screening out students who have already mastered the knowledge or skills indicated in the objectives of instruction. Researchers like Hartley and Davies (1976), however, contend that pretests are likely to sensitize the students to the objectives of instruction and are, therefore, a learning aid.

As noted earlier and as illustrated in Figure 2.1, the CR test is a very critical aspect of systematic instruction. The CR test is viewed as a learning aid because it helps the learner focus on the intent of instruction. Furthermore, it is intended to be a precise instrument because it is based on this intent of instruction and is, in fact, sensitive to instruction (Haladyna & Roid, 1981b).

As we examine features of CR tests, it may be useful to understand three types of test interpretations that are derivable from any set of educational or psychological measurements. Because these interpretations provide the meaning of measurement, we will examine them carefully before describing CR tests more completely and examining the steps by which such tests are developed.

THREE LEVELS OF TEST INTERPRETATION

Regardless of the particular way an achievement test is used in systematic instruction, one can extract three kinds of interpretations from such test: (*a*) norm-based, (*b*) criterion-based, or (*c*) domain-based.

A *norm-based comparison* involves the comparison of an examinee to a specified group of examinees. The purpose of a norm-based comparison is presumably to (*a*) group students for instruction, (*b*) assign honors for high achievement, (*c*) select for special programs, or (*d*) evaluate an instructional program. Particular statistical transformations of test scores are often used to develop norm-based comparisons: for example, percentiles, z-scores, T-scores, and stanines. It is important to note that these can be calculated on all measurements that deal with observable student behaviors representing traits such as achievement. That is, one can develop norm-based comparisons with achievement tests as well as with physical measurements involving time, space, distance, and weight.

A *criterion-based* interpretation follows from the establishment of an absolute standard. For example, in the following achievement test scale, which varies from 0%—indicating no correct responses—to 100%—indicating all responses are correct—a standard is set at 80%.

```
----------------------------------------------------------------┴---------------
0%                                                               80%       100%
```

Terms used for this standard include *criterion level, cutting score, pass–fail, go–no go,* and *passing standard*. Every student test score is given a criterion-based interpretation relative to this criterion level. One student may score 85% and another 95%. Both have passed the criterion and are treated the same way.

Conversely, two students who have scored 55% and 75%, respectively, are treated as not having met the criterion. The distance from a student's score to the criterion level has particular importance, in that it suggests that a lower scoring student, such as the one who got 55% must spend more time in instruction than the one who got 75%. Some writers (e.g., Millman, 1974b) have suggested developing a band around the criterion level. This band serves to separate students who are close to mastery and thus may need only review work from those (below the band) who need reassignment to more appropriate instruction or reinstruction (see Figure 2.4).

A *domain-based* interpretation is possible only when a domain or universe of items has been created and the test is based on a sample from this domain. This is a more infrequent type of test interpretation but one of great importance in systematic instruction, and it is the heart of what is currently known as CR testing. Although the term *criterion-referenced* is semantically confusing, it is clear from recent accounts of the topic by Hambleton, Swaminathan, Algina, and Coulson (1978), Millman (1974a), Popham (1978), Berk (1980), and Baker, Linn, and Quellmalz (1980) that domain-based interpretations are what is really intended. A domain-based interpretation involves the use of the test score to estimate the level of achievement relevant to the entire domain of test items. For instance, from a score of 85% on a test one can infer that the student can successfully complete about 85% of the several hundred or thousand tasks (or test items) in the domain that was the target of instruction. Thus, the domain-based interpretation is the only one that provides meaningful information about the student with respect to how much that student has learned and the degree of effectiveness of instruction. Further, the setting of a criterion level is meaningless without the

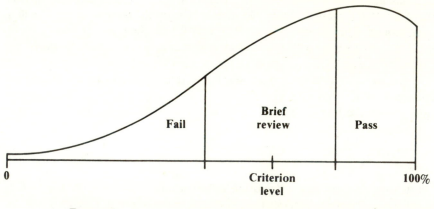

Figure 2.4. An uncertainty band.

establishment of a domain-based interpretation. Instructors can use both criterion-based and domain-based interpretations to make meaningful statements about the consequences of teaching and learning—statements which will help the student toward a more focused attempt to achieve the objectives that are the target of instruction. In other words, by using both types of interpretation, instructors can assess not only whether students pass or fail a test, but what proportion of the domain they have mastered.

Domain-based interpretations of scores have a strong statistical foundation. When a test is a random sample of items from a domain, the proportion of correct items is an unbiased estimator of the hypothetical, true domain score. The domain score would be that obtained by the student if all items in the domain were answered. Lord and Novick (1968, p. 234) point out that the proportion of correct answers to a random sample of items from a domain is a sufficient statistic for estimating the student's ability.

THE CRITERION-REFERENCED TEST

Glaser (1963) was among the first to discuss the use of the criterion-referenced test in systematic instruction. Long an advocate of systematic instruction, Glaser described the role of the test in determining the adequacy of instruction with respect to the criterion level and the specific behaviors that a student can perform as reflected in his or her score.

Although *domain-referenced* would probably describe this test more accurately, the term *criterion-referenced* is widely used, and there is far too much history behind the test movement to suggest a change in name (Hambleton *et al.*, 1978; Popham, 1978). Moreover, domain-based and criterion-based interpretations are both achievable for many purposes of testing in systematic instruction. When a domain can be specified for a test, a criterion-based interpretation of pass–fail can be applied to domain scores, using judgmental standards as suggested by Meskauskas (1976), Millman (1974a), or Shepard (1976). In this way, the scores have maximum interpretability and usefulness.

Leaving the semantic problem, we can look at the steps involved in CR test development (as illustrated in Figure 2.5) to get an impression of the role that item development plays and of how we can best develop items that are appropriate for the types of interpretations that are needed.

Step 1: Instructional Intent

Before instruction is planned or delivered, the instructor or designer of instruction must have an idea of the content of instruction. This idea may be purely abstract (''to understand the mechanics of a centrifuge'') or it may be very concrete (''to be able to operate a centrifuge to extract gold dust from sand''). A

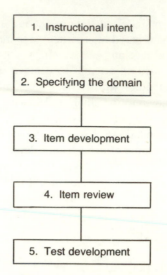

Figure 2.5. Five steps in the ideal development of a CR test.

continuum ranging from abstract to concrete may characterize all of instructional intent, with the above examples serving to anchor the end points:

understand   operate

ABSTRACT   CONCRETE

Regardless of what level of abstraction–concretion comprises the instructional intent, the instructor or designer of instruction will have to "operationalize," or make more concrete, the intent of instruction. Several forms of job analysis and task analysis can be used to operationalize the instructional problem or intent of the instruction. This process is described more completely elsewhere (e.g., Foley 1973). Thus, Step 1 is viewed as a starting point from which all planning of instruction and testing occurs. It is important at this point to observe that testing is viewed as part of instruction and not a separate operation. Testing, when used properly, is a powerful tool in teaching as well as in evaluating the results of teaching.

Step 2: Specifying the Domain

This next step involves the clarification of the instructional intent. We have used the term *operationalize* to suggest that whatever was intended in instruction needs to be made more concrete. The most common way to do this is to develop a single learning objective or a set of learning objectives that represent the intent of instruction logically. For the mechanics of the centrifuge, the instructor may list four or five important concepts—such as centrifugal force—and several facts and principles that all students must know before they can "understand the mechanics of a centrifuge." Thus, the learning objective serves as a guide to the instructor both in the development of specific instruction and in the development of appropriate tests. The objective also serves the students with respect to helping them focus on what they must learn. Research on the utility of objectives thus far has been impressive (Duchastel & Merrill, 1973; Hartley & Davies, 1976; Melton, 1978). Baker (1974) and Popham (1975) have provided excellent guidelines for expanding objectives to include elements of domain specification such as the wrong-answer population for multiple-choice items or the range of content to be sampled by essay questions.

An alternative method to using instructional objectives has been given much recent attention. Through such comments as those of Bormuth (1970) on the biases that exist in item-writing practices, it has become clear that although objectives have many good properties, they may result in great variability of interpretation between item writers. In fact, some studies (e.g., Roid & Haladyna, 1978; Roid, Haladyna, & Shaughnessy, 1979) have shown that objectives lead to differences between item writers that confound the difficulty level of a test. As a consequence, many persons who work to study and improve CR tests have turned to domain specifications that use a wide variety of means to clarify the intent of instruction through rules for writing items. These rules lead teams of item writers to produce items that have a minimum of discrepancy between writers. Although these item-generating rules vary from theory to theory, and although some techniques are more efficient than others, there are several at present that may provide help to item writers. Several of these developing approaches are introduced in Chapters 6–11.

The areas that have received the least attention, and yet are most needed, are the first two steps in CR test development. There have been advances in the military and industrial fields in defining instructional intent, but American public education has suffered for lack of specific methods for developing specifications for instructional domains. One possible approach was suggested by Messick (1975), who maintained that educational measures need to have construct meaning. The construct validation of educational measures requires careful formulation of instructional domains, explication in terms of measures, and empirical data to support our interpretation of those measures. Although such procedures may seem tedious, they have the impact of adding theoretical significance to our interpretations of educational achievement measures as well as meaning. On the other hand, operationally defined measures, such as a test score on a universe of test items, are rather limited in interpretation and meaning due to the fact that the universe is typically not developed from an abstract construct that is part of a network of constructs. Messick's paper, as well as the original treatise on construct validity by Cronbach and Meehl (1955), provides the substance of this kind of thinking about domain specifications.

Step 3: Item Development

This step involves the identification of the item format and the selection or creation of actual items to be used. Step 3 is the basis for the technology of test-item writing. A fundamental principle of item development states that the test item must correspond logically to the intent of instruction and that test-item data should follow predictable and understandable patterns of student responses when used in instruction.

One alternative in item development is to tap already existing item banks that represent well-known domains. For example, the National Assessment of Educational Progress (NAEP) has extensive collections of items that have been used with national samples. Organizations such as the Northwest Evaluation Association have developed collections of test items in reading, mathematics, and language arts that are goal-referenced and equated to common achievement scales by means of the Rasch testing model (Forster, 1977; Rasch, 1980).

These item collections provide the basis for usual measurement concerns in public-school, basic skills areas, but the large specialized needs in most subject matter areas and at most educational levels require the use of technologies of test-item writing of the kinds that are described in subsequent chapters. Also, these technologies have the added feature of providing potentially theoretically relevant descriptions of content that are publicly testable and understood.

Step 4: Item Review

A major goal in CR test development is to establish a domain of items that reflects the intent of instruction adequately. Adequacy is determined in two ways, each of which is viewed as complementary to the other. The first involves logical review of items by subject-matter experts; the second involves empirical item review based on item analysis and field tests.

Logical item review involves the use of subject-matter experts or instructors to identify possible item flaws and to judge the consistency between objectives (or domain specifications) and the test items. Items are accepted, rejected or revised in accordance with the judgments of these reviewers. The process may be informal or it may be quite elaborate, depending on the adequacy of resources and time and the importance of the instructional material. Ideally, logical item review is a process in which items are carefully scrutinized to insure that the test is characterized by this important quality of item-objective consistency. This topic is covered in Chapter 12.

The process of *empirical item review* is seen as an important step in reviewing and editing items. Patterns of student response before or after instruction are examined to determine if instruction has been adequate or if test items have failed to detect what they were designed to detect. Through a reasoning process that is supported by actual test-item data, items undergo empirical review. This topic is covered in Chapter 13.

Step 5: Test Development

As suggested earlier, there is a need for a great many criterion-referenced test forms for pretests, posttests, and retests. In addition to these summative evaluations, or CR tests, there is a need to produce shorter tests as part of formative evaluations. As you can see, the testing needs are great, and if all three types of interpretations are needed, test development is a crucial step.

Fortunately, test development is the easiest and most clerical in nature. The way to develop randomly parallel test forms for summative evaluations that yield legitimate domain-based interpretations is to randomly sample items from the domain. If a summative evaluation of several objectives is required, the test developer may draw a sample of 20–30 items for each objective—or to economize, he or she may wish to draw a smaller sample of items for each objective. The latter practice yields a shorter test, but there is a danger in certifying mastery for a student based on a small sample of items.

There is one interesting alternative to the test model that employs random sampling procedures. This alternative is a direct application of latent-trait test models (Hambleton & Cook, 1977; Wright, 1967). The model states that all test items are calibrated on a common scale, so that any subset of items can be used to create tests. Regardless of which set of items a student receives, a score can be generated on this common scale. Thus, the problem of equating test results from form to form is said to be solved (Wright, 1977). Research by Haladyna and Roid (1981a) reveals that this alternative is viable if the information required is global rather than specific to instructional objectives. Also, this alternative allows the difficulty of subtests to be tailored to the functioning level of the student, thereby reducing potential error of measurement due to subtests that are too difficult or too easy.

RELATIONSHIP OF ITEM-WRITING TECHNOLOGY TO GENERALIZABILITY THEORY

Cronbach, Gleser, Nanda, and Rajaratnam (1972) extended the theory of test reliability to include the analysis of the many possible components of error variance in tests. These researchers have used analysis of variance and multivariate techniques to estimate the generalizability of test scores across facets such as people, items, times, raters, test forms, and other conditions of testing. The development of generalizability theory has led Cronbach into a consideration of the universe or domain of items that a test represents. Stated in more general terms, ''a central concept of generalizability is that the observation is a sample from a universe, or, more formally, that any condition is sampled from a universe of conditions [Cronbach *et al.*, 1972, p. 316].'' The arguments against generalizability theory have centered around the way universes are defined and the methods of sampling items or conditions. These arguments are similar to those that might be levied against domain-based testing and the technology of test-item writing.

Several measurement researchers (e.g.,Loevinger, 1965; Thorndike, 1967) have questioned the notion of random sampling on at least two grounds: (*a*) that a pure random sample from a complex domain can produce an odd combination of items; and (*b*) that, in actual practice, most tests are far from random samples. The first objection may be overcome by stratified random sampling with respect to content or task classifications for items. The result, random sampling within strata, still allows for the application of the mathematical model of generalizability theory.

The objection that tests are rarely true random samples would have been correct before the advent of the technology of item writing. Samples of items were determined by expert selection, item-format constraints and item-selection procedures. Loevinger (1965) claimed, apparently without knowledge of the works of Hively, that ''no system is conceivable by which an index of all possible tests could be drawn up; there is no generating principle [p. 147].'' This opinion reminds one of the skeptical view that, in the eyes of experts who lived before the Wright brothers, ''flying machines'' were impossible. From the perspective of the item-generation technology to be presented in this book, it seems understandable that the objection that universes cannot be defined occurred before new inventions were widely known.

More serious objections have to do with the meaningfulness of definable universes of items. Thorndike (1967) commented that ''a really adequate definition of the universe from which we have sampled will become so involved as to be meaningless [p. 289].'' With the benefit of today's perspective, the reader need only examine the item forms of Hively, Maxwell, Rabehl, Sension, and Lundin (1973) as presented in Chapter 7, to decide if Thorndike's objection still holds true.

At a deeper philosophical level, Kaplan (1964, pp. 40–41) has criticized the use of strict operationism by any scientist. Kaplan's objections are essentially that an overly specific definition of the conditions of measurement becomes trivial if it does not allow a *class* of conditions to be described. As applied to test development, this concern is that an item-generation method must define a class of items, not a set of items discriminable from one another only in a trivial way. The reader need only read Chapter 9, on concept-based item writing, to appreciate the inventive, nontrivial domain specificiations now possible for items that measure concept learning.

Clearly, the operational definition of item universes is simple in some content areas, and difficult or seemingly impossible in others. We hope, in this book to delineate the subject-matter areas and the types of item writing that show potential for the application of rigorous generalizability analysis. At a minimum, the essential link between generalizability and item-writing technology will surely become clear as the reader progresses through Chapters 6–11.

Summary

In this chapter, we have tried to provide a context for the technology of test-item writing. Two general and prevailing ways of thinking about learning are represented in behavioral and cognitive theories. While there are many distinguishing characteristics of these two philosophies, systematic instruction appears to embody features that are accommodated by each. Two recent descriptions of school learning provide a good theoretical background for systematic forms of instruction and criterion-referenced testing. Six forms of systematic instruction were reviewed, and criterion-referenced testing was described as a critical component in all systematic forms of instruction.

Five steps in the development of criterion-referenced tests were described. Steps 2 and 3 involve the technology of test-item writing and provide the basis for one of the most important kinds of test interpretations desired—the domain-based interpretation. When we have a sufficient description of our instructional intent in terms of test items, we may develop test construction plans that provide adequate sampling of the domain of knowledge we are testing. Mapping the domain through domain specifications becomes critical, and the development of items follows. Any test developer may employ a number of approaches. The technology of test-item writing contains the means by which item domains may be created. As item domains are defined, the applicability of generalizability theory as a means of assessing test reliability becomes clear.

References

Ausubel, D. P. *Educational psychology: A cognitive view.* New York: Holt, 1968.

Baker, E. L. Beyond objectives: Domain-referenced tests for evaluation and instructional improvement. *Educational Technology,* 1974, *14* (6), 10–16.

Baker, E. L., Linn, R., & Quellmalz, E. S. *Knowledge synthesis: Criterion referenced measurement.* Los Angeles: Center for the Study of Evaluation, Univ. of California, 1980.

Bandura, A. *Principles of behavior modification.* New York: Holt 1969.

Berk, R. A. (Ed.) *Criterion referenced measurement.* Baltimore: Johns Hopkins Univ. Press, 1980.

Block, J. H. (Ed.). *Mastery learning: Theory and practice.* New York: Holt, 1971.

Bloom, B. S. Learning for mastery. *Evaluation Comment,* 1968, *1,* 1–12.

Bloom, B. S. Time and learning. *American Psychologist,* 1974, *29,* 682–688.

Bloom, B. S. *Human characteristics and school learning.* New York: McGraw-Hill, 1976.

Bormuth, J. R. *On the theory of achievement test items*. Chicago, Illinois: Univ. of Chicago Press, 1970.

Branson, R. K. Implementation issues in instructional systems development: Three case studies. In H. F. O'Neil, Jr. (Ed.), *Issues in instructional systems development*. New York: Academic Press, 1979.

Burton, N. W. Societal standards. *Journal of Educational Measurement*, 1978, *15*(4), 263–271.

Cronbach, L. J., Gleser, G. C., Nanda, H., & Rajaratnam, N. *The dependability of behavioral measurements*. New York: Wiley, 1972.

Cronbach, L. J., & Meehl, P. E. Construct validity in psychological tests. *Psychological Bulletin*, 1955, *52*, 281–302.

Duchastel, P. C., & Merrill, P. F. The effect of behavioral objectives on learning: A review of empirical studies. *Review of Educational Research*, 1973, *43*, 53–69.

Flanagan, J. C. Program for learning in accordance with needs. *Psychology in the Schools*, 1969, *6*, 133–136.

Flanagan, J. C. The PLAN system for individualizing education. *NCME Measurement in Education*, 1971, *2*, 2.

Foley, J. P. Job task analysis for ascertaining precise objectives for maintenance instructions and related training. *Improving Human Performance*, 1973, *2*, 27–40.

Forster, F. *RASCH: An item analysis program*. Portland, Oregon: Portland Public Schools, 1977.

Gagné, R. M. *The conditions of learning* (3rd ed.). New York: Holt, 1977.

Glaser, R. Instructional technology and the measurement of learning outcomes: Some questions. *American Psychologist*, 1963, *18*, 519–521.

Glaser, R. Adapting the elementary school curriculum to individual performance. *Proceedings of the 1967 Invitational Conference on Testing Problems*. Princeton, New Jersey: Educational Testing Service, 1968, 3–36.

Glass, G. V Primary, secondary and meta-analysis of research. *Educational Researcher*, 1976, *5*(10), 3–8.

Glass, G. V Standards and criteria. *Journal of Educational Measurement*, 1978, *15*(4), 237–261.

Haladyna, T. Measurement issues related to performance standards. *Florida Journal of Educational Research*, 1976, *18*, 33–34.

Haladyna, T., & Roid, G. *A comparison of two item selection procedures for building criterion-referenced tests*. Paper presented at the annual meeting of the American Educational Research Association, Los Angeles, 1981. (a)

Haladyna, T., & Roid, G. The role of instructional sensitivity in the empirical review of criterion-referenced test items. *Journal of Educational Measurement*, 1981, *18*, 39–53. (b)

Hambleton, R. K. Testing and decision-making procedures for selected individualized instructional programs. *Review of Educational Research*, 1974, *11*, 371–400.

Hambleton, R. K., & Cook, L. L. Latent trait models and their use in the analysis of educational test data. *Journal of Educational Measurement*, 1977, *14*, 75–96.

Hambleton, R. K., Swaminathan, H., Algina, J., & Coulson, D. B. Criterion-referenced testing and measurement: A review of technical issues and developments. *Review of Educational Research*, 1978, *48*, 1–47.

Hartley, J., & Davies, I. K. Preinstructional strategies: The role of pretests, behavioral objectives, overviews and advance organizers. *Review of Educational Research*, 1976, *46*, 239–265.

Hively, W., Maxwell, G., Rabehl, G., Sension, D., & Lundin, S., *Domain-referenced curriculum evaluation: A technical handbook and a case study from the MINNEMAST project*. Los Angeles: Center for the Study of Evaluation, Univ. of California, 1973.

Johnston, J. M. *Behavior research and technology in higher education*. Springfield, Illinois: Thomas, 1975.

Kaplan, A. *The conduct of inquiry*. San Francisco: Chandler, 1964.

Keller, F. S. Goodbye, teacher . . . *Journal of Applied Behavior Analysis*, 1968, *1*, 79–89.

Klausmeier, H. J. Instructional design and the teaching of concepts. In J. R. Levin & V. L. Allen (Eds.), *Cognitive learning in children: Theories and strategies*. New York: Academic Press, 1976.

Klausmeier, H. J. *Individually guided elementary education: A new kind of schooling*. Paper presented as an invited address at the annual meeting of the American Educational Research Association, New York, 1977. (a)

Klausmeier, H. J. Instructional programming for the individual student. In H. J. Klausmeier, R. A. Rossmiller, & M. Saily (Eds.), *Individually guided elementary education: Concepts and practices*. New York: Academic Press, 1977. (b)

Klausmeier, H. J., Morrow, R. G., & Walter, J. E. *Individually guided education in the multiunit elementary school: Guidelines for implementation*. Madison: Wisconsin Research and Development Center for Cognitive Learning, 1968.

Klausmeier, H. J., Rossmiller, R. A., & Saily, M. (Eds.). *Individually guided elementary education: Concepts and practices*. New York: Academic Press, 1977.

Kulik, J. A., Kulik, C., & Cohen, P. A. A meta-analysis of outcome studies of Keller's personalized system of instruction. *American Psychologist*, 1979, *34*(4), 307–318.

Loevinger, J. Person and population as psychometric concepts. *Psychological Review*, 1965, *72*, 143–155.

Logan, R. S. A state-of-the-art assessment of instructional systems development. In H. F. O'Neil, Jr. (Ed.), *Issues in instructional systems development*. New York: Academic Press, 1979.

Lord, F. M., & Novick, M. R. *Statistical theories of mental test scores*. Reading, Massachusetts: Addison-Wesley, 1968.

Melton, R. F. Resolution of conflicting claims concerning the effect of behavioral objectives on student learning. *Review of Educational Research*, 1978, *48*, 291–302.

Meskauskas, J. A. Evaluation models for criterion-referenced tests: Views regarding mastery and standard-setting. *Review of Educational Research*, 1976, *46*, 133–158.

Messick, S. The standard problem: Meaning and values in measurement and evaluation. *American Psychologist*, 1975, *30*, 955–966.

Millman, J. Criterion-referenced measurement. In W. J. Popham (Ed.), *Evaluation in education: Current applications*. Berkeley, California: McCutchan Publishing Company, 1974. (a)

Millman, J. Sampling plans for domain-referenced tests. *Educational Technology*, 1974, *14*, 17–21. (b)

Neisser, U. *Cognitive psychology*. New York: Appleton, 1967.

O'Neil, H. F., Jr. (Ed.). *Issues in instructional systems development*. New York: Academic Press, 1979.

Oregon Department of Education. *Minimum standards for Oregon public schools*. Salem, Oregon: Oregon Department of Education, 1974.

Popham, W. J. *Educational evaluation*. Englewood Cliffs, New Jersey: Prentice-Hall, 1975.

Popham, W. J. *Criterion-referenced measurement*. Englewood Cliffs, New Jersey: Prentice-Hall, 1978.

Premack, D. Reinforcement theory. In D. Levine (Ed.), *Nebraska symposium on motivation*. Lincoln: Univ. of Nebraska Press, 1965.

Rasch, G. *Probabilistic models for some intelligence and attainment tests*. Chicago: Univ. of Chicago Press, 1980.

Robin, A. Behavioral instruction in the college classroom. *Review of Educational Research*, 1976, *46*, 313–354.

Roid, G. H., & Haladyna, T. M. A comparison of objective-based and modified-Bormuth item writing techniques. *Educational and Psychological Measurement*, 1978, *35*, 19–28.

Roid, G., Haladyna, T., & Shaughnessy, J. *Item writing for domain-referenced tests of prose learning.* Paper presented at the annual meeting of the American Educational Research Association, San Francisco, April 1979.

Rosenshine, B. & Berliner, D. Academic engaged time. *British Journal of Teacher Education,* 1978, *4,* 3–16.

Shepard, L. Setting standards and living with them. Paper presented in the symposium *Measurement Issues Related to Performance Standards in Competency-Based Education* at the annual meeting of the National Council on Measurement in Education, San Francisco, April 1976.

Sherman, J. G. *Personalized system of instruction: 41 germinal papers.* Menlo Park, California: W. A. Benjamin, 1974.

Shoemaker, D. M. Toward a framework for achievement testing. *Review of Educational Research,* 1975, *45,* 127–148.

Skinner, B. F. *The technology of teaching.* New York: Appleton, 1968.

Spady, W. G. Competency-based education: A bandwagon in search of a definition. *Educational Researcher,* 1977, *6*(1), 9–14.

Thorndike, R. L. Reliability. In Anastasi, A., *Testing problems in perspective.* Washington: American Council on Education, 1967.

TRADOC (U.S. Army Training and Doctrine Command). *Interservice procedures for instructional systems development* (TRADOC Pamphlet 350–30). Ft. Benning, Georgia: TRADOC, 1975.

Walberg, H. J. A psychological theory of educational productivity. In F. H. Farley & N. Gordon (Eds.), *Perspectives on educational psychology.* Chicago, Illinois and Berkeley, California: National Society for the Study of Education and McCutchan Publishing, 1980.

Wright, B. D. Sample-free test calibration and person measurement. *Invitational Conference on Testing Problems.* Princeton, New Jersey: Educational Testing Service, 1967.

Wright, B. D. Solving measurement problems with the Rasch model. *Journal of Educational Measurement,* 1977, *14,* 97–116.

II

PRACTICAL GUIDELINES
FOR ITEM WRITING

3

A Practical Framework for Item Development in Criterion-Referenced Testing

To provide a theoretical context for the technology of test-item writing, systematic instruction has been introduced and described, and the criterion-referenced (CR) test was identified as a major component of systematic instruction. The CR test is viewed as highly sensitive to instruction and as appropriate for many purposes including research on learning, program evaluation, and monitoring of student progress through instructional units. One of the primary needs of good CR tests is CR test items; thus we need a technology of test-item writing. This chapter is devoted to more practical considerations of preexisting conditions leading to the development of test items. These preconditions constitute a practical framework for the technology of test-item writing.

As stated in Chapter 2, the first three steps in CR test development are (*a*) stating instructional intent, (*b*) specifying achievement domains representing this intent, and (*c*) developing items. The third step may involve the technology of test-item writing; the former two steps involve the preexisting conditions that must be carefully considered—the nature of the instructional intent and the specification of that intent, typically in the form of instructional objectives. There are two fundamental types of instructional intent in the cognitive domain: knowledge and skills.

The next decision involves the type of test format to be used. We will describe a logical process that allows the test developer to decide which type of test format is appropriate to the instructional intent. After the test format has been selected, practical guidelines for good item writing can be applied, regardless of the exact method of item generation.

Finally, we will describe how each of the technologies to be presented in Chapters 6–11 pertain to the types of instructional intent and testing formats presented here. The selection of an item-writing technology should be governed by the type of cognitive behavior desired and by the ability of that technology to yield items for that cognitive behavior type.

The Cognitive Domain: Knowledge and Skills

The cognitive domain represents student behaviors that are intellectual in nature. Fundamentally, these cognitive behaviors are generally classified into one of two categories, knowledge or skills. Along another dimension, we can classify objectives and items by level of cognitive complexity. The most familiar frame work for describing cognitive behaviors along this complexity dimension is the cognitive taxonomy of Bloom and colleagues (Bloom, Engelhart, Furst, Hill, & Krathwohl, 1956). Six categories exist in this taxonomy, each dealing with specific aspects of cognitive behavior. At the lowest level of complexity is simple recall. Other types of behaviors in the cognitive domain are comprehension, application, analysis, synthesis, and evaluation. This approach is one of several that attempt to define the full range of behaviors that represent the cognitive domain.

In his review of this taxonomy, Seddon (1978) quotes Bloom: "The taxonomy must be accepted and used by workers in the field if it is to be regarded as a useful tool [p. 304]." This taxonomy is well-known among most educators and psychologists but, according to Seddon, the research base is not conclusive as to the evidence for or against the taxonomy. An attempt by Miller, Snowman, and O'Hara (1979) to improve on earlier research on the taxonomy was equally perplexing. The results obtained by these researchers who used different tools of analysis, were not clear as to the factorial structure of measures of different levels of the taxonomy. In fact, interpretations of the results suggested fluid and crystallized intelligence. Thus, this recent study of the taxonomy does not provide the level of empirical support that is needed to promote the use of the taxonomy.

Several item-writing technologies employ structures that are viewed as alternatives to the taxonomy of Bloom and his colleagues. For instance, Chapter 10 deals with a typology for higher level thinking that permits the classification or writing of items by various types of higher level thinking (Miller, Williams, &

Haladyna, 1978) and Chapter 11 deals with the Instructional Quality Inventory (Ellis & Wulfeck, 1978) which includes a structure that is useful for classifying as well as for preparing items.

Achievement tests are intended to measure learning that occurs in the cognitive domain. As noted previously, the two terms *knowledge* and *skills* are often used to designate two distinct and mutually exclusive areas in the cognitive domain. We will distinguish between knowledge and skills with respect to the intent of instruction and the nature of the material to be learned. Once you know whether your instructional intent is knowledge or a skill, the item development phase is ready to begin.

Generally in this chapter, *knowledge* will refer to an awareness (understanding) of facts, concepts, or principles. In traditional instruction, most knowledge is transmitted visually, orally, or in writing—in the latter case, mostly through books and training manuals. We can characterize knowledge this way, but it is difficult, if not impossible, to tell exactly what it is, because knowledge is essentially abstract. We can not really observe knowledge directly, but we can observe indicators of knowledge. The process of observing behavior and making inferences about the degree to which persons or things have or do not have a trait is what measurement is all about. The most common method of measuring knowledge employs the analysis of responses to paper-and-pencil test items. One good way to think about situations that represent knowledge, as opposed to skills, is to think about how one observes the behavior. If a paper-and-pencil test is used, the particular behaviors manifested very likely fall in the category of knowledge. In such instances, we are prone to infer degree of knowledge through frequency of correct responses to test questions. A distinction is made between skills that have a cognitive element and those that are strictly motor. Athletic movements in sports, such as the jumpshot in basketball, are all body movement and timing, and during execution they require little cognitive planning or recall of facts or concepts. In contrast, the assembly and correct use of science laboratory equipment requires much cognitive activity.

The instructional intent may often focus on how the student is performing or on what is produced from a skill. The orientation in measuring any skill, therefore, is on performances or products. The performance is a sequence or set of behaviors that comprises a process in which the student is an active participant. The product is the outcome, result, or consequence. A product is tangible. When we measure a performance, what we really mean is that we are interested in aspects of a performance. Quite often, through such procedures as task analysis or the like, we are able to break down performances into isolated segments. The problem then is to determine what aspects of the performance were completed or, in some circumstances, to determine how well they were performed. For example, in the assembling of a table saw, there may be nine critical steps. We could observe whether each of these nine steps were completed as instructed.

With a product, there is a slightly different orientation. A product has many defining characteristics or dimensions that may serve as the basis for measurement. First, we must define the dimensions of the product before we impose some form of rating system or observation method for the measurement of the dimensions of that product. For example, a child's work of art may be examined for originality, use of color, detail, and completeness. Each of these are dimensions of the product and constitute that which we measure with respect to the skill that is represented by that product.

None of the first five item-writing technologies bear on the measurement of skill. The reason for this is that the measurement of skills is typically achieved through the use of rating scales, checklists, or observation methods. These techniques continue to be the "stock in trade" of skills measurement; little has evolved beyond them. We will review these methods for measuring skills in Chapter 5; in addition, the reader is referred to the numerous excellent texts that deal with the subject of measuring skills (see, e.g., Cronbach, 1970; Ebel, 1972; TenBrink, 1974).

Once a statement of instructional intent has been logically analyzed, decisions must be made as to whether the behavior is cognitive or noncognitive in nature and, when cognitive, as to whether it entails knowledge or a skill. Discriminating between knowledge or a skill from statements or instructional intent is a most difficult task. It is important, however, to make this discrimination, as the decision eventually leads to the use of a particular test format (e.g., paper-and-pencil) or of other methods appropriate for skills.

To develop the distinction between knowledge and skills, a few examples are presented and discussed.

1. *The student will use a jigsaw properly.*

The objective stresses how a jigsaw is used. There is no implication that we want to know about a student's knowledge of the working parts of a jigsaw or of the variety of uses of a jigsaw in carpentry. The objective emphasizes how the student uses the jigsaw—that is, properly—and therefore we are concerned about the process that the student uses in the performance of a skill rather than the end product. *Properly* suggests that some criteria for adequate performance exist. If the objective were rewritten to show some understanding of the jigsaw's operation or safe practices with a jigsaw, then knowledge would be the part of the cognitive domain requiring testing.

2. *Using algebraic theorems and the transformation process, the student will explain why the equation of a line in the form $Ax + By + C = 0$ can be transformed to fit the equation $y = mx + b$.*

In this example, a process in mathematics where two expressions can be equated is described. It is implicit that the student will have to explain in writing or orally the reasons why two expressions are exchangeable. By doing this the student displays knowledge about the process.

3. *Field-strip and assemble an M-16A rifle under conditions of **total darkness**.*

The third example is clearly a skill, but the problem is distinguishing between the process of performance and the created product. For a performance, we are concerned with *how* the rifle was assembled. Was a certain set of procedures followed? With a product, we want to know if the rifle operates as we expected it to operate. Does it work? The focus is the product, the rifle itself. Thus, the instructional intent of the person who wrote the objective is not clear without an explanation of what constitutes adequacy. Such an explanation will allow us to decide whether the skill is one of performance or of creating a product.

4. *Correctly spell all words on the list of 50 basic terms from organic chemistry.*

This fourth example, commonly misnamed "spelling skills," requires the student to display knowledge of spelling in written form. Although it is easy to display the domain of test items for spelling, we are still testing for knowledge.

Types of Testing Formats

Once a statement of instructional intent has been analyzed and the decision has been made that it suggests the measurement of knowledge or a skill, the task of identifying a type of testing format follows. Sometimes with a particularly difficult statement of instructional intent, this process works in reverse. The type of testing format that appears appropriate, may lead to a conclusion regarding whether the concept being represented by that statement of instructional intent is cognitive, affective (attitudes), or psychomotor (motor skills).

We shall continue to focus on the cognitive domain, as all our writing technologies are germane to that domain. Our orientation is toward the knowledge part of that domain rather than the skill part, because most instructional programs emphasize the knowledge area and it is in that area that the need for test items is greatest.

There are two major types of test formats for knowledge in the cognitive domain. The *selected-response* format requires the student to choose the correct answer; in the *constructed-response* format, the answer is provided by the student. There have been numerous discussions of the differences between selected-response and constructed-response testing that will not be repeated here. Virtually every text on educational testing presents a discussion of these differences. The major thrust of many discussions leads to the false belief that selected-response testing leads to measures of one type and constructed-response testing to measures of another. Such a conclusion is not well founded in research, as either a selected-response or a constructed-response test will provide reasonably accurate indicators of levels of achievement. What is important to test builders is the relative validity and reliability of an achievement test.

Generally, a test should be representative of the domain of achievement, as described by our statement of instructional intent. Achieving adequate representation is a matter of content validity (Cronbach, 1970; Helmstadter, 1964), and the most appropriate type of testing format is one that allows the maximum number of items to be sampled in a given time period. Therefore, selected-response testing and the "completion" format of constructed-response testing are generally regarded as providing the best opportunity for more complete sampling of the domain. In many cases, selected-response testing provides more opportunity for achieving higher content validity.

Issues of reliability are discussed in numerous basic texts, so a lengthy discussion will not be given here (Nunnally, 1967; Lord & Novick, 1968; Stanley, 1971).

Reliability is estimated by coefficients that describe the relative degree of error of measurement in test scores. Measurement error is believed to be the difference between any score and a true score (the true score would be the result obtained if all items in the domain were administered). Statistically, reliability is represented by the ratio of true score variance to observed score variance. Reliability is also theoretically described as the squared correlation between true and observed scores. In practice, reliability is maximized when a set of similar items is given to a wide ranging group of examinees; the more items given, the higher the reliability estimate. From one point of view the standard error of measurement, which is an estimate of the average error that might occur for any given true score, is a more important concept than reliability. Based on the perspective of error of measurement, selected-response testing gives the best opportunities for high reliability and smaller standard errors. Therefore, from the standpoint of content validity and reliability (measurement error), one is compelled to recommend selected-response testing in situations where the measurement of knowledge is required. Nunnally (1967) concisely summarizes this argument: "Since the multiple-choice test typically is much more reliable than the essay test, the conclusion is inescapable that the objective test is more valid [p. 239]."

Summary

We have described the cognitive domain, delineating two specific subareas of this domain: knowledge and skills. The technology of test-item writing deals principally with the measurement of knowledge, and consequently the emphasis will be on types of testing formats that are suitable for testing knowledge. The two major alternatives are the selected-response and constructed-response test-item formats. it was argued that in many cases selected response offers greater potential for achieving good content validity and higher reliability.

References

Bloom, B. S. Engelhart, M. D., Furst, E. J., Hill, W. H., & Krathwohl, D. R. *Taxonomy of educational objectives*. New York: Longmans, Green, 1956.

Cronbach, L. J. Review of *On the theory of achievement test items* by J. R. Bormuth. *Psychometrika*, 1970, *35*, 509–511.

Ebel, R. *Essentials of educational measurement*. Englewood Cliffs, New Jersey: Prentice-Hall, 1972.

Ellis, J. A., & Wulfeck, II, W. H. *The instructional quality inventory: IV. Job performance aid* (NPRDC Special Report 79-5). San Diego: Navy Personnel Research and Development Center, 1978.

Helmstadter, G. C. *Principles of psychological measurement*. New York: Appleton, 1964.

Lord, F. M., & Novick, M. R. *Statistical theories of mental test scores*. Reading, Massachusetts: Addison-Wesley, 1968.

Miller, H. G., Williams, R. G., & Haladyna, T. M. *Beyond facts: Objective ways to measure thinking*. Englewood Cliffs, New Jersey: Educational Technology Publications, 1978.

Miller, W. G., Snowman, J., & O'Hara, T. Application of alternative statistical techniques to examine the hierarchical ordering in Bloom's taxonomy. *American Educational Research Journal*, 1979, *16*(3), 241–248.

Nunnally, J. *Psychometric theory*. New York: McGraw-Hill, 1967.

Seddon, G. M. The properties of Bloom's taxonomy of educational objectives for the cognitive domain. *Review of Educational Research*, 1978, *48*, 303–323.

Stanley, J. C. Reliability. In Robert L. Thorndike (Ed.), *Educational measurement* (2nd ed.). Washington, D.C.: American Council on Education, 1971.

TenBrink, T. D. *Evaluation: A practical guide for teachers*. New York: McGraw-Hill, 1974.

4

Characteristics of Quality
Test Items

Practical guidelines for writing test items have been presented by Coffman (1971), Conoley and O'Neil (1979), Ebel (1972), Gronlund (1968), and others. These guidelines typically include lists of characteristics, such as having answer alternatives that are brief in multiple-choice items. Frequently, examples and nonexamples of item construction are presented as illustrations. This chapter summarizes the accumulated conventional wisdom of test developers and measurement researchers. Two major types of test items are discussed: selected-response and constructed-response items.

Selected-Response Items

The technology of test-item writing discussed in this book pertain fundamentally to the measurement of knowledge in the cognitive domain. The type of test format we most typically employ is that of the selected response. The three types of selected-response formats—multiple-choice, true–false and matching—are reviewed here to provide a summary of existing knowledge regarding test-item writing. Many of these principles of item writing are helpful in or apply to the implementation of the technologies of test-item writing that are discussed in subsequent chapters. More comprehensive discussion on this topic can be found in Ebel (1972).

MULTIPLE-CHOICE TEST ITEMS

All multiple-choice items have the same elements: (*a*) an item stem that is the beginning statement, the stimulus for the test examinee; (*b*) options (choices), one of which is the correct response; and (*c*) *foils,* or distractors— incorrect options that are supposed to be reasonably attractive to the student who has not yet mastered the objective the item is intended to tap.

The multiple-choice item normally takes one of two possible forms:

Type 1—Question
STEM: Which one of the following is most typical of a malfunctioning exylizer?
    FOIL: a. blue gas
    CORRECT
      RESPONSE: b. whining noise   } OPTIONS
    FOIL: c. grating sound
    FOIL: d. periodic "thud"

Type 2—Question
STEM: A typical malfunctioning exylizer will emit a
    FOIL: a. blue gas.
    CORRECT
      RESPONSE: b. whining noise.   } OPTIONS
    FOIL: c. grating sound.
    FOIL: d. periodic "thud."

You should note that in Type 1, a question is asked and the options form responses that are grammatically parallel. Type 2's item stem is part of a sentence of which the options form grammatically correct completions.

PROCEDURES IN WRITING GOOD ITEMS

Here are four steps to follow in writing multiple-choice items:

1. Make sure your statements of instructional intent are very clear and that the item requires the student to identify the correct response.
2. Write an item stem using one of the two multiple-choice forms presented in the preceding section.
3. Write the correct response, one of four options you will use.
4. Write foils that are parallel in grammatical construction and appealing to the student who has not yet mastered what you are trying to teach.

You will find that Step 4 is, by far, the most challenging. The essential in foil writing is to provide options that are incorrect yet attractive to *un*knowledgeable students. Students who truly possess knowledge should select the correct answer. Those who lack this knowledge should select a foil.

COMMON FAULTS AMONG ITEM WRITERS

This section contains advice on how *not* to write test items. As you will see later, some of these problems are avoided by the application of a technology of test-item writing.

Grammatically Incorrect Statements

A very common fault among some item writers is the use of poor grammatical structure, as shown below:

A typical malfunctioning exylizer will emit a
  a. It gives out a blue gas.
  b. whining noise.
  c. nonoperational.
  d. hard to say without more information.

An item of this type often confuses the student, thus increasing the chance that the student will respond incorrectly even if he or she has learned the objective and possesses knowledge.

Include as much of the item as possible in the item stem so as to avoid unnecessary repetition.

The best way to test for specific gravity of a solid is
  a. through the use of a graduated cylinder.
  b. through the use of a beaker.
  c. through the use of a platform balance and a graduated cylinder.
  d. through the use of a beaker and a platform balance.

A better format would be:

The best way to test for the specific gravity of a solid is through the use of a
  a. graduated cylinder.
  b. beaker.
  c. platform balance and a graduated cylinder.
  d. beaker and a platform balance.

In the second example, the student spends less time reading through foils and the item has a better, leaner appearance.

Multiple-Multiple-Choice Format

Another common problem is the use of the multiple-multiple-choice format (* signifies correct answer throughout):

Noah's brother was thinking of
I. ice cream; II. a trip to the zoo; III. a new bike; IV. girls.
  a. I, II, and III
  b. II and III
  c. III and IV
 *d. all of these

This type of format is unnecessarily complex. Moreover, it is often easy for the crafty test taker. For example, the chance of guessing the right answer is one in four (25%). Consider the possibility that the test taker knows that IV is a right answer. The student can then reduce the choices to (c) and (d), thereby increasing the chances of guessing correctly to one in two (50%). Items should not test a student's test-taking skills but the knowledge gained by the student. The multiple-multiple-choice format is not useful and does not contribute to effective test-item writing. It would be far better to rephrase the item thus:

> Among other things, what was Sara's brother thinking of?
>   a. his science test
> *b. girls
>   c. taking a nap
>   d. a trip to the zoo

In this example, only one answer is correct and the item is direct and to the point.

Long Correct Option

Another common mistake is to use a long correct option in contrast to short foils.

> The main reason for the Civil War of Utopia was
>   a. the discontent of a few.
>   b. the tribulations of the Euphorians coupled with growing dissatisfaction of the people with the prime minister's foreign policy.
>   c. bad times.
>   d. inflation.

This happens when the item writer completes the first three steps of multiple-choice item writing satisfactorily and then impatiently thinks up three plausible yet brief wrong answers that become foils. The intelligent test taker notices the length of one response and chooses it even without knowing the right answer. Such items contribute to increasing the test-wise person's score instead of accurately reflecting knowledge acquired as a result of instruction.

Excessively Long Test Items

Such items require more reading and therefore more time, try the patience of a test taker, and emphasize reading comprehension rather than achievement. The item writer should avoid such lengthy foils as much as possible. An excessively long test item is illustrated below:

> The healthy, free gingiva aids in the self-cleaning process by its
>   a. tendency to direct food particles toward occlusal surfaces.
>   b. tendency to force particles away from the proximal space.
>   c. tendency to deflect particles away from free gingiva onto the interdental papillae.
>   d. close adherence to the tooth surface below the height of contour of the cervical enamel.
>   e. propensity of erosion from the bolus.

Ridiculous Foils

The use of ridiculous foils may often relieve test anxiety, but such foils make the probability of the selection of the correct answer by the unknowledgeable student higher. Thus, the item fails to measure what it was designed to measure.

Which of the following is best known for his contribution to mathematics?
   a. Archie Bunker
   b. Robert Hogg
   c. O. J. Simpson
   d. Abraham Lincoln

Clue in the Item Stem

Another common fault is the use of a clue in the item stem to tip the student to the correct option:

The famous Four Hundred were
   a. a vaudeville team
  *b. four hundred soldiers who perished in the Battle of Calories
   c. the results of a systematic search for socially prominent persons in New York City
   d. a group of persons dedicated to becoming famous

While all four choices may be plausible in the context of the instruction, the correct response, (b) repeats the clue, the "four hundred."

Similar Foils

Another common fault is the use of similar foils. The item below provides a good example:

The most common form of recreation in Utopia is
   a. a computer game.
   b. an electronic game.
  *c. soccer.
   d. an automated TV game.

The three options that are very similar in content are all incorrect answers (foils). As always, care should be taken in constructing foils for all items.

Specific Determiners

Another item-writing fault is the use of specific determiners, or foils that reveal the correct answer by phrasing the incorrect options in absolute terms while leaving the correct option in less absolute terms. For example:

The tendency for persons to wish for happy things is
   a. totally absent.
   b. completely present.

*c. occasionally troublesome.
 d. never a reason for that type of action.

A test-wise person with no knowledge could conclude that the only option that deals with the phenomenon in a less than absolute manner is the correct answer.

"All of the Above"

"All of the above" is a poor option because, if one of the other options is known to be true, then the correct answer may be one of only two options. For example:

In the story, "Boris and Morris Go to the Circus," who told Boris and Morris that the circus was looking for a funny-looking moose and bear?
   a. Elise
   b. Mark
   c. Eric
   d. Angie
   e. all of the above

If the student knows that Eric told Boris and Morris, then either (c) or (e) are possible right answers, and this parital knowledge improves the student's chances of correctly choosing the answer.

"None of the Above"

The option "none of the above" can be effectively used if it is the correct answer about one time in four. In fact, for the item writer who has difficulty conceiving of options, the use of "none of the above" may be an effective tool.

"I Don't Know"

One of the most unusual foils used in test-item writing has been the option, "I don't know." If a student doesn't know and is willing to admit it, this option can be used effectively. In fact, it has been effectively used in statewide assessments (Oregon Department of Education, 1974) as well as in the National Assessment of Educational Progress. On the other hand, this option could defeat its purpose if the situation for testing is highly competitive or there is a reward for obtaining a high score. Therefore, this form of option should be used with caution.

Negative Statements

The use of negatives in item stems or options is sometimes very confusing to the student. Whenever possible, phrasing items in this manner should be avoided. An achievement test should not resemble an IQ test, in which the student must analyze the logic of the questions. Items should be direct and should elicit the responses intended in order to reflect the achievement of the objective the item was intended to tap.

An example of a confusing, negatively worded item follows:

Which of the following is *not* recommended for an accident victim?
  a. Do not leave the victim unattended.
  b. Do not move the victim.
  c. Notify the authorities.
  d. Do not talk to the victim.

When the negative is used, you should underline or write it in capital letters for emphasis so that the reader will understand that the reverse is intended. It is very easy to read through a test item with a negative in it and overlook that negative. The meaning is then reversed and the student may miss the item for the wrong reason—carelessness.

Multiple-choice test items should not measure the student's cleverness at analyzing items to extract correct answers. They should be direct and meaningful indicators of a student's learning. Faulty items, when used in tests, often discourage or confuse students, who may react emotionally, and justifiably, against such tests. These poor items also contribute to lower degrees of content validity, reliability, and efficiency.

A Final Word

Another important aspect of options in multiple-choice testing is the order of placement of the correct answer. Good test-item writers make certain that correct responses are randomly distributed across option positions. One experienced test taker said: "When in doubt, choose Charley." He meant, "I always choose (c) when I don't know the answer." If the order of correct responses is varied among the options in a test, then this experienced test-taker will no longer take advantage of tests.

TRUE-FALSE TESTING

It is generally known that multiple-choice test items are the most prominent and well-accepted type of item because of their qualities of content validity and reliability. Much neglected is the true–false format. Ebel (1972) has done the most to advance this item format's acceptability, and his book contains an excellent treatment of the subject for the reader interested in exploring this topic in depth. Our position is that the true–false item is occasionally appropriate, and that the item writer should not shy away from true–false formats.

Among the several advantages of true–false questioning are:

1. More questions can be asked and answered in a typical testing period and therefore more coverage can be given to a topic.

2. True–false questions are easy to write.
3. It does not take long to respond to a true–false question.
4. Questions can be highly reliable.
5. True–false items take up less space on paper, thereby saving testing materials.
6. Different types and levels of content are adaptable to true–false items.

To summarize, true–false items contribute to tests of high content validity, reliability, and greater efficiency, if properly constructed and reviewed.

Among their disadvantages are the following:

1. True–false items tend to measure trivial or irrelevant things.
2. The probability of guessing successfully is quite high: 50%.

As with the multiple-choice items, these disadvantages can be overcome. With respect to the first disadvantage, the item writer needs to be careful about what each question asks. The use of the approaches in Chapters 10 and 11 protects against the practice of using true–false items to measure trivial aspects of learning.

With respect to the second disadvantage, guessing is not a problem if a sufficient number of questions are used because the probability of guessing all items correct diminishes. Also the scale upon which test interpretation occurs can take into account the fact that a score of 50% correct on a true–false test is very much like 25% on a four-option multiple-choice test. A score of 54% on a true–false test is quite low; 54% on a four-option multiple-choice test is moderate. Our standards and ways of interpreting test data from true–false tests should be governed by the fact that 50% is a lower bound for the test scale.

Guessing is more of a problem with true–false items, but it is really not something to affect test results greatly. For example, in a 30-item true–false test, guessing 20 items correct (67%) or better will happen about twice in a million occasions. Rarely will someone be classified as knowledgeable on the basis of pure guessing.

Below is advice on constructing true–false items for tests:

1. *Avoid shades of meaning; deal with things that are dichotomous in nature.*

GOOD: A well-adjusted Type 245 engine has an engine speed idle of between 700 and 900 RPM's.
BAD: One of the best characteristics of higher altitude training is in the recovery of oxygen deficit.

The first item is factual, coming from a training manual that states these limits. The second is disputable, dealing more with a set of characteristics and human judgment. It is best to avoid such potentially controversial or debatable issues in true–false questioning.

2. *Avoid negatives and double negatives.*

As in the case of multiple-choice, the use of negatives makes questions harder to read and thus lengthens response time. Since you want to ask more questions in a time period, ask them in a positive way.

GOOD: A dangerous reaction will occur when you pour water into a hot frying pan.
BAD: You should not pour water into a hot frying pan.

In testing situations, where many students are test-anxious, they are likely to overlook the word *not* and answer the question incorrectly. The first example is stated more clearly and is factual.

If negatives appear necessary in writing the true–false item, emphasize it in the sentence. For example, ''A thermofropple should *not* be installed with the arrow pointing up.''

3. *Avoid long sentences.*

Long sentences are difficult to read and understand, and the student can lose sight of what is actually being tested.

BAD: Among the parenchym cells, which are thin-walled cells making up the bulk of the pulp of fruits, and the vascular cells can be found the supporting cells, such as fibers.
GOOD: Parenchym cells make up the bulk of the pulp of fruits.

4. *Only a single idea should be contained in a true–false item.*

BAD: A rectangle has four right angles and two sets of adjacent and equal sides.
GOOD: A rectangle has four right angles totaling 360°.

The second example tests a single concept. The first tests several concepts in a complicated way. If the student misses the first item, we cannot determine what the student is lacking. It would be better to rewrite the first item as three separate items:

A rectangle has four right angles.
Opposite sides of the rectangle are equal.
A rectangle is distinguished from a square by the fact that the square has four equal sides.

As you can see, true–false items are easy to prepare and use and are *not* subject to serious disadvantages if properly constructed. These items, like multiple-choice items, are subject to item review to determine (*a*) whether they measure what they were intended to measure in a logical sense and (*b*) whether student responses to items follow consistent and predictable patterns.

MATCHING TEST ITEMS

There is always some subset of content that is subject to more than four or five options and that lends itself nicely to multiple-choice testing of a unique kind, namely matching. Matching has all of the advantages and disadvantages of multiple-choice items (of which it is a variety). An example is provided to show the format for matching and the type of knowledge to which it may be applied.

_____ 1.	farthest from the sun	a.	Mercury
_____ 2.	satellite of the earth	b.	Venus
_____ 3.	largest planet	c.	Earth
_____ 4.	smallest planet	d.	Mars
_____ 5.	many moons	e.	Jupiter
_____ 6.	two moons	f.	Saturn
_____ 7.	closest to the sun	g.	Uranus
_____ 8.	slowest rotation, longest days	h.	Neptune
_____ 9.	satellite of the star Alpha Centauri	i.	Pluto
_____10.	habitable	j.	None of these

As you can see, the number of items for testing knowledge about the planets can be quite large. Thus, the matching format lends itself quite nicely to this body of knowledge. One major advantage of the matching over the multiple-choice format is that efficiency—and ultimately content validity—is higher with the former. You can ask more questions and thereby attain greater coverage of the domain or objectives you are testing.

The rules for creating matching test items really do not vary from those for the conventional multiple-choice test items. The matching format has many varieties and applications. The interested reader is invited to consult more comprehensive texts on measurement, such as Gronlund (1971) and Ebel (1972).

Principles of Constructed-Response Item Construction

A constructed-response test question allows the student to create rather than simply select the answer. Despite this major difference, both constructed-response and selected-response techniques are useful for measuring the complete range of knowledge typically encountered.

The constructed-response format is useful in a number of settings where the instructional intent requires the student to plan and create a response to a question as opposed to simply selecting an answer. If the objective is written in a manner to suggest that the student will explain, describe, define, state, or write, then a constructed-response format is appropriate. On the other hand, identifying, distinguishing, and matching are processes that suggest selected-response questioning. The dilemma facing any test-item writer is which format to select, given the instructional intent. Often we choose to use the selected response when the intent clearly suggests the constructed-response format, believing that when a student correctly supplies an answer that student can, with equal facility, select the correct answer from a series of options. If, however, there is a need to follow your intent strictly, and that intent suggests constructed response, then that format can be effectively used.

THREE TYPES OF CONSTRUCTED-RESPONSE FORMATS

Generally, there are three kinds of constructed-response formats: (*a*) completion item, (*b*) short-answer essay, and (*c*) extended-answer essay. Each will be described and more fully discussed.

Generally, the constructed-response technique lends itself nicely to higher level questioning. In cases where objectives call for higher level cognitive behavior, questions must go beyond factual recall or comprehension to tap higher levels such as analysis, application, synthesis, or evaluation (from Bloom's cognitive taxonomy). The following objective illustrates higher level thinking:

Given the mass of each body and the distance between them, the student will determine the gravitational pull that the earth has on other planetary bodies.

This objective requires a question with a short response. The student must identify a formula that is appropriate and use it correctly to produce the correct response. An exercise could be constructed using a multiple-choice format, but it appears simpler (more efficient) and appropriate to test with a completion format where the correct response is provided by the student.

COMPLETION ITEMS

The steps employed in writing completion items are similar to those employed in writing multiple-choice items. Completion items are easier to write because options are not given and the student is asked to provide a key word or phrase to either answer the question or complete the sentence. Questions should be stated so that responses are specific as opposed to general. General responses lead to ambiguity in scoring the responses and, hence, to more measurement error.

Form of Items

Completion items will take three general forms:

1. List four persons who assumed the presidency in times of peril to the United States.
2. Who were the four presidents who assumed their office in times of peril to the United States?
3. The four presidents were _____, _____, _____, and _____.

Completion items can be constructed by identifying an important sentence in a prose passage and then paraphrasing or transforming the sentence into a question by removing its key word or phrase and having the student supply the response. Chapter 6 presents more information on some new approaches for taking prose materials and creating completion items as well as multiple-choice items.

Thorndike and Hagen (1969, pp. 88–90) offer this advice on writing completion items:

1. Be sure that each item deals with important content; do not measure trivia.
2. Be sure the question or statement poses a specific problem to the examinee.
3. Be sure that the answer that the student is required to produce is factually correct.
4. Be sure the language used in the question is precise and accurate in relation to the subject matter area being tested.
5. If the problem requires a numerical answer, indicate the units in which it is to be expressed.
6. In a completion item, omit only key words.
7. In an achievement test, do not leave too many blanks in a completion statement.
8. In a completion item, put blanks near the end of the statement rather than at the beginning.

Scoring Completion Items

If a word or phrase is omitted from a sentence and a completion question is formulated, then the missing word or phrase is the correct answer. One could insist on the exact answer in judging the correctness of a response to a completion item, but most examiners tend to accept answers that are reasonably close to the acceptable answer. Cocks and Bormuth (1975) provide some guidelines for scoring completion items. One of the methods accepts any *superordinate* or general term as a correct replacement for the specific term; for example, the answer "hammer" could be replaced by the superordinate "tool."

The practice of accepting reasonably close answers creates a problem for persons scoring a test because there are many shades of meaning and what may seem correct to one person who scores the test may seem entirely different to another. In general, it is advisable to provide the desired answer and several alternative right answers so that the person scoring the completion item has a good idea of the range of acceptable responses.

WRITING A SHORT-ANSWER ESSAY QUESTION

The short-answer essay is intended to elicit a brief response to a question or instruction. The essay question takes two general forms:

1. State two reasons why night flying is dangerous.
2. What are two reasons why night flying is dangerous?

Short-answer essays are usually the choice in constructed-response testing, because one can ask a few more questions in a typical testing period than one can using the extended-response essay. The short-answer essay thus gives greater coverage to the instructional intent and insures a higher degree of content validity. Further, these questions are relatively easy to write.

Considerable effort and skill are required in scoring student responses. Typically, inconsistencies arise between scorers of the same exam question. Even with a single scorer, error may occur in rescoring a test item. As a result, test scores from short-answer essays are less reliable than one would like them to be. If, on the other hand, recommended procedures for scoring are followed, these tests can be made reliable.

The short-answer essay can be used to cover a wide range of cognitive behaviors, from recall to evaluation. Short-answer essays may elicit different kinds of cognitive behavior than are elicited by selected-response tests. Atlas (1979) has suggested that expert writers generate more ideas, personalize their opening paragraphs more, and depart more often from their own outlines than novice writers. This suggests a wealth of cognitive activity during constructed writing tasks that would presumably be missing, particularly in most selected-response items. Further research is needed to document such differences.

Five guidelines are listed in writing the short-answer essay question. For some guidelines, examples are provided:

1. *First identify the statement of instructional intent and make certain that an essay is appropriate.*

BAD: Objective: Describe the role of white blood cells in the body's defenses.
BETTER: Objective: The student will define and provide examples of the following phenomena in relation to white blood cell function: blood coagulation, bacterial invasion, antibody activity.

2. *Identify a specific focus for the question:*

If possible, systematically sample prose materials, paragraphs, or key sentences, from which to construct questions. Paraphrasing of prose material may help to provide key sentences that summarize important ideas.

3. *Use such verbs as **compare, contrast, describe, distinguish, illustrate**, and phrases such as **give examples of, explain how**, so the student has a good idea of the nature of the task required.*

BAD: Trace the development of the selective service system.
BETTER: Give examples of major events and their probable causes in the development of the selective service system.

4. *Make the question as unambiguous and clear as possible.*

All students should have the same general interpretation of what the question is asking. Being specific is one way to achieve this end.

BAD: Discuss inflation.
BETTER: Describe how the supply of newly printed money affects American inflation.

5. Sample the content as fairly as possible.

Describe the full range of questions that would be possible for each statement of instructional intent (objective), and then provide a sampling plan.

6. Tell the student about the answer desired.

Is it long or short? What details are needed? Leaving these kinds of things unsaid invites serious departures from expected responses. The purpose of a test question is to determine the student's level of knowledge. If the question confuses the student, it obscures the measurement of the knowledge that the student possesses.

BAD: What is the theorem of Pythagoras?
BETTER: State the theorem of Pythagoras and its usefulness in the mathematical science of trigonometry. List at least four applications.

7. Write a model answer.

This often helps you understand the strengths and weaknesses of your question and can be the first step toward creating a checklist of attributes of a good answer. Later the model answer is useful in scoring the test.

WRITING AND SCORING THE EXTENDED-ANSWER
ESSAY QUESTION

This form of constructed-response technique is used only when the instructional intent is broadly focused on a single objective, and the response to a question is considered the whole of instructional intent. These are rarer occasions, but there are times when instruction is geared not to various aspects of knowledge but a holistic body of knowledge. For example, an objective might be:

The student will describe the major conclusion of the staff study of communications in Sector G-16 indicating present status and what changes might be made to improve all communications.

The purpose of the above question is to test how well the student understands the major conclusion of a report on a communication system in an office or plant. The response called for in the objective should be extensive and comprehensive. You should note that such an extended-anwer essay is not creative in nature but incorporates a definable answer on which subject matter specialists or the instructor will commonly agree.

Thus, the extended-answer essay is intended to apply to situations where comprehensive knowledge is to be tested, and the key to this choice of testing technique is to make certain that the cognitive knowledge desired is general and extensive rather than specific and highly focused, as it is with short-answer essay questioning.

The principles and steps for writing the item are the same as for the short-answer essay. More important, however, is the preparation of the model answer. Besides serving as a guide to score the result, the model answer serves to educate the students about any deficiencies in their responses.

With selected-response testing, scoring is objective, that is, two persons scoring the same exam question for any student should get the same result. With any form of essay, two persons scoring the same item for any student may get discrepant results, unless the scoring process is carefully done. Therefore, great effort should be given to planning the scoring of essays.

As stated earlier, a model answer is essential to proper scoring. The model answer should contain the major content elements of the essay question. If the content is to be organized in a certain way, the model answer should reflect this organization. It is also wise to list the major points that the answer should contain and to assign values for each.

In most cases, we use one of two devices to evaluate a response to an essay question. Both of these devices are described as tools to measuring skills. They are the *rating scale* and the *checklist*.

The rating scale simply requires that a response be given a point value ranging typically from low performance (zero) to some higher level (e.g., 10). This device is used in what is called the "holistic" method of evaluating writing skill (Diederich, 1961). In other approaches, each test question is given a number of assigned points, depending on the weight of the question. The rating scale is a device for determining the value of the response along that scale. In some cases, we may want to use several rating scales representing dimensions of the response. For example, if an essay question asks for a definition and examples of a complex idea, we may want to assign five points for the adequacy of the definition and five points for the reasonableness of the examples.

The checklist is more commonplace in evaluating essay items. We simply note the presence or absence of critical aspects of the essay response. When present, we assign points; when absent we do not assign points. Therefore, a response to an essay question is evaluated in terms of the number of critical points contained as outlined in the model answer.

For example, if an essay question requires an explanation of factors contributing to inflation in the American economy, we may look for the naming of four valid factors and a brief description of each. We may assign two points for naming each factor and two points for describing each. The question may have a total value of eight points. We merely check the answer for the presence or absence of these critical features.

Summary

In this chapter, we have reviewed methods for writing selected- and constructed-response items. This review has been intentionally brief. It is intended to present the major principles in item construction and, in the case of the constructed response form, scoring. For a very comprehensive treatment of selected-response testing, Ebel (1972) provides one of the most authoritative and comprehensive accounts. For essay testing, the chapter by Coffman (1971) is one of the best. These references are intended for those seeking more comprehensive treatments of this subject.

This material has been presented in the context of an emerging technology of test-item writing. Traditional item-writing wisdom has been helpful to an extent, but the emerging technology has made possible the careful specification of test formats and the writing of test items that are more closely geared to the intent of instruction.

In the past, item writing was largely dependent on the consummate skill of the item writer. The technology of test-item writing reduces differences in skill in test-item writing, by restricting the item writer from injecting his or her personal bias into the item-writing process. Therefore, the item writing becomes more objective, and we hope, so does the ensuing measurement of knowledge.

References

Atlas, M. *Expert–novice differences in the writing process*. Paper presented at the annual meeting of the American Educational Research Association, San Francisco, April, 1979.

Cocks, P., & Bormuth, J. R. *Rules for classifying scoring responses to wh-completion questions*. Paper presented at the annual meeting of the American Educational Research Association, Washington, D.C., March–April 1975.

Coffman, W. E. Essay examinations. In R. L. Thorndike (Ed.), *Educational measurement*. Washington, D.C.: American Council on Education, 1971.

Conoley, J. C., & O'Neil, H. F., Jr. A primer for developing test items. In Harold F. O'Neil, Jr. (Ed.), *Procedures for instructional systems development*. New York: Academic Press, 1979.

Diederich, P. B. *Factors in judgments or writing ability* Princeton, New Jersey: Educational Testing Service, August 1961. (ERIC Document Reproduction Service No. ED 002 172)

Ebel, R. *Essentials of educational measurement*. Englewood Cliffs, New Jersey: Prentice-Hall, 1972.

Gronlund, N. E. *Constructing achievement tests*. Englewood Cliffs, New Jersey: Prentice-Hall, 1968.

Gronlund, N. E. *Measurement and evaluation in teaching* (2nd ed.). New York: Macmillan, 1971.

Oregon Department of Education. *Minimum Standards for Oregon Public Schools*. Salem, Oregon, 1974.

Thorndike, R. L., & Hagen, E. *Measurement and evaluation in psychology and education*. New York: Wiley, 1969.

5

Measuring Skills: Rating Scales, Observations, and Checklists

In Chapter 3, two indicators of skills, performances, and products, were described. Additionally, three kinds of techniques used in measuring aspects of performance or the qualities of products were discussed. These were the (*a*) rating scale, (*b*) observational method, and (*c*) checklist. In this chapter, we will review the distinction between knowledge and skill and provide a number of practical suggestions for each of the techniques used to measure skills.

Overview

Except for a few examples, such as a marksmanship test described by Hively (1974), little has appeared on domain-based skill measurement in the literature. Because of the potential for a technology of domain-based skill-item development, the techniques are discussed here to suggest areas for research and development in the future.

DEFINITION OF SKILL

Skills are learned abilities to perform competently and they are inferred from the characteristics of a performance or the qualities of a product. A skill is directly observable, but the characteristics and qualities of a skill are often inferred from the observation of a performance or a product. A product is a tangible result that you can touch, see, smell, taste and/or hear. A performance is a sequence or set of actions that students carry out that must be observed *in progress* because the behavior itself is the focus of interest.

The list below helps to define this interpretation of a skill by giving examples of statements of instructional intent.

1. **Statement:** *Solve the algebra problems on page 31, involving two unknowns.*
   Type: Knowledge. The student must solve problems displaying knowledge about the algebra involved. It is a paper-and-pencil completion exercise that reflects knowledge.
2. **Statement:** *Predict the chances of getting a "7" on a set of dice.*
   Type: Knowledge. Although the student speaks or writes the answer, this behavior involves knowing and applying the rules of probability to a situation. It is also a completion exercise.
3. **Statement:** *Complete all exercises on the par course quickly, resulting in a par score of 35 or more.*
   Type: Skill performance. It is the judgment of how *well* the behavior is done and the final score—which measures speed and quantity of exercise—that are of interest.
4. **Statement:** *An audience of ten or more people do an oral reading of a poem using pace, clarity and expressiveness that is judged to be of acceptable quality.*
   Type: Skill performance. The focus is on the qualities that must be rated by trained judges during the actual performance.
5. **Statement:** *Assemble a working model of a steam engine. Success is determined by whether or not the model produces visible steam.*
   Type: Skill product. The emphasis is on whether or not the engine—the product—works. No standards of procedure, assembly, or quality of appearance are stated.

In many instances, it may be difficult to identify knowledge and skills until the statement of instructional intent is improved. Forging ahead and trying to select an appropriate measuring technique without a clear statement of instructional intent is similar to attempting to go south by heading east. If the learning objective effectively communicates the intent of instruction, the type of measure required should become clear.

METHODS TO MEASURE SKILL

First, the methods for measuring skill will be described and suggestions for selecting each method will be provided. Then, each technique will be described in greater detail.

The Rating Scale

The rating scale is used when the aspect of performance or the quality of a product varies from low to high, best to worst, good to bad, or on some other implicit continuum (see Figure 5.1). When any aspects or qualities are somewhat abstract and it is thought that they may vary in degrees, the rating scale is

Low   Medium   High

Figure 5.1 A continuum representing an aspect of performance or quality of a product.

probably the method to use. As we will see, rating scales have advantages and disadvantages. By and large, rating scales are very useful in measuring many important types of outcomes of instruction and training.

Some examples of statements of instructional intent that suggest the use of rating scales follow:

1. The student will compose an original piece of music demonstrating counterpoint.
2. Given appropriate materials with which to work, the student will construct a cabinet. The complete cabinet will be evaluated in terms of (*a*) overall workmanship, (*b*) adequacy of finish, and (*c*) detail work.
3. The mechanic will clean all pistons in an internal combustion engine and perform a ring job. Both must pass a quality inspection based on the following characteristics: (*a*) cleanliness, (*b*) thoroughness, and (*c*) workability.

It is important to note that all three examples require judgment by an observer in terms of degrees, necessitating a rating scale.

Observation

Observation is employed when the performance or product to be measured is binary, that is, present or absent. Observation applies particularly to physical skills. With observation, nothing abstract is implied. We are dealing with tangible and directly observable events.

Following are some examples of direct observation as it applies to the measurement of products or performances:

1. The student can carry a 50-pound pack for 1 mile without any support or aid.
2. The student will construct a working exylizer.
3. In a 25-meter pool, the student will swim 50 meters in less than 3 minutes.
4. The student will activate, charge, and install a new car battery.

Checklists

This form of measurement of skills is most like observation, because a checklist is used in a situation where a number of correlated observations must be made. A good example of a checklist is brewing a pot of coffee, as given by Mager (1973):

√ 1. Disconnects coffee pot
√ 2. Disassembles coffee pot
√ 3. Cleans components and pot
√ 4. Inspects components
√ 5. Fills pot with water
√ 6. Reassembles components
√ 7. Fills basket with coffee
___ 8. Reconnects coffee pot
√ 9. Sets dial on coffee pot
√ 10. Reports pot is perking properly [p. 11].

The student, in this example, failed to reconnect the coffee pot (No. 8). Thus, coffee was never made, despite the fact that 90% of all desired behaviors were achieved. The point to be made is that observations are useful for a summative question. For example, Did the student produce drinkable coffee? No. However, the checklist is more valuable in process-oriented instruction, so we can employ checklists to measure a skill as well as diagnose learning problems. In this example, we must remind the student to connect the coffee pot.

Summary

Up to this point, we have reviewed definitions of knowledge and skills and strengthened our understanding of the techniques used to measure skills, whether they be the aspects of performance or the qualities of products. The next step in the process is to select the appropriate measuring technique. Will it be a rating scale, an observation, or a checklist?

Constructing and Using Rating Scales Properly

To develop appropriate and useful criterion-referenced (CR) tests requires that one maintain a close relationship between instructional intent and testing—that one make teaching and testing virtually synonymous. If one's intent is to teach people to perform with certain qualities that are somewhat abstract, then a rating scale may be desirable. For example, if the quality to be learned is balance, form, or creativity in completing a task, a rating scale would be recommended, whereas if one is only interested in completion of a task, observation is more appropriate. If the intent is to teach people to create products that possess certain abstract qualities, rating scales are also indicated.

This section is devoted to building a better understanding of the construction and use of rating scales. When the decision about what measuring technique to use leads you to a rating scale, the next step is to build a rating scale and insure its proper use. This section provides advice, guidelines, and examples with respect to the use of rating scales in measuring aspects of performance and qualities of products. A more extensive treatment of this topic can be found in TenBrink's excellent book (TenBrink, 1974). Also, Cronbach (1970, pp. 571–607) provides many important concepts and references. For information on job-skill assessment, a text such as Dunnette (1966) may provide a starting point for further study.

The advantages of a rating scale are as follows:

1. It is simple to construct and use.
2. It is easy to interpret.
3. It can be adapted to statistical analyses or data summaries.

The disadvantages of a rating scale include the following:

1. It is subject to lack of agreement among those who use it.
2. It is time consuming to administer individually.
3. It usually involves human judgment with respect to abstract ideas, and judgment is subject to lack of agreement among raters.
4. It is subject to biases as well as halo effects.

Each of these disadvantages needs to be discussed because many of them can be overcome. Overall, the rating scale is one of the most useful techniques for measuring skill and should be used whenever appropriate. However, there are a good many pitfalls to avoid along the way. The following discussion will suggest techniques for avoiding the pitfalls and disadvantages.

FOUR PROBLEMS IN USING RATING SCALES

Lack of Agreement among Raters

Most of us have observed this kind of problem when viewing such Olympic Games competitions as gymnastics, ice skating, and diving, where rating scales and rater judgment are important. Experts often disagree about the superlativeness of performances. This lack of agreement among raters contributes to a form of measurement error and hence reduces the reliability of the measurement involved. The error occurs in ratings among judges (*interrater* agreement), but more often there is a lack of consistency in a single rater viewing the same objects. This intrarater inconsistency is especially perplexing.

One of the most effective ways to overcome this problem is to define the instructional intent clearly. If the skill to be rated is well defined, raters will converge in their judgments and ratings will be reliable. Another preventive action is to train raters before they engage in rating. If the ratings are important, then sufficient time should be allocated to train raters and insure that there is agreement about what they are rating. If we have two objects to be rated, one inherently high and the other low on the scale, all raters should agree, and ratings

Table 5.1
Examples of Good and Poor Interrater Agreement

Good interrater agreement	Objects being rated[a]	
	Object 1	Object 2
Rater 1	5	2
Rater 2	4	2
Rater 3	5	1
Rater 4	4	1
Poor Interrater Agreement		
Rater 1	5	3
Rater 2	4	2
Rater 3	2	4
Rater 4	5	1

[a] On a rating scale of 1 to 5, 1 = superior, 2 = above average, 3 = average, 4 = below average, and 5 = inferior.

should be consistent from rater to rater. Table 5.1 provides a good example of this. If there is a lack of agreement, the training session should either focus on problem raters or go back over the entire process of rating. Often the problem is one of definition. Clarity of purpose (instructional intent) is again the key.

A second cause of lack of agreement may be that raters have not been given a sufficient amount of time to learn criteria or to develop their skills at rating. Although such training sessions are costly, they are invaluable in eliminating many of the problems of interrater inconsistency.

A third cause might be a lack of sufficient time for the raters to observe the performance or product. If the time to examine the performance or product is too brief, then we might reasonably expect a poor distribution of ratings.

Inefficiency

As we will see, putting together rating scales is a simple matter. What is difficult is to administer the scale. If you have 25 performances or products to observe, you must spend sufficient time with each one to achieve a good rating. Thus, the use of rating scales, as well as of observation and checklists, requires time. Many will argue, however, that the rating of performances or products is quite important and well worth this investment. Too often, we take shortcuts and use the convenient written test of knowledge as a substitute for skill measurements. Too often the substitute is a poor one because the student may be able to write a description of performance without being able to perform competently, and we miss the point of the CR test—to measure precisely what we teach.

Judging Abstract Variables

As we have noted earlier, rating scales typically involve abstract variables. A scale is created and labeled with an abstraction, for example, originality, beauty, durability, quality, emphasis, tone, or texture. These terms may vary in meaning to many raters. The problem again is one of definition. Any time we deal with an abstraction, it is the responsibility of the instructor or designer of instruction to clarify the instructional intent—the variable to be rated. Following is an example that illustrates the distinction between clearly stated traits and those that are less than clear.

Bad Example:
Rate the originality expressed in the following photographs.
Good Example:
Originality is defined as (1) use of a wide range of tones, (2) asymmetrical composition, and (3) realism. Each will be explained in detail....

An excellent example of methods for clearly stating traits for performance ratings is the work of Fogli, Hulin, and Blood (1971). They used a structured interview questionnaire of on-the-job personnel as a means of collecting descriptors to anchor points along rating scales. The interview elicited descriptions of critical incidents in job performance (Flanagan, 1954). This method allows those people who will actually do the rating to use their own words and standards in the definitions of excellent and poor performance. Using this method, Fogli, Hulin, and Blood (1971, p. 5) obtained reliabilities of .97 to .99 for seven different rating scales.

Bias in Rating

When raters are inconsistent, we have a problem of reliability. When one rater commits errors in a particular direction, we have a validity problem. We know from studies and our own experiences that raters fall into certain traps that are natural and almost unavoidable. For example, there is a tendency to be lenient, to give ratings that are too high. Once in a while a rater will be too strict and will differ considerably from other raters in his or her ratings. Each of five common types of bias will be discussed next and ways of correcting for bias will be suggested.

Lack of interest If a rater is not motivated or fully involved in the process of rating an aspect of performance or a quality of a product, that rater is likely to perform inconsistently. It is more important to ask who the rater is and why that person is rating than to ask if that person is qualified to rate. Training raters will help you assess their quality. But if a person simply is not committed to excellence in performing the ratings, then the results will have questionable value. One must either relieve the person of the responsibility or provide some incentives for good work.

Personal bias Personal bias is the extent to which a single rater will overrate or underrate consistently. That is to say, a single rater may assign higher rating for one type of performance than for other comparable types. This is most manifest in Olympic Games competitions where raters from Country A will give high ratings to their performers and low ratings to all others. This is a very unfortunate kind of bias, which not only produces errors of measurement but makes the entire rating process questionable.

One can, of course, dismiss such raters, or one can retrain raters in whom one has detected biases. A third solution is as follows: We can obtain a series of ratings, perhaps five or more, and not count the highest and lowest ratings. For example, if a performance were given the five ratings of

$$\cancel{1} \quad 3 \quad 4 \quad 4 \quad \cancel{5}$$

we would cancel scores 1 and 5, producing an average rating of 3.67. Including the two extreme ratings, the average would be 3.4. As you can see, one or two extremely biased raters can seriously change the ratings. If there are even more biased raters, the entire process of rating becomes invalid.

Generosity–toughness Two extremes in ratings are the tendency to rate everyone very generously or very strictly. Often raters work without the cover of anonymity. The persons rated know the raters' names, and there is a tendency on the part of the raters to overrate the performance or the product. Whether the rater is known or not, generosity is a major problem in rating. If the ratings given have consequences for a student's progress and the rater is personally or emotionally involved in the instructional program, the problem is even greater.

Generosity or stringency can be overcome by an adequate training program where performances or products of both high and low quality are viewed as part of the training. Raters who are well trained and motivated can overcome this generosity. Stringent raters may respond to feedback showing their tendency; if they are entrenched in their methods, their replacement may be the only alternative.

The halo effect Halo differs from generosity yet the two are similar as well. The *halo effect* refers to the tendency to give either (*a*) a high rating based on the reputation of the student who is performing or who has created a product or (*b*) high ratings for all traits being rated when actually only one was critically analyzed. The weakness here is natural for many persons and difficult to avoid. A student who is well known or has a pleasing personality will receive higher ratings than other students, regardless of their skill demonstration. If a student performs well in one area, there is a tendency to believe that the student will perform well in other areas.

Again, the training program should discuss this form of rating problem and, by alerting raters to the halo effect, reduce the possibility of future problems.

Central tendency On occasion, raters who are overly conservative will tend to choose options that fall in the middle of the scale, regardless of how widely distributed the persons being rated really are. The *error of central tendency* can be combatted by either (*a*) using a 4-point scale with no neutral option or (*b*) changing extreme options so that they will be more frequently chosen by raters.

Summarizing our discussions, it should be pointed out that we have offered a relatively brief treatment of rating scale development. This chapter is not intended to give you a comprehensive treatment of the subject, replete with statistical methods for diagnosing rating problems or evaluating interrater reliability. The reader who wishes to follow this topic more fully and comprehensively should turn to such books as TenBrink (1974), Cronbach (1970), and Mehrens and Lehmann (1973). Also, empirical studies such as those of Thomson (1970), who applied multitrait–multimethod validity analysis to managerial ratings, provide additional techniques.

FOUR STEPS IN CONSTRUCTING A RATING SCALE

Define What Is To Be Rated

It is essential to define the aspects of performance or the quality of the product to be rated. As we have emphasized throughout this book, instructional intent is the key to appropriate CR test construction, use, and interpretation. Without adequate definition, the rating scales we use will not be useful. Spurious ratings have significant consequences for individuals in educational and training programs. Misclassifying students on the basis of ratings can dismiss persons from programs or force them to repeat instruction. Therefore, we cannot over-emphasize this point about clarity of definition of instructional intent in minimizing errors in the classification of students.

Create a Scale

A scale for each aspect or quality must be created. For example, if creativity has four qualities, we want a single rating scale for each quality.

There are generally three types of ratings scales one can employ: (*a*) simple numerical, (*b*) simple graphic, and (*c*) descriptive. Table 5.2 provides examples of these three types. The three form a good range of options for the user of rating scales; however, each is uniquely advantageous for certain situations.

Table 5.2
Examples of Three Types of Rating Scales

Simple numerical
Use the following scale to rate the qualities listed:
  1 = very good 2 = good 3 = fair 4 = poor 5 = very poor

  ———size   ———coordination
  ———speed   ———motivation

Simple graphic
Rate the trainee with respect to the following traits:
  Ability to repair defective units

  ☐   ☐   ☐   ☐   ☐
  very   above   average below   very
  high   average   average low

  In terms of on-the-job performance, how did the student do?
    ☐ very well   ☐ well   ☐ as well as most   ☐ poorly   ☐ very poorly

  To what extent does the finished work show good attention to details?
    ☐ never   ☐ seldom   ☐ sometimes   ☐ often   ☐ quite frequently

  This student performs routine office tasks quite well.
    ☐   ☐   ☐   ☐   ☐
  strongly   agree   neither agree   disagree   strongly
  agree   nor disagree   disagree

Descriptive

Meets all criteria for a trainee	Meets some of the criteria of a trainee	Meets none of these criteria
☐	☐	☐
Excellent performance on the course	An average performance	Performance was poor as compared with established standards
☐	☐	☐

The simple numerical scale is very efficient and probably the most popular type of rating scale. Numbers are used to represent degrees, and the rater merely assigns a number to each object or performance being observed in terms of the quality or aspects of interest. If the trait is well understood, then this numerical system serves quite well. If, however, the trait being observed is not well understood, the raters are likely to disagree, and errors of measurement are introduced.

An improvement over the numerical scale is the simple graphic scale. For each item, the rater is confronted with three to seven terms representing degrees on the rating scale. This model provides a little more information and allows the rater less chance for deviation from other raters. One danger is that if the options on the rating scale are too extreme (e.g., "always," "never") they are unlikely to be chosen and restrict the effective range of the scale. The simple graphic scale is viewed as a slight improvement over the simple numerical scale in terms of descriptiveness, but it is also slightly less efficient because it requires more time for writing the answer options and more space on the pages on a questionnaire.

The descriptive scale describes the points on the rating scale more fully and is useful to those who are not trained to rate or who need more information about what is being rated. It takes more time to develop a descriptive scale, but users of such a scale can derive more meaning from its options.

It is reasonable to assume that most raters will be able to use a 5-point scale, making as many as 5 discriminations. A 7- or 10-point scale is a little too broad for making that many discriminations, whereas a 3-point scale is too narrow.

Arrange Scales Clearly

Scales should be arranged on a form to be clear and readable. Scales can be arranged in a number of ways, as shown in Table 5.2. Fundamentally, any scale will assume one of two forms:

Positive to negative:

| very good | good | fair | poor | very poor |

or

Negative to positive:

| very weak | weak | average | strong | very strong |

Some test developers prefer a neutral mid-point, others do not. There is no hard and fast rule about either position; it is essentially a matter of personal preference. Generally speaking, the more options on a scale the better, up to a limit of seven.

Write Directions

Persons using rating scales must have a clear notion of how to use the rating-scale forms. Any source of confusion will eventually enter into the rating process and create problems that result in measurement errors of bias.

Following are examples of directions to the rater:

1. All exhibits to be judged must be rated with respect to four criteria. Each criterion is described below, and examples are given of how each applies to every option of the rating scale. Complete one of these forms for each criterion.
2. Circle the number corresponding to the phrase that most accurately describes the quality being rated. At the bottom of the page, add your ratings to obtain a total. Write this total in the box at the lower left.

Directions such as these make the rating process clearer and more under-standable. Directions are often thought to comprise a trivial aspect of construct-ing rating scales, but if they are overlooked they may contribute to confusion when the rating scales are used.

Measuring Skills through Observation

When the statement of instructional intent suggests to us that an aspect of a performance or a quality of a skill to be measured can be directly observed, we need to employ appropriate *observation* techniques. Observation takes one of two forms. The first involves simply noting the presence or absence of an aspect or quality. The second involves noting the degree to which that aspect or quality exists. Observation is performed either by a trained observer or through a record-ing device. The rating scale is used when the aspect or quality being measured exists in degrees but must be inferred, because that aspect or quality is essentially abstract. Observation is used when something is directly observable and requires no inference.

DEFINITIONS

The first step in designing an observation measure for a skill is to make sure that the instructional intent, or learning objective, specifies clearly the type of behavior expected. Lack of content validity or reliability in an observation can be traced back to lack of clarity in the intent of instruction or the learning objectives.

Whether we are viewing a performance or a product, two forms of observa-tion are always possible, as shown in Table 5.3. In each of the examples in Table 5.3, it is assumed that all aspects and qualities are tangible and thus directly observable rather than abstract and thus requiring inferences. In each example, the procedure that created the product or motivated the performance can vary, but the procedure for observation is often simple, direct, and error-free. As you can imagine, there are relatively few situations in which performances and products can be observed without some concern for their quality. Therefore, this particular category of skill measurement has a limited but nonetheless important applica-tion.

DEVELOPMENT OF OBSERVATION MEASURES

Hand-Written Records

The most basic direct observation measures are those in which a human observer makes a record of the presence or absence of a performance or product

Table 5.3
Examples of Situations for Which Direct Observation Is Appropriate

	Aspect of a performance	Quality of a product
Indicating presence or absence	1. Completion of a 25-mile bicycle tour	1. Building a food dryer
	2. Completing a report on Monday	2. Supplying photo-graphs for an exhibit
Indicating degrees	1. Rate of travel during a 25-mile bicycle tour	1. Cost of building a food dryer
	2. Time it takes to complete a report	2. Number of photo-graphs supplied for an exhibit

on a hand-written document. The best written documents of this kind require only that the observer make a check mark to indicate the presence or completion of a task or product. A group of observations resembles a checklist. The document, of course, will have undergone systematic development, including field tests, so that the performance or product to be observed is well defined. The document must be closely aligned with the instructional intent or learning objective of the training program.

Rather than use a prepared document, the observer may be required to produce a hand-written narrative describing the performance or product. The obvious drawback here is that the observer's judgment and subjective reporting of the events may be affected by personal bias or may be misinterpreted by readers of the resulting report. To prevent these biases, a very specific scoring document should be produced prior to the test. Table 5.4 provides examples of items on such a document.

Given a well-defined record or scoring of the observation, the method of observation may vary: (*a*) The observer may be present and visible to the student; (*b*) The observer may be present but unseen by the student; (*c*) The observer may be absent but able to indirectly infer that the product has been produced. Indirect observation would seem possible only in the case of enduring products that can thus be inspected at any time. Direct observation of a performance would require that the action be observed "live," unless it were recorded on a video tape, time-lapse photograph, audio tape, or other recording device.

Table 5.4
Examples of Guides for Scoring by Observation: First-Aid Training

For Measuring the Presence or Absence of a Performance

Yes	No		
☐	☐	Performance:	Begin mouth-to-mouth artificial respiration in a simulated test.
		Criterion:	Begun within 2 min of collapse of victim (actor) in simulation test.

For Measuring the Degree or Rate of a Performance

Yes	No		
☐	☐	Performance:	Gives mouth-to-mouth artificial respiration to child or adult in simulated test.
		Criterion:	Rate is, at least, once every 5 sec (12 times per min) for adult or, at least, once every 3 sec (20–25 times per min) for child.

Inappropriate Narrative Record
ITEM: Describe the student's use of artificial respiration in a simulated test.

Recording System

The second major method of observing a performance or product is by the use of mechanical or electronic recording devices. Such devices make it possible to assess an aspect of performance or a quality of a product with great precision and objectivity. One of the oldest devices is the employee's time clock, which measures the time of attendance on the job. The time clock is a good example of a method that does not require a human observer (unless it is to check the reliability of the device). We have much excellent equipment for assessing psychomotor skills. for example, measures of reaction time, speed, or strength and error counters. A great many technical skills can be assessed with simulators. Examples of complex recording equipment are such things as aircraft simulators and computer-aided testing. For example, Isley and Caro (1970) used 16-mm films of instrument panel readings to evaluate flight performance in helicopters.

Behavior Observation

There are basically two kinds of behavior-observation systems (Medley & Mitzel, 1963, pp. 298–299). The *category system,* is used when several different types of behavior or actions are being observed. The *sign system* of observation is used to determine whether the behavior is present ($+$) or absent ($-$) in a given time frame. Category systems are essentially checklists; therefore, they will be discussed in the next section.

Sign systems of behavioral observation are used to assess either the presence or absence of a behavior or its frequency of occurrence within a given time. Frequency of a behavior may be important in such situations as the assessment of a signalman's response capabilities. It may be important to know how consistently he or she can respond rapidly to warning messages. The criterion for the presence or absence of behavior may be that personnel must respond within 10 seconds of a warning message appearing on a teletype machine. A systematic time sample of observations could be collected to note the consistency of this behavior.

PASSIVE VERSUS ACTIVE OBSERVATION SYSTEMS

Observations can be made of either naturally occurring behavior or of simulated behavior, in which the occurrence of the behavior has been specifically prompted. In both cases, behavior must be observed passively without disrupting the ongoing action.

An example of very passive observation systems would be those in which a direct observer is hidden or in which equipment is used to measure a naturally occurring event. Examples would be the concealed observation of safety practices in a weapons storage facility, the unannounced inspection of Telex messages, or the request for a printout of a computer file in order to check for the presence of an update.

Active observation methods might include the development of simulations. Examples include simulations of strategic defense movements in a war game and observations of performance in first-aid treatment simulations. Another example would be the use of a computer display, after a trainee had completed an exercise, in order to detect presence or absence of appropriate settings of switches on computer-controlled equipment. Frederiksen (1965) describes several evaluation methods for eliciting "lifelike behaviors." An example is the week-long simulation-game for school administrators who receive messages concerning situations and emergencies in a hypothetical school and must respond with memoranda describing their advice and reactions.

Evaluating Skills through the Use of Checklists

Checklists will be the method of choice when a set or sequence of observable behaviors in a performance or a product must be examined. A checklist is literally a list of behaviors that can be checked by an observer. It can be a simple list of a few sequential and related elements or a complex observational system involving precise behavioral definitions for each element. The most important idea introduced in this section is that checklists should be empirically derived from a job analysis, a task analysis, and/or field testing with actual students.

CHARACTERISTICS OF CHECKLISTS

Checklists are useful because they allow for a clear-cut determination of whether or not the student has performed various steps in a performance or has included essential elements in a product. Further, the checklist may be used to identify deficient steps or elements, and it is simple to use. Its primary disadvantage is that because it does not apply to a great many learning objectives its usefulness is limited. Another disadvantage is that it applies only to observable events whereas rating scales allow for the measurement, and by inference, of abstract qualities like completeness, fineness, goodness, clarity.

We present here a checklist for an instructor who is determining whether a CR test is being properly developed for a course.

In evaluating your classroom achievement test, please check (√) any of the following that can be answered yes.

_____ 1. Was the instructional intent specified?
_____ 2. Were domain specifications or objectives used?
_____ 3. Was item development systematic?
_____ 4. Did a logical item review occur?
_____ 5. Did an empirical item review occur?
_____ 6. Were items found to be representative of all aspects of the domain?
_____ 7. Were items from the universe drawn with a stratified, random-sampling plan?

DESIGN OF CHECKLISTS FOR MEASURING
ASPECTS OF PERFORMANCE

Suppose your objective is to teach a student to execute some sequential performance like the triple-jump in track and field, to conduct a survey interview, or to play a musical instrument. Here are some steps recommended for generating a performance checklist (Geis, 1970):

1. List in sequence the steps a skilled expert completes when executing the performance. You might do this from recall, but a better way would be to conduct a study while observing one or more skilled performers.
2. Refine your checklist by observing several skilled experts perform the behavior.
3. Have a skilled expert go through a performance while using the checklist. Have that person think ''out loud'' to discover whether additional steps must be added to the checklist and whether others may be unnecessary or irrelevant. Stop at that point, discuss such steps and, if

you agree, add or delete them. If the wording of some checklist items is not clear, revise it.

4. Have a trainee go through the performance step by step. Revise the checklist as you proceed, based on whether or not the trainee can understand the steps and directions. He or she will be unable to perform some items in the checklist without teaching. You might have available a manual that describes in detail how to carry out a particular step.

5. Give the checklist to a third party and ask him or her to use it to check the performance of the skilled expert. Ask this third party to judge (*a*) when a step is completed and (*b*) whether it is completed correctly. Emphasize that the checklist, not the performer, is on trial. This whole process should help to identify unclear words and phrases in the checklist. Make notes to yourself during these observations if you need to edit it more extensively at a later time.

Some examples of performance checklists would be the evaluation of a building inspector who identifies each of the on-site visits and each item of the building code as correctly or incorrectly inspected. Another would be the evaluation of a pilot's preflight inspection of an airplane. A final example would be an evaluation of a student's sequence of actions in a laboratory experiment.

DESIGN OF CHECKLISTS FOR MEASURING QUALITIES OF PRODUCTS

Although some tasks can best be evaluated by performance checklists, many others involve tangible products. Examples of products that can be evaluated by checklists of qualities or characteristics include (*a*) a good instructional program, (*b*) an effective filing system, (*c*) a good political campaign, (*d*) a safe and efficient high-altitude snow camp, (*e*) a complete weather report, and (*f*) a well-documented computer program. Here are some steps recommended for generating a product-oriented checklist (Geis, 1970):

Step 1. Collect as many examples as you can of *good* and *bad* instances. For example:
  • The top 5 (best) essay answers on your examination and the bottom 5 (worst).
  • A set of carpentry projects you judge "good, imaginative, skillful, etc." and a set you judge to be "very poor."
  • Some tape-recordings of good and bad debates.
  Then, separate your collection into two sets.
Step 2. Go through all of the good examples, noting qualities that the good examples have in common.
Step 3. Put the common qualities of the best students' work on your checklist.

Step 4. Do the same kind of analysis as you did in Step 2, only with the poor examples.

Step 5. Put the common attributes of your worst students' work on your checklist in negative form (e.g., "There will be no spelling errors.").

Step 6. Eliminate the entries you made in Step 4 that are simply the converse of a positive statement made in Step 3. For example, if an attribute of your best students' performance is "Spelling is accurate," eliminate "There will be no spelling errors" from the items you added in Step 4.

Step 7. In this step, you submit your checklist to test:

- Ask a student to take your checklist and tell you as many ways as he can think of to "beat" the system—that is, to fulfill all of the positive requirements on your list and still produce a poor, or outlandish, assignment;

  and/or

- Ask a colleague to do the same thing.

  For Step 7 use the following instructions (or some close approximation): "Here is an assignment that I will be giving to my trainees [insert directions for the assignment]. I have decided that I will give *any* student an A, *no matter what else is done,* so long as he or she follows the directions and meets the criteria listed [insert attribute checklist]. Tell me all the ways that you can think of to get an A by doing work that we would otherwise call 'poor' or 'absurd.' Try to beat the system. For example: Take the statements in the attribute checklist literally; do anything that is not specifically prohibited."

These seven steps should help make your checklist and items observable and relevant. The last criterion, agreement among observers, can be checked as follows:

Step 8. Ask a student or colleague to take the most recent revision of the checklist and go through the batch of examples you used to generate the list (in Step 1, above). Do not let this person see your original sort. (You can keep track of your sort by numbering or coding the products before mixing them up.) The two sorts should be in agreement. If they are not, more revision is needed.

Field-Testing Considerations for Observations and Checklists

Fortunately, observations and checklists deal with simpler behaviors that can be reliably seen by raters of who may vary in their rating ability. Because behaviors are either present or absent, it is quite simple to detect deviant obser-

Table 5.5
Percentage of Students Performing Behaviors That Are Judged
To Be the Intent of Instruction

Aspects of performance observed	Students performing as intended	
	Pretest (%)	Posttest (%)
1	20	20
2	30	80
3	80	85
4	70	50

vers who do not agree with other observers. The very same distribution of responses holds true for observations and checklists as applies to knowledge items and rating scales—most students will not perform well prior to instruction and most will do well after instruction.

For example, Table 5.5 shows student performance as recorded in four observations done with pretests before instruction and posttests after instruction. Observation 1 shows no growth; Observation 2 shows more satisfactory change. Observation 3 indicates the presence of the behavior on both occasions, suggesting that instruction was probably unnecessary for most students. Observation 4 shows an unusual decline in a skill from pretest to posttest. In any instance where the results are less than desirable (e.g., Observations 1, 3 and 4), we have to question whether (*a*) instruction was ineffective or (*b*) the observation was faulty in some way.

Some additional considerations that should be made in the development of observations and checklists are (*a*) field testing with *masters* and *nonmasters*, to insure adequate sampling of component skills; (*b*) studying the effects of time sampling and sampling across conditions; and (*c*) examining the effects of human observers. The foregoing are common concerns among military and industrial evaluators (e.g., Wilson, 1965, p. 354).

MASTERS VERSUS NONMASTERS

If observations or checklists are based on rigorous job analyses or task analyses, they should discriminate between *masters*, individuals who can truly perform a job or task, and *nonmasters*, individuals who have no experience or skill. This requirement suggests the usefulness of field tests in which masters and nonmasters are observed while performing the skill. Some direct observations may be so obvious that no formal test of their accuracy is required, but if there is any doubt, a tryout should substantiate the accuracy of the observation instrument. For example, a skill such as vertically climbing a 20-foot rope, hand-over-hand, can be directly observed without a study of the validity of the observation. However, a complex skill, such as the monitoring functions of an air traffic controller, may require a job analysis and field testing to establish the accuracy of using a particular checklist as a valid assessment of the skill. Comparing a group of experienced traffic controllers with a group of trainees would constitute an excellent validation study for a checklist.

The study of masters versus nonmasters parallels the use of pretest and posttest data, as described earlier in reference to Table 5.5. The pretest item difficulty is equivalent to the proportion of nonmasters that successfully complete a task, and the posttest difficulty would apply to masters. Thus, the most accurate indicator of skilled performance would show that all masters can do the behavior, whereas none of the nonmasters can.

TIME SAMPLING

The appropriateness of an observation or checklist may be affected by the conditions under which the behavior is occurring. For example, observations made during sports practice and actual games situations may vary; actual public speaking may involve more anxiety than rehearsal. If any of these conditions are suspected to influence an observation, field testing should attempt to evaluate the observation's appropriateness under a sampling of times and conditions.

Field testing under a variety of times or conditions can lead to revision of the observation system or checklist. The best times for observations can be established by noting the times at which the behavior shows the greatest variation. Directions to the observer may be revised to reduce variations across time or conditions.

OBSERVER EFFECTS

The issue of agreement among different observers should not be as serious in the use of direct observation or checklists as it is in the use of rating scales. However, if a checklist is lengthy, requires fine discriminations, or involves close observation of rapidly occurring events, a field test with a team of observers can provide a check on the clarity and wording of checklist items.

Although a discussion of the statistical methods for verifying the effects of observers or conditions on observation systems is well beyond the scope of this book, one approach is recommended. The most complete information on behavioral observation methods can be obtained by analysis of variance procedures, such as those described by Cronbach, Gleser, Nanda, and Rajaratnam (1972). Analysis of variance methods provide more information than is given by a single index of observer agreement (Medley & Mitzel, 1963, p. 310). By using a sample of observers, times, conditions, and items as factors in an analysis of variance design, it is possible to compute several indexes of dependability. These indexes summarize the reliability of observations across observers, times, conditions, items, or other factors of interest. Also, interactions between factors, such as the interaction between observers and conditions, can be examined. Statistical consultation should be requested for the application of this method to complex observation systems.

Summary

The rating scale has been defined and illustrated, and examples have been provided for three different types of rating scales: numerical, graphic, and descriptive. Four steps in the creation of rating scales were listed and discussed. The overarching concern in the design of rating scales has been the clarification of instructional intent. It has been asserted that when intent is clear, the potential for properly using a rating scale in a CR test is increased.

Although direct observation may be less widely used than rating scales or checklists, it forms an essential part of the measurement of skills. Observations can be very accurate, because the observer is noting only the presence or absence of a performance aspect or a product quality. Reliability will be high unless observers must identify a behavior in a rapid series of events. The reliability of observing a product may be higher than that of observing a performance, because a tangible product can usually be examined for a longer period of time. Direct observations are highly efficient in construction and require only a clear and specific description of the precise behavior or product to be observed. Direct observations are individually administered and may involve complex arrangements or costs if expensive equipment or complex conditions must be present, as in the computer sciences. Scoring of direct observations is very efficient in that only presence or absence needs to be noted by a plus or minus, check mark, or other symbolic notation.

Direct observations vary as to whether they (*a*) are passive examinations of naturally occurring behaviors or products or (*b*) involve active intervention that prompts a behavior or product. Time-lapse photography, audiotapes or videotapes, counters, timers, error-detecting devices, and other recording systems are examples of excellent direct observation tools.

Checklists have a wider application than simple, direct observation, and they can be highly accurate and precise. Their only real limitation is that they may require extensive work in initial development and validation. However, development of an accurate checklist for a task will serve over and over again to provide an objective means of assessing performances or products that will

Table 5.6
Types of Testing Formats for the Cognitive Domain[a]

	Cognitive	
Domain[a]	Knowledge	Skills
Aspects	Recall comprehension higher level thinking	Performances products
Nature of trait	Inferred in a paper-and-pencil instrument	Inferred or directly observed
Testing formats	Selected response Multiple choice True–false Matching Constructed response Completion Short-answer essay Extended-answer essay	Observation rating scales Numerical Graphic Descriptive Checklists

[a] Scoring methods: Knowledge-testing formats—Score selected-response test by number of correct answers; score constructed-response tests by means of a rating scale or checklist. Skills-testing formats—Score performance by (1) observing and recording presence or absence of particular behaviors; (2) assigning observed behaviors positions on a numerical, graphic, or descriptive rating scale; or (3) checking items on a list to record the performance of behaviors in a correct, or prescribed, sequence.

remove some of the subjectivity from more informal systems. Checklists can be domain based if the elements of a good performance are large enough that they form a large universe of items.

Table 5.6 summarizes the uses of observations, rating scales, and checklists as measures of cognitive skills and contrasts them with the types of test formats used to measure knowledge.[1] As a summary of the material presented in Chapter 4 on the measurement of knowledge, Table 5.6 also displays the types of testing formats for selected and constructed response items as well as the recommended scoring methods for each format.

Armed with the practical guidelines and basic concepts discussed in previous chapters, we can now examine the technology of item writing. The next part

[1] Beyond the scope of this book is a discussion of assessing attitude (affective) or psychomotor domains. However, the methods of observation, rating scales, or checklists are clearly the predominant types of measures used in these domains, and, for that reason, some of the material in this chapter is relevant to their assessment.

Table 5.7
Location of Discussion of Item-Writing Technologies and Instructional Material for Which They Are Appropriate

Chapter	Item-writing technology	Relevant instructional material
6	Linguistic-based item-writing algorithms	Prose material
7	Item forms	Quantitative–objective material
8	Mapping-sentence method	A wide range of material
9	Concept learning	Concepts
10	Typology of higher level thinking ⎫	Any instructional material
11	Instructional Quality Inventory ⎭	

of this book presents a description of six major methods of item writing. Each of these methods is described in a separate chapter, beginning with Chapter 6 and ending with Chapter 11. For quick review and reference, Table 5.7 lists the item-writing technologies and relevant instructional material discussed in each of the six chapters that follow.

References

Cronbach, L. J. *Essentials of psychological testing* (3rd ed.). New York: Harper, 1970.

Cronbach, L. J., Gleser, G. C., Nanda, H., & Rajaratnam, N. *The dependability of behavioral measurements*. New York: Wiley, 1972.

Dunnette, M. D. *Personnel selection and placement*. Belmont, California: Wadsworth, 1966.

Flanagan, J. C. The critical incident technique. *Psychological Bulletin*, 1954, *51*, 327–258.

Fogli, L., Hulin, C. L., & Blood, M. R. Development of first-level behavioral job criteria. *Journal of Applied Psychology*, 1971, *55*, 3–8.

Frederiksen, N. Proficiency tests for training evaluation. In R. Glaser (Ed.), *Training research and education*. New York: Wiley, 1965, pp. 323–346.

Geis, G. L. (Ed.). *Designing more effective college instruction* (Book 1). Ann Arbor, Michigan: Center for Research on Learning and Teaching, Univ. of Michigan, 1970.

Hively, W. Introduction to domain-referenced testing. *Educational Technology*, 1974, *14*, 5–10.

Isley, R. M., & Caro, P. W., Jr. Use of time-lapse photography in flight performance evaluation. *Journal of Applied Psychology*, 1970, *54*, 72–76.

Mager, R. F. *Measuring instructional intent or, Got a match?* Belmont, California: Lear Siegler, Inc./Fearon Publishers, 1973.

Medley, D. M., & Mitzel, H. E. Measuring classroom behavior by systematic observation. In N. L. Gage (Ed.), *Handbook of research on teaching*. Chicago: Rand McNally & Company, 1963.

Mehrens, W. A., & Lehmann, I. *Measurement and evaluation in education and psychology*. New York: Holt, 1973.

TenBrink, T. D. *Evaluation: A practical guide for teachers*. New York: McGraw-Hill, 1974.

Thomson, H. Comparison of predictor and criterion judgments of managerial performance using the multitrait–multimethod approach. *Journal of Applied Psychology*, 1970, *54*, 496–502.

Wilson, C. L. On-the-job and operational criteria. In R. Glaser (Ed.), *Training research and education*. New York: Wiley, 1965.

III

ITEM-WRITING TECHNOLOGY:
SIX PROMINENT METHODS

6

Items for Prose Learning

Learning often involves the reading of textbooks and other prose material by students. For this reason, tests of comprehension require a logical connection between test items and prose material. Bormuth (1970) has suggested that the most rigorous connection will exist where items are created as transformations of segments of prose. This includes the transformation of sentences or groups of interrelated sentences.

Cronbach (1970), in reviewing Bormuth's work, has commented that, "One might conclude, wrongly, that Bormuth is only interested in low level responses.... Bormuth does show how intersentence syntax is used to form questions on paragraphs [p. 510]." In other words, the logic of transforming segments of prose need not necessarily limit one to the most trivial sentence rearrangement. In fact, a wide variety of transformations, from sentence-based to higher level arrangements, will be the topic of this chapter.

Anderson (1972) added a new dimension to the measurement of prose learning by emphasizing the importance of testing at the comprehension level rather than at the level of recall. Specifically, Anderson advocated that any application of Bormuth's methods should employ paraphrase. Paraphrase produces a new sentence for each original sentence so that the two sentences have no substantive words (nouns, verbs, modifiers) in common and yet are equivalent in meaning. The reason for using paraphrase is to ensure that students have truly comprehended the ideas in prose material, that they have not just recalled the wording at a surface level. As Anderson (1972) explains, "in order to answer a question based on a paraphrase, a person has to have comprehended the original sentence, since a paraphrase is related to the original sentence with respect to meaning but unrelated with respect to the shape or the sound of the words [p. 150]."

Of course, paraphrasing is not universally possible (e.g., for proper names), and it can be done well or poorly. Also, the subjectivity of the writer can influence the choice of substituted words. With young readers (e.g., third-graders), care must be taken in substituting paraphrased material that the original reading level of the prose material is not exceeded by substituted words that are unfamiliar or quite different from the vocabulary used in instruction.

Whether we are discussing verbatim transformations of prose or paraphrase, the rationale for generating items from prose remains essentially the same—to operationalize the process of item writing so that tests of comprehension of prose material match the intended instructional goals.

Rationale for Prose Transformations

Bormuth (1970) gives the most complete presentation of the rationale for a technology of item writing for prose learning. For him, operational definitions are the specifications of the rearrangements in wording necessary to create test items from instructional text. A summary of some of Bormuth's (1970, pp. 2–17) ideas follows:

1. In order to justify huge expenditures of public funds for educational programs, heavy demands are being made on specialists responsible for developing tests. The test specialist must provide test items that are operationally defined so that the items can be reproduced in other experiments where researchers can then determine the kinds of student cognitive abilities that underly the responses to those items.

2. One can simply accept the assertion that a test measures what the test developer says it measures. However, more rigorous standards require that the developer describe the set of steps by which an item writer has rearranged segments of instruction to create items of a given type for testing a stated cognitive skill or knowledge.

3. Traditional approaches to item writing appear to confound both the writing of items and their selection for inclusion on a test. Achievement tests should be assembled by conceiving of every possible item of a given type and then choosing a sample to compose a test form. Screening out items that appear too simple and stopping when one has "enough items on a certain topic" are examples of the subjectivity that can enter into test design.

4. The purposes of formative and summative evaluation and research in

instructional theory can be aided by the clarity of item-writing methods that are based on publicly defined operational methods. The underlying theme of Bormuth's theory is that tests should be viewed as measuring devices that form a part of scientific inquiry, not just a collection of convenient questions. Anderson (1972) provides evidence from a survey of the educational research literature that researchers have not adequately indicated how their achievement tests were derived. In 51% of all cases, no information was provided about the relation of test items to instruction. In 67% of the cases, no information was provided about procedures for selecting questions. Anderson concluded that these studies failed to meet a criterion of reproducibility—that is, the reader could not create tests to replicate the experiments.

The most persuasive rationale for the benefits of using transformations of prose for item writing comes from a commonsense, logical analysis of school learning. As nearly everyone who has ever taken a course of instruction knows, the numbers of pages assigned to be read fill volumes. Because of this quantity of written material, a technology of item writing that could be keyed to this prose would achieve two important things. Such a technology would (a) match the content of tests to the content of the courses in very direct ways, and (b) provide a very large number of useful items. For instance, if a mastery learning approach were used in instruction, the difficulty of the test and the difficulty of the instruction could be matched. If the test were much more or less difficult than the instruction, the passing standard on the test must be adjusted to correct for this bias.

One of the criticisms of prose transformation is that it can lead to the generation of trivial items. It is feared that items will be keyed to relatively unimportant ideas or to the verbatim-recall level exclusively. Just as any technology or tool can be used inappropriately, the transformation of prose material into test items can be done in a mindless way; any sentence, no matter how trivial or poorly written, can be transformed into a question. This was clearly not the intention of Bormuth (1970) nor of any of the subsequent investigators such as Roid, Haladyna, Shaughnessy, and Finn (1979). What if the technology could be applied in a sensitive and accurate way to the important ideas in a prose passage? What if subject-matter experts indicated a consensus on important sentences from a passage that held key ideas and these key segments were then transformed? What if paraphrase were used to ensure that a higher level of mental processing was taking place, not just rote memory? All of these steps are possible and when properly applied make the technology attractive and promising rather than something to be dismissed as "just rote learning."

A Review of Relevant Literature

A review of the literature on item writing for prose learning demonstrates four important points: (a) The methodology is feasible; (b) it creates items that have reasonable statistical characteristics, with a control on item-writer bias; (*c*) it creates tests of important content when important segments of prose are chosen and when paraphrase is used; and (*d*) there are currently practical limitations and particular applications best suited for the method.

FEASIBILITY OF THE METHOD

Some of the earliest tests for comprehension of prose material used the cloze (a variation of "close") procedure, the methods of which are reviewed more extensively elsewhere (Culhane, 1970). Cloze tests are designed in a variety of ways, but are basically segments of prose in which words have been removed and the student is asked to fill in the blanks. A typical cloze method is to delete every fifth word from a 100-word segment chosen at random. Other methods delete only substantive words such as nouns and modifiers, not prepositions or conjunctions. These refinements are said to increase the validity of the tests and to retain the ease of construction that marks all cloze methods. Cloze tests have been used extensively and are clearly an example of the feasibility of prose transformations.

Bormuth, Manning, Carr, and Pearson (1970) experimented with four types of questions constructed from paragraphs given to fourth-graders. In one case, verbatim sentences from the prose paragraphs were transformed into items. The *wh*-transformation was used when a word such as *who, what, where,* or *when,* was substituted for a subject in a sentence. For example, the text sentence, *The boy rode the steed* was transformed to, *Who rode the steed?* It was found that 77% of the students answered these items correctly. In a second type of item, the subject and verb in the sentence were transformed. *By whom was the steed ridden?,* was answered by 71% of the students. Two item transformations were subject–object transformations such as, *Who rode the horse?,* and a subject–verb–object transformation such as *By whom was the horse ridden?* These paraphrased items showed percentages correct of 69% and 67%, respectively. This experiment shows the feasibility of item transformation as a research tool, in that effects on item difficulty of variations such as paraphrasing can be detected empirically.

Bormuth's seminal work (1970) was an excellent logical and theoretical analysis that begged for more detail on actual item-writing methods. It was with the continuing work of Finn (1975, 1978) in collaboration with Roid and Haladyna (1979) that the sentence-based methods were substantially refined. Finn's original elaboration of sentence transformations involved an 82-step algorithm (Finn, 1975). This algorithm was subsequently refined to a much simpler procedure (Roid & Finn, 1978; Roid, 1979, pp. 79–83). The most current refinement of these procedures is detailed in a later section of this chapter.

The purpose of these refinements was to make the method feasible for teachers and other test developers who may not have linguistic training. In fact, the study by Roid, Haladyna, and Shaughnessy (1980) involved the training of three teachers who were previously unfamiliar with the method.

STATISTICAL CHARACTERISTICS OF PROSE
TRANSFORMATION ITEMS

The reliability of various types of Cloze tests is well documented and appears high enough to permit their use in numerous reading-comprehension studies. In one study (Finn, 1977), an index called *Cloze difficulty* was found to be useful as a characteristic of words appearing in prose material. The cloze difficulty index reflects the percentage of subjects that will guess a word when it is deleted as a part of a cloze test. Finn found this index highly useful as a predictor of the "information" that a word provides to a reader. A word that is easy to supply in a cloze task contains relatively less information in the sense of providing meaning to a prose passage than a difficult word. A difficult word, when it is included rather than deleted in a cloze test, reduces more uncertainty about the meaning of a passage than does an easy word.

Hively, Patterson, and Page (1968) produced domain-based items and conducted an analysis of variance on item data to show that items generated from a particular transformation were more similar to each other than they were to items from other transformations. In other words, items from a given transformation can demonstrate internal consistency.

In a series of related experiments, Roid and Haladyna and colleagues have demonstrated the item characteristics and control of item-writer differences that occur with the use of prose item transformations. Roid and Finn (1978) and Roid and Haladyna (1978) studied several variations of sentence transformations used to create tests for a science passage given to high school students. Sentences were chosen from the passage by selecting keywords that met criteria of text frequency and relative frequency in American English. A relative-frequency index for American English words was taken from Carroll, Davies, and Richmond (1971). This *standard frequency index* (SFI) measures whether a word is very common or relatively unique. The use of SFI was successful in identifying several very key technical terms that occurred in the passage. (Further discussion of this technique of word identification will be found on pages 101–102.) After words and their sentences were selected, verbatim transformations were used to create test questions. Also, several clerical methods of writing foils for multiple-choice items were used by Roid and Haladyna (1978), and Roid, Haladyna, Shaughnessy, and Finn (1979). These studies concluded that the method of selecting the "question word" (a noun or adjective in the sentence) played a crucial role in determining the pattern of pretest and posttest item difficulties of the resulting items. The use of nouns that occur frequently in a passage was shown to create items that are too easy if the sentence in which they first occur is used. "Rare singleton nouns," which are relatively rare in American English but appear only once in a passage, were found to be the most effective question words in the study. An example of a rare singleton noun (actually a noun phrase) in the previous pages of this book would be *cloze difficulty index*. It appears only once and is indeed rare in American English! Rare singletons created items that were relatively free from item-writer differences in difficulty.

In a subsequent study, Roid, Haladyna, Shaughnessy, and Finn (1979) used prose transformations for two stories from a popular wildlife magazine. Four different item writers created items using rules for transforming sentences from stories, that were read by 423 fourth-graders and fifth-graders. The fact that no significant item-writer differences were found in this study suggests that the methods for controlling item-writer differences that normally occur are quite powerful (Roid & Haladyna, 1978). This study also showed that the statistical characteristics of items were affected by several factors: (a) the method of writing foils, (b) the information density (number of sentences judged important by teachers) in the passage, (c) the parts of speech of the question words, and (d) verbatim versus paraphrase transformations.

In another study, Roid, Haladyna, and Shaughnessy (1980) experimentally compared three types of items: (a) items written with informal methods, (b) items written from objectives, and (c) items written by transforming sentences. A science story from a children's magazine was read by 364 elementary school students, who completed pretests and posttests on the unit. The study showed the influence of item-writing methods and foil-construction techniques on the difficulty of items. Informal methods showed wide differences between the six item writers in the study. The most rule-based sentence-transformation method, involving a clerical method of assembling foils, proved to create items that were too easy. The method with the best pattern of pretest and posttest item difficulties was a noun-based sentence transformation in which item writers chose their own wording for foils within certain constraints. The study indicated the importance of field testing and analyzing items to identify possible differences between item writers of CR tests.

CREATION OF TESTS OF IMPORTANT CONTENT

Refinements of the Bormuth method of transforming sentences have emphasized the selection of important sentences from a prose passage. A simple random sample of sentences, although it has the intuitive appeal of creating a true, domain-based, criterion-referenced (CR) test (where all the sentences in a passage represent the universe of possible items), creates some items that are nonsense. Therefore, several methods of sentence selection, as refinements of the Bormuth method, have been tested. Roid and Finn (1978) used word frequency analyses to choose important words and their sentences. And Roid,

Haladyna, and Shaughnessy (1980) used a combination of teachers' ratings of important sentences and the standard frequency indexes (Carroll, Davies, & Richman, 1971) to select sentences. They asked 17 teachers to underline the important sentences in a science story, and their ratings were tabulated to identify key sentences. Then, the standard-frequency index of each of the nouns and adjectives in the chosen sentences were obtained, and those with low indexes (relatively rare words in American English textbooks) were chosen. The logic of this method is that a consensus of teachers should be a reliable index of content importance. Because specific words must then be selected from these sentences in order to transform them into questions, the word frequency analysis provides an objective method of choosing the question words.

As Anderson (1972) has emphasized, paraphrasing is one of the best techniques for ensuring that nontrivial items are created from prose. It would seem that paraphrasing could be combined with methods for selecting important sentences or segments of prose material. For example, a textbook could be reviewed by a team of instructors who would note important segments. Summarizing sentences that would integrate the important principles in the text could be written by the instructors if no single sentences provided good definitions or statements. Or, as suggested by Anderson (1972), a mediating sentence could be written, an example of which is a mediating sentence that gives a general model for the principle of intermittent reinforcement: "In all cases, given an organism w, in environment x, intermittently reinforced with y for response z, when y no longer follows (z of w in x), then w will continue z (in x) at a relatively high rate for a relatively long period of time [p. 156]." The italicized letters in the foregoing sentence represent variable elements that can be inserted to produce an example of the principle. For example, "If a student in a discussion session is intermittently reinforced with a smile from an admired instructor for volunteering personal experiences, when that smile no longer follows, the student will continue to volunteer personal experiences for a relatively long period of time." The point of this example is that it is possible to construct a model sentence that summarizes important prose material and that provides a skeleton item that can be used to create many parallel, but different, test items.

The methods of concept testing and higher level thinking that are discussed in Chapters 9 and 10 can also be adapted, in the opinion of the authors, to prose-transformation technology. To elaborate this claim, however, will require considerable additional research and development.

PRACTICAL LIMITATIONS AND APPROPRIATE USES OF PROSE TRANSFORMATIONS

The state of the art of item transformations for assessing reading comprehension is still relatively primitive. Hence, item transformation is open to the criticism that it does little more than test at the comprehension level. On the other hand, the importance of comprehension in school curricula is sometimes underrated. Certainly, basic terminology and concepts must be understood before higher level thinking is possible in an academic discipline. Therefore, it seems that basic exercises in comprehension will always be needed. An objective method of identifying the important terms and concepts in prose will be appreciated by busy educators.

The most obvious limitation of the method is that it is restricted to prose material. However, when one considers all the instructional content that is or can be presented in prose, the quantity is staggering. The scripts of audiovisual programs or computer-assisted instruction, as well as of lectures or panel discussions that have been recorded and transcribed, are also amenable to this type of item writing.

Another more subtle limitation that becomes apparent only when one is actually transforming segments of prose is that the material must be reasonably well written. Ambiguous or lengthy and involved sentences are difficult to transform. The main ideas, principles, and concepts of the material need to be prominently and concisely explained. If one were to write prose material expressly for item transformations, such material would contain many well-stated, concise sentences that highlighted the important ideas in each segment—in the tradition of the well-written topic sentence.

The challenge for those who are motivated by the precision and logical design of item transformations is to push the frontier of the methods to the edges of the domains of higher level thinking. Referring to items developed from intersentence syntax, Bormuth (1970) has stated, "Colleagues seem to place higher subjective values on the knowledge tested by questions testing the higher nodes in the discourse-tree structure. They often describe these questions as getting at the basic ideas of the instruction or something similar [p. 55]." Commenting on this passage from Bormuth, Cronbach (1970) has remarked that "To unpack this idea is likely to require ten years of investigation, but it will be worthwhile [p. 592]."

Procedures for Transforming Sentences into Test Questions

What follows is a practical guide to one of the prose-transformation methods, based on the research of Roid, Haladyna, Shaughnessy, and Finn (1979).

Textbooks, instructional materials, and the scripts of lectures or audiovisual presentations contain important sentences that explain important ideas to the student. Because the sentence is a basic unit of communication in instruction, a technology of item writing is developing that is based on the transformation of sentences into questions.

A fundamental problem in basing test questions on any prose passage is that all sentences are not instructionally relevant. Most paragraphs contain a topic sentence and one or two sentences that amplify the meaning of the topic sentence. Often, depending on the quality of the prose, there is extraneous, irrelevant, and even meaningless material that contributes little to the instructional intent of the author of the prose or of the instructor who has chosen the prose as a basis for instruction. Our experience with translating prose passages into test questions has shown that randomly selecting questions from a prose passage is a highly questionable practice. The problem with this practice is that often sentences will be selected that will *not* be instructionally relevant, and the resulting test items may be dysfunctional.

Clearly, not every sentence will produce an important question; therefore, selection of key sentences will be crucial in making the method practical. In creating CR tests as defined in Chapter 2, the universe of items comprises all the possible questions that can be transformed from the key sentences, and the domain can be described as "comprehension" or "recall of key ideas" from prose material, for example, comprehension of the basic terminology of energy conservation as applied to residential property.

Most educational and training programs will have, at least as initial or enabling objectives, the learning of terminology or basic facts that are presented in written material. Therefore, the application of sentence transformation techniques should be possible in a wide variety of instructional areas.

There are a number of advantages to using sentences as a source of items:

1. The reading level of the resulting items can be made to match the reading level of the course materials so that tests are fair and matched to the instruction.
2. The actual content of instructional materials can be systematically rather than subjectively sampled.
3. Through the use of paraphrase, a strong test of both reading comprehension and recall can be made.
4. A large number of items can be constructed rather quickly that will be closely matched to the intent of instruction as reflected in course materials.

In summary, the technology of making questions from sentences in instructional materials, when it is properly used to create CR tests, has a number of advantages and applications. There are, of course, practical limitations to the method, and these will be discussed after the method is introduced.

STEP 1: SCREENING FOR INSTRUCTIONALLY RELEVANT KEY SENTENCES

As we have pointed out, unless a conscious attempt has been made by an author to make his or her prose entirely instructionally relevant, most prose contains many useless sentences. There will be directions to the reader such as "Consider the steps in this process," or "Now, examine Figure 3.4." Transforming these sentences into test questions might be fun for us, but very surprising for students. So, the first step in sentence-based question writing is to screen out the instructionally irrelevant, or "contentless" material. If some sections are difficult to judge, use a team of readers and take a consensus judgment of what should be screened out.

STEP 2: SELECTING IMPORTANT SENTENCES

A crucial step in the use of sentence-based methods is to make sure that only the most important ideas in a prose passage are tested. Clearly, this technology of item writing could degenerate into a testing of trivial points—footnotes or other items—which would reinforce memorization of trivial details, a pointless affair. At present, sentence transformation methods provide three basic ways of selecting sentences: (*a*) having subject matter experts choose the sentences, (*b*) having experts write summary sentences keyed to objectives, and (*c*) using a keyword search. Each of these options will be described in turn.

Selection of Sentences by Subject Matter Expert

A subject matter expert can read prose materials and highlight (simply by underlining) the important sentences in relation to the learning objectives of the instructional system. Or another criterion, such as topical sentences of paragraphs, can be used as a guide. In a study by Roid, Haladyna, Shaughnessy, and Finn (1979), 17 teachers marked two science passages known to differ in reading difficulty, and significant differences between the number of sentences underlined in each passage were found. In other words, teachers effectively discriminated between passages that varied in terms of the number of important sentences they contained.

The crucial part of this approach to selecting sentences is that the method of choosing sentences must be operationally defined if a CR test is to result. For example, if one subject matter expert were to underline sentences in an informal way, without criteria, his or her method could not be easily duplicated by another subject matter expert. However, if a group of experts were to underline those sentences, a new person attempting to duplicate the method would probably identify a pattern of underlined sentences that was similar to the group consensus. Also, criteria for selection of sentences can be written and given to each judge. If topic sentences are selected, an even more objective measure can be obtained.

Writing Summary Sentences

An alternative to selecting important sentences is to write summarizing sentences that abstract the important ideas from the prose passage. This can be done after some objective method of identifying important sentences has been devised. For example, after experts have underlined the important sentences in a passage, they can go back and write summarizing sentences for the underlined sentences. This method provides a rigorous test of comprehension. Anderson (1972) has argued that questions in paraphrased form will test a student's real understanding of the passage. Clearly, care must be taken that the meaning and nature of the domain underlying the prose passage is not changed by the summarizing. Therefore, one should use the rules of paraphrase offered by Anderson (1972, p. 150): (a) All substantive words must be replaced by synonyms, and (b) the meaning of the original sentences must be preserved. A third important rule in our view is that paraphrase should not change the reading level of the original passage or introduce new, unfamiliar vocabulary.

Clearly, the summary-sentence method relies on the creative writing ability of the person doing the abstracting and summarizing. Because this ability varies greatly among people, steps should be taken to control the resulting variation in sentence writing. However, the advantages of this method in identifying the truly important elements in a passage would seem to outweigh its disadvantages and to encourage further experimentation.

Keyword Search

A very objective method of identifying important sentences is the procedure that involves identifying important keywords in a prose passage. The technologies of library indexing and of computerized keyword searches can be used in this endeavor. Research by Roid and Finn (1978) has shown that nouns are the best keywords for use in writing items. Verbs and adverbs create very unusual, sometimes unclear, transformations of sentences. Adjectives can be effective at times but have somewhat poorer statistical qualities when transformed into test questions.

The following is a list of ways in which important nouns in a prose passage can be identified:

1. Identify the key nouns in the statement of a learning objective in a training manual or other materials.
2. Have a group of subject matter experts highlight the important nouns.
3. Conduct an objective word frequency count to identify *rare nouns*. Rare

nouns are those that are infrequently found in the average American English textbook, and the method for identifying them will be explained next.

The study by Roid and Finn (1978) revealed the necessity for caution with the use of nouns as keywords. Using the first occurrence in a passage of a highly frequent noun may produce an item that is too general or easy. Therefore, when a noun occurs in several sentences in a passage, choose a noun and sentence at random.

Word Frequency Analysis

One method of identifying important nouns in a passage involves using a word frequency index such as the *standard frequency index,* or SFI (Carroll, Davies, & Richman, 1971), referred to in the second major section of this chapter. The SFI was developed from a study of millions of sample words taken from textbooks written in American English. A word that has a standard frequency index lower than 60 is a relatively rare word. Therefore, all nouns in a passage that have a standard frequency of 60 or less can be identified and highlighted. This can be done clerically with the book in hand or through the use of a computer tape (obtainable from the publisher of Carroll, Davies, and Richman, 1971). The logic of this method is that a rare word is probably an important and/or new technical term that the student needs to learn. In addition, some research has indicated that rare words (SFI<60) that occur only once or twice within a given passage may be important words to select for questions (Roid & Finn, 1978).

STEP 3: TRANSFORMING THE SENTENCES

The transformation of important sentences, once they have been identified, into test questions follows six steps, or rules:

Rule 1: Copy the Sentences

All the chosen sentences, or the sentences in which the important nouns have been identified, should be copied onto worksheets, cards, or some other recording form.

Rule 2: Clarify References to Other Sentences

Sometimes if a sentence is taken directly from a text, it may contain a pronoun (e.g., *this, they, that, it*) that refers to a previous sentence or segment of prose. If the meaning of the sentence is unclear without this other segment, insert a noun phrase from the earlier sentence that clarifies the sentence in question. For example, consider the following two sentences: *There are a few methods of stopping thermal runaway;* and *The most common method uses an emitter resistor.* If *emitter resistor* is the keyword noun and the second sentence is copied, then the phrase *of stopping thermal runaway* should be inserted after the word *method* so that the sentence reads, *The most common method of stopping thermal runaway uses an emitter resistor.*

Rule 3: Simplify the Sentences

Some sentences contain more than one idea. Others contain several clauses. Still others are composed of two or more sentences joined by conjunctions. The sentence segment that contains the important noun in one case should be separated and the remainder of the sentence eliminated, if possible. To screen out extraneous clauses or sentences, answer the following questions:

1. Does this part of the sentence limit the meaning of the larger sentence?
2. Would elimination of this part make the larger sentence ungrammatical?
3. Would elimination of this part make the larger sentence an incomplete thought?
4. If the answers to Questions 1, 2, and 3 are all yes, retain the part being examined. If the answers are all no, eliminate the extraneous clause or sentence.

For example, in the sentence, *The simplest type of amplifier is the **single-ended amplifier** and it is also the least expensive,* the last segment refers to cost and is a second idea that can be deleted. However, in the sentence, *The best choice of sound equipment would include an **XA-1 amplifier** if you were going to be in a remote location where equipment would be hand-carried,* the segment following *if* is necessary because the question, *What would be included in the best choice of sound equipment?* would be far too general.

Rule 4: Replace the Keyword Noun

First, circle the noun or the entire phrase that includes the keyword noun. Noun phrases are made up of nouns plus adjectives, other modifiers, and articles such as *the, a,* and *an.* The entire phrase should be removed from the sentence.

Here are some examples with all the nouns, including any phrases in which they occur, in boldface.

1. **Chromium oxide** is used as **a polishing agent** for **stainless steel.**
2. **Tripoli** is obtained from **certain siliceous rocks** and is **a mild abrasive.**
3. **Pumice** has **a high silica content** and is used either as **an abrasive** or **a polishing agent.**
4. **Tin oxide** is **a pure white powder** used extensively as **a polishing agent** in **dentistry.**
5. **A large proportion** of **the stones** used for grinding in **dentistry** are made of **silicone carbide.**

After the noun or noun phrase has been identified and removed from the sentence, an appropriate word beginning with the letters *wh* is substituted to form the question. For example, the words *who, what, which, when, where,* or *why* can be used depending on the type of noun and position of the noun in the sentence.

Rule 5: Rewrite the Sentence in a Question Format

The best questions will begin with the *wh-* word that replaces a noun. Therefore, an original sentence must be turned around so that the replacement *wh-* word can be near the front of the sentence. Study the following examples taken from the above examples of noun and noun phrase identification.

1. **Key noun:** *chromium oxide*
   Transformed sentence
   What is used as a polishing agent for stainless steel?
2. **Key noun phrase:** *siliceous rock*
   Transformed sentence
   What is the mild abrasive and polishing agent tripoli obtained from?
3. **Key noun:** *pumice*
   Transformed sentence
   Which abrasive or polishing agent has a high silica content?
4. **Key noun:** *tin oxide*
   Transformed sentence
   Which polishing agent, used extensively in dentistry, is a pure white powder?
5. **Key noun:** *silicone carbide*
   Transformed sentence
   What are a large proportion of the stones used for grinding in dentistry made of?

The overriding rule in all of these transformations should be to stay as close as possible to the original wording and meaning of the original sentence unless paraphrase is purposely being used as an item-writing technique. Clearly, different item writers will come up with slightly different transformations of sentences at this point. It is, therefore, important for item writers as a team to work together on a number of sample sentences, to compare notes, and to come to agreement on their procedures prior to conducting a large-scale item-writing effort. The following are examples taken from a first-aid course.

Sentence:
The only way you can stop severe bleeding from a wound in a victim's side is by applying direct pressure.

Item:
What is the only way you can stop severe bleeding from a wound in a victim's side?

Sentence:
A salt and soda solution should be given to a shock victim if medical help will be delayed.

Paraphrase item:
What drink should be administered to a person in shock if a doctor is not coming immediately?

Rule 6: Stay As Close to the Wording of the Original Sentence as Possible

Unless paraphrase is purposely being used in order to create a test item of a specific comprehension level, stay as close to the original wording of the passage as possible. This will retain the exact meaning of the original instruction and will also ensure that the reading level of the test question exactly matches the instructional materials. If the original sentence is truly a key idea in the course, the students will not be reinforced for memorizing small details.

STEP 4: CONSTRUCTION OF FOILS FOR MULTIPLE-CHOICE FORMAT

Up to this point, we have discussed the method of turning sentences into questions that then become completion items. When the keyword noun is removed, for example, and a question is formed, the student can be asked to write out the correct noun answer. We will now examine the transformation of sentences into multiple-choice items.

The wrong-answer alternatives, or foils, of multiple-choice questions are an extremely important element of such items. Therefore, careful attention to the way in which foils are created is crucial. Moreover, if the item writer has a completely free hand in the wording of foils, large differences between item writers may be found (Roid & Haladyna, 1978). Thus, a team of item writers that is producing a test, should consider writing out rules for the construction of foils. This will not only help to control for differences among item writers but will provide permanent documentation of how the test was developed. There is some evidence that automated or clerical methods of creating foils may reduce differences among item writers (Roid, Haladyna, Shaughnessy, & Finn, 1979). However, it should be pointed out that these methods produce easier items than do methods that allow the item writer freedom of choice in respect to some of the wording of the foils. We will review three methods of foil construction, two in which the item writer has some choice in foil wording and a clerical method.

Using Field Tests to Create Foils

A very objective method of creating foils for multiple-choice questions is to first write foils as completion items and then try them out with students. If a wide range of student ability is represented in the field-test sample, a large number of plausible wrong answers will be obtained. These wrong answers will usually make good foils for multiple-choice versions of the completion items. Such answers are usually grammatically correct and may reflect students' underlying misconceptions or confusions. This method is very simple to use and amounts only to tabulating all of the wrong answers for each question in the field test.

Item-Writer Selection of Foils from a
Fixed List of Keywords

If a sentence-based method of item writing is being used for a given set of instructional materials or a prose passage, the original list of all the key nouns in that material can be provided to item writers. In constructing multiple-choice versions of transformed sentences, the item writers can select the foils from the lists provided. This procedure provides an operationally defined and reproducible method of creating foils. If no list were used, it would be impossible to describe what process item writers had used to select their foils. A list is particularly appropriate when a reasonably long passage or set of materials has a large number of technical terms that are interrelated and/or may be confused in the mind of the beginning student. This list method has been experimented with and found to create reasonably good items that are slightly easier than those written from learning objectives (Roid, Haladyna, & Shaughnessy, 1980).

There is one case in which the transformation of sentences into multiple-choice format requires an additional step. When the noun phrase that is deleted from a sentence is lengthy, it is necessary to move a part of the phrase into the stem of the question so that foils are not too long. A portion of the phrase is moved to the stem and a blank space inserted for the keyword noun. Examples of this type of transformation, from a course in computers, follow.

Example sentence
In a modern computer, the main storage is composed of tiny, magnetic, doughnut-shaped ferrite elements called "cores."

Transformed sentence
What is the main storage of a modern computer composed of? Tiny, magnetic, doughnut-shaped ferrite elements called _____.
    a. "binaries"
    b. "cores"
    c. "CPUs"
    d. "flip-flops"

Example sentence
A magnetic disc pack is an example of a nonsequential, direct access device. (Keyword phrase: direct access device)

Transformed sentence
What is a magnetic disc pack an example of? A nonsequential _____ *device.*
    a. remote communication
    b. peripheral output
    c. direct access
    d. file editing

Clerical Method of Foil Construction

A completely operationally defined method of creating foils is available. In using such a technique it should be kept in mind that it will create items that are easier than a typical multiple-choice question. Just as in the case of true–false items, one should be aware that the guessing factor may be closer to 50% than to the 25% of the normal four-option multiple-choice item. With this caution in mind, this section contains an account of this automated method.

Step I: List key nouns The entire passage or set of materials must be examined to identify key nouns. Rather than list every possible noun in the passage, either a subject index or a glossary can be used to identify these nouns or a team of subject matter experts can highlight them. Alternatively, the method of identifying nouns that have a standard frequency index (Carroll, Davies, & Richman, 1971) of less than 60 could be used to ensure that the nouns are the nontrivial nouns of the passage. Also, the list of nouns can be further grouped by using the method of Roid and Finn (1978), who suggested that the rare nouns that occur infrequently in a passage are "high information" words.

Step II: Categorize the nouns In order for an appropriate substitution to be made, nouns should be grouped according to some method of categorization. A method that has proved effective in several studies is adapted from Frederiksen (1975). Nouns are classified as either dynamic or static. *Dynamic* nouns have some implied movement, life, or process underlying them. *Static* nouns refer to objects or unchanging quantities and things. Using the matrix provided in Table 6.1, one can further classify nouns as either *animate, symbolic, nonsymbolic,* or *abstract;* the table gives several examples of each class of noun.

A team of item writers can be used to check the interjudge reliability of these classifications, and training can be conducted to ensure that reasonable agreement is obtained.

Step III: Select foils In this step, the keyword noun removed from the original sentence is also classified by means of the matrix in Table 6.1. Then, a random sample of three other words that can be assigned to the same cell of the matrix are selected for foils. The multiple-choice item is constructed by writing out the transformed sentence and then randomly placing the correct keyword noun in the position of alternative (a), (b), (c), or (d). The selected foil words are then placed in the other wrong-answer alternative positions as shown in the following example:

Table 6.1
Classification of Nouns

	Dynamic	Static
Animate	*animal, man, insect, John*	
Symbolic	*movie, game, song*	*book, picture, letter*
Nonsymbolic	*wind, noise, pressure*	*rock, house, shovel*
Abstract	*love, hope*	*length, size, pounds*

Original sentence
Pumice is a polishing agent that has a high silica content.

Words from the passage (nonsymbolic-static)
pumice, tripoli, tin oxide, chromium oxide, diamond chips, sand, chalk, iron oxide.

Transformed sentence and question:
Which polishing agent has a high silica content?
  a. tripoli
  b. tin oxide
  c. chromium oxide
  d. pumice

Practical Limitations of the Sentence Method

The method of making sentences into questions presented here has an application to special cases where the terminology and basic facts in written or verbal material needs to be learned by the student. The advantages of the method are that it can be completely operationally defined and thus available to public inspection. It can match the reading difficulty level of the instructional materials and can help to produce a large number of excellent factual items.

Clearly, this method of item writing would not be the only one used in tests in an instructional system. Because this method can assess only a limited level of cognitive knowledge, it would not be used exclusively. For this reason, some of the emerging techniques for prose transformations that measure higher level thinking are now discussed.

Prose Transformations for Tests of Higher Level Thinking

Bormuth (1970, pp. 50–55) outlines methods for what he calls ''discourse-derived'' items. These are items generated from relationships between sentences. Two types are described—those developed from analyses of both *anaphora* and *intersentence syntax.*

ANAPHORA ITEMS

Anaphora is the use of structures in prose that refer back to or substitute for structures that appear in a previous clause (antecedent). For example, *When I saw Tom, he was running,* includes an antecedent pronoun, *he.* Anaphoric expressions can involve pronouns such as these, or other structures such as deleted modifiers, for example, *Tom was extremely fast. (This) fast a player was needed.*

These kinds of anaphora and others (Bormuth, 1970, pp. 51, 147–150) appear frequently in any text (such as just occurred here—"These kinds of anaphora" at the beginning of this sentence is an anaphoric substitute for the preceding paragraph). Without anaphoric expression, writing would be extremely repetitive and very odd indeed. For example, the sentence, *Mary's friends liked Mary because Mary helped Mary's friends* is very unusual. In comparison, the more acceptable sentence is, *Mary's friends liked her because she helped them.*

A sample paragraph shows how anaphoric analysis can assist in creating items that seem to measure the basic idea in a prose segment.

Tests are an important part of any instructional system. Objective-based tests are designed to include several items measuring each learning objective. Such [objective-based] tests are an important part of the Instructional Systems Development or ISD model. The model [ISD] employs these [objective-based] criterion-referenced tests to evaluate student performance. Also, the tests [objective-based/criterion-referenced] are used to validate the instructional methods used in the [ISD] model.

Working from the last two sentences in this paragraph, and using anaphoric analysis as shown in brackets, an item can be written. Using *wh*-transformation and paraphrase we can construct an item like the following:

Item
What kinds of assessment instruments are used in the Instructional Systems method to measure trainee achievement and teaching effectiveness?
Possible Correct Answers
  1. objective-based tests
  2. tests that include several items measuring each learning objective
  3. criterion-referenced tests

Clearly, the reader must really understand this prose in order to complete the question. As the example shows, anaphoric analysis leads to a tracking of the evolution of meaning of a term (tests) in a prose segment. Also, the possibility of more than one correct answer is demonstrated. Bormuth (1975) and Cocks and Bormuth (1975) have elaborated on methods for scoring answers to completion questions.

INTERSENTENCE SYNTAX

Bormuth (1970, pp. 53–55 and 150–155) describes a relatively new and untapped area of item writing for prose material, intersentence relationships. There are about nine basic kinds of intersentence relations, examples of which are listed below.

  1. *Connective relations (conjunctions—**and, but, or**): Domains are specified, **and** CR tests are designed to measure them.*
  2. *Time relations (**same time, after, before**): CR tests are designed. This is done **after** domains are defined.*

3. *Causal relations (cause, effect): Posttest scores were low. This drop was **caused** by some confusions in a training session.*
4. *Concessional relations: Posttest scores were not high. **Nevertheless,** the students were positive about the course.*
5. *Illustrative relations: Some item-writing methods are computerized. **Examples,** are the chemistry items of Johnson and the spelling items of Engel.*
6. *Sequential relations: The ISD Model has five phases. **The first is** analysis ... **The second is** design ... **The third is ...***
7. *Parenthetical relations (incidental, explanatory): Cloze tests are used in reading research. **Incidentally,** this type of test was not invented by a person named Cloze.*
8. *Topic–comment relations:* A topic sentence in a paragraph is usually followed (or preceded) by comment sentences that elaborate on the idea in the topic sentence. Although little is known about how to identify and use topic sentences for item transformations, such sentences are one of the most prominent elements in intersentence (and interparagraph) relations.
9. *Dialog: Tom phoned Harry and asked, "Can the deadline be extended?" Harry said, "How much of an extension do you mean?" Then Tom said, "One month will do it."*

This list of types of intersentence relations is provided so that the first step in item writing can be accomplished—identification of the intersentence links. Table 6.2 shows an example of intersentence analysis, leading to item transformations.

The kind of intersentence analysis outlined in Table 6.2 is a model for much more elaborate, real-life examples. The method remains in a rather crude state of development at this point due to the need for more applications of the analysis to curriculum materials. This can probably be done best with the help of someone trained in linguistic analysis. Cronbach (1970), for one, expressed support for this line of research, and expected it to be a worthwhile effort, perhaps requiring ten years of work.

APPLICATION ITEMS

Conoley and O'Neil (1979, pp. 122–127) have outlined methods for prose item writing at the application and analysis levels. Only the application level will be discussed here due to the fact that analysis items are at the very edge of the state of the art of item writing. It may be years before a full development of these methods has been accomplished.

Table 6.2
An Example of Intersentence Analysis

1. *Original sentences*
   a. Joan read the story.
   b. She identified the keywords.
   c. Then, she chose the sentences for items.
2. *Make the sentences into noun phrases*
   a. Joan's reading of the story . . .
   b. Joan's identifying of the keywords . . .
   c. Joan's choosing of the sentences for items . . .
3. *Map the intersentence relations*
   a. *B* occurred during *A*
   b. *C* occurred after *A–B*
4. *Embed the phrases using the map*
   a. Joan's identifying of the keywords occurred during her reading of the story.
   b. Joan's choosing of the sentences for items occurred after her identifying the keywords while reading the story.
5. *Derive the items*
   a1. What occurred during Joan's reading of the story?
   a2. When did Joan's identifying of the keywords occur?
   b1. What occurred after Joan's identifying of the keywords (and/or reading of the story)?
   b2. After what did Joan's choosing of the sentences for items occur?

Application-level items test the student's ability to apply a learned principle to a new situation not described in the instruction. This is to be done without prompting as to which principle is involved. If the principle is named, the item can be considered a comprehension item in which the student is demonstrating understanding of the principle.

Principles are statements of the interrelationship between two or more concepts (Gagné, 1965, p. 141; Tiemann & Markle, 1978; also see Chapter 9 for a more complete discussion of concepts). Also, principles usually occur as propositions or scientific laws (Anderson, 1972, p. 155). A principle can usually be stated in an *if–then* form in which a specific precondition (stated in a conditional clause) is followed by a specific consequence (stated in the main clause). For instance, Premack's differential probability hypothesis in reinforcement theory states that, "For any pair of responses, the more probable one will reinforce the less probable one." This principle involves the interrelated concepts of response, high and low probability behaviors, and reinforcement. The classic illustration uses *Grandma's Law*. Grandma's Law states that if you eat your meat and potatoes (you do the low probability behavior) you can have your dessert (you can do the high probability behavior).

In order to write items for statements of principle, superordinate terms must

Table 6.3
An Example of Transforming a Statement of a Principle into a Question

---

Statement of principle: Given any pair of responses, the more probable one will reinforce the less probable one.

Examples used in instruction: Grandma's Law (dessert only after meat); watch TV as soon as you finish homework; buy a new magazine after your garage is cleaned; go to Hawaii after you finish your book.

STEP 1: Replace Superordinate Terms
Given a difficult work assignment and an enjoyable diversion, the diversion will reinforce the work assignment. Or, more particularly, given the task of stacking two cords of wood and watching a championship football game, the game will reinforce the wood stacking.

STEP 2: Paraphrase the Statement
When there are two activities, stacking two cords of wood and watching a championship football game, watching the game after stacking the wood will increase the chances that wood stacking will be repeated in the future.

STEPS 3 and 4: Form the Question
When there are two activities, stacking two cords of wood and watching a championship football game, which activity will increase the chances that the other will be repeated in the future?

---

be identified. A superordinate term is one that subsumes a class of things that can be described without repeating the superordinate term. For example, the term "high probability behavior" is a superordinate term for all the fun things we enjoy doing such as going to a good movie, reading a good book, walking on a beach, etc. *Reinforce* is, however, not easily replaced or paraphrased. The word *reward* for example, does not completely replace *reinforce*. Other terms such as *intermittent reinforcement, positive reinforcement* and *negative reinforcement* repeat the original term. Gagné (1965, p. 142) gives another example of a principle with one superordinate term, *round things,* in the statement *round things roll.* Particular terms are things that replace the superordinate term, for example, baseballs, bowling balls, furniture casters, and barrels, all of which roll. The word "roll," however, is not easily replaced and is not a superordinate term.

Conoley and O'Neil (1979, pp. 122–123) list the steps in actually deriving items: (*a*) replace every superordinate term in the statement of the principle with a particular term, (*b*) paraphrase the remainder of the statement, (*c*) delete a segment to create a completion item, or (*d*) form a *wh*-question. As Anderson (1972, p. 155) has pointed out, it is crucial that the example of the principle used in a test not repeat an instance used in instruction.

Anderson (1972) successfully applied this method to tests designed to measure application of the principle of intermittent reinforcement.

An example of the use of this method with Premack's hypothesis is given in Table 6.3.

Summary and Directions for Future Research

Considerable research and development has been conducted on item writing for prose learning. Early work grew out of research on reading and readability indexes. Bormuth (1970) has made the most comprehensive statement of the logic and theoretical nuances of item-writing methods that involve transformations of prose. These methods promise to provide tests that are logically and judiciously related to text material. Also, such tests will be matched to the readability level of the material. Operationally defined methods can be described easily to other researchers and others so that achievement tests can be designed to advance the technologies of instruction and evaluation. Clear definitions of the cognitive tasks set before the student will help to advance our knowledge of the processes in learning from text. These are all powerful promises. All that remains is the continued, perhaps gradual, application of the methods to actual instructional materials such as textbooks. This application may be waiting upon two important future developments—computerization of the algorithms for creating items and progress in the linguistic analysis of higher level test items.

Computerization could begin immediately with implementation, in at least a computer-assisted mode (e.g., Schulz, 1979), in the identification of keywords and their repetition in a passage (examples of anaphora). Perhaps at least part of the sentence-transformation method outlined in the present chapter can be programmed. Surely, interesting analyses can be performed if entire textbooks are prepared for computer processing and keyword analyses.

Advances in the linguistic analysis of intersentence and even interparagraph relationships may reveal methods for "getting at the basic ideas" in written instruction. Clearly, such phenomena as anaphora and intersentence syntax are not well enough understood to provide the detailed rules required for computerized item writing. These are challenging and uncharted areas for new research and development.

The prose transformation certainly proves to be more substantial as a practical methodology as one becomes familiar with its nuances and wide applications. As Conoley and O'Neil (1979) remarked in the conclusion of their primer on item transformations, the process of writing about transformations and constructing examples of them convinces the writer of their utility.

References

Anderson, R. C. How to construct achievement tests to assess comprehension. *Review of Educational Research*, 1972, *42*, 145–170.

Bormuth, J. R. *On the theory of achievement test items*. Chicago, Illinois: Univ. of Chicago Press, 1970.

Bormuth, J. R. *Anaphora: Their structure, taxonomy, and questioning.* A paper presented at the annual meeting of the American Educational Research Association, Washington, D.C., March–April 1975.

Bormuth, J. R., Manning, J., Carr, J., & Pearson, D. Children's comprehension of between- and within-sentence syntactic structures. *Journal of Educational Psychology*, 1970, *61*, 349–357.

Carroll, J. B., Davies, P., & Richman, B. *Word frequency book.* Boston, Massachusetts: Houghton, 1971.

Cocks, P., & Bormuth, J. R. *Rules for classifying scoring responses to wh-completion questions.* Paper presented at the meetings of the American Educational Research Association, Washington, D.C., March–April 1975.

Conoley, J. C., & O'Neil, H. F., Jr. A primer for developing test items. In Harold F. O'Neil, Jr. (Ed.), *Procedures for instructional systems development.* New York: Academic Press, 1979.

Cronbach, L. J. Review of *On the theory of achievement test items* by J. R. Bormuth. *Psychometrika*, 1970, *35*, 509–511.

Culhane, J. W. Cloze procedures and comprehension. *The Reading Teacher*, 1970, *23*, 410–413.

Finn, P. J. A question writing algorithm. *Journal of Reading Behavior*, 1975, *4*, 341–367.

Finn, P. J. *Word frequency, information theory and cloze performance: A lexical-marker, transfer-feature theory of processing in reading.* Unpublished paper, State University of New York at Buffalo, School of Education, 1977.

Finn, P. J. *Generating domain-referenced, multiple-choice test items from prose passages.* Paper presented at the meetings of the American Educational Research Association, Toronto, March 1978.

Frederiksen, C. H. Representing logical and semantic structure of knowledge acquired from discourse. *Cognitive Psychology*, 1975, *7*, 371–458.

Gagné, R. M. The analysis of instructional objectives for the design of instruction. In R. Glaser (Ed.) *Teaching machines and programmed instruction II: Data and directions.* Washington, D.C.: National Education Association, Dept. of Audio–Visual Instruction, 1965.

Hively, W., Patterson, H. L., & Page, S. A "universe-defined" system of arithmetic achievement tests. *Journal of Educational Measurement*, 1968, *5*, 275–290.

Roid, G. The technology of test-item writing. In Harold F. O'Neil, Jr. (Ed.), *Procedures for instructional systems development.* New York: Academic Press, 1979.

Roid, G. H., & Finn, P. J. *Algorithms for developing test questions from sentences in instructional materials* (NPRDC Tech. Rep. 78-23). San Diego: Navy Personnel Research and Development Center, 1978.

Roid, G. H., & Haladyna, T. M. A comparison of objective-based and modified-Bormuth item writing techniques. *Educational and Psychological Measurement*, 1978, *35*, 19–28.

Roid, G. H., & Haladyna, T. M. *Handbook on item writing for criterion-referenced testing.* San Diego, California: Navy Personnel Research and Development Center, 1979.

Roid, G. H., Haladyna, T. M., & Shaughnessy, J. *A comparison of item-writing methods for criterion-referenced testing.* Paper presented at the annual meeting of the National Council on Measurement in Education, Boston, April 1980.

Roid, G. H., Haladyna, T. M., Shaughnessy, J., & Finn, P. J. *Item writing for domain-referenced tests of prose learning.* Paper presented at the annual meeting of the American Educational Research Association, San Francisco, 1979.

Schulz, R. E. Computer aids for developing tests and instruction. In H. F. O'Neil, Jr., *Procedures for instructional systems development.* New York: Academic Press, 1979.

Tiemann, P. W., & Markle, S. M. *Analyzing instructional content: A guide to instruction and evaluation.* Champaign, Illinois: Stipes Publishing Company, 1978.

7

Item Forms for Technical and Quantitative Items

In factual, scientific, technical, and quantitative areas, an important item-writing method is available that can be operationally defined. Items can be constructed using steps or rules that specify the structure, format, and even some of the wording of resulting items. In many cases these steps or rules can be programmed for a small computer. If a large pool of items can be created by a set of rules, the domain to be measured is defined as the knowledge or skill measured by the pool of items. A computer or a clerical staff can randomly assemble items if the rules are programmed or made sufficiently clear. Methods like this are in use in many locations where computer-assisted instruction is used in universities, industries, and the military, particularly in scientific and quantitative areas. With the increased availability of small computers, this method is feasible even in most public school settings.

In this chapter, we will define the characteristics of an *item form* and describe the background of the development of this method of generating items in the work of Hively (1974) and Osburn (1968). Also, examples are given of how and where item forms can be found.

Rationale

Most achievement tests are scored by adding up the number of items correct as an estimate of how well students are performing in an area of knowledge or skills. Usually we are interested not only in this observed score on items in a particular test but in what the score represents with respect to performance on a larger content domain. Thus, it is often said that we would not want to "teach to a test," (train specific responses to particular items) but rather teach a verbal or behavioral repertoire that can be assessed by a given test. Therefore, the primary objective of testing appears to be generalization from a sample of items to a larger "universe of content" (Osburn, 1968).

Facing the need to define the universe of content, test developers have devised a number of techniques over the years. For a long time one of the primary techniques used a two-way grid, or table of specifications, showing content areas by behavior levels (Tyler, 1950). Items were written for each cell in the grid to ensure coverage of curriculum elements at each cognitive or behavior level. Another approach is to invoke a latent achievement continuum underlying a set of items (Lord & Novick, 1968, p. 359; Wright & Stone, 1979). Items are drafted and field tested, and then statistical analyses of test data are used to fit these items to a statistical model that represents the hypothetical underlying continuum of achievement. In addition to content–behavior tables and latent trait models, task analyses and behavioral objectives have been used in several ways to define an instructional content area. Bloom, Hastings, and Madaus give an excellent review of these techniques (1971, pp. 19–41).

Hively, Patterson, and Page (1968) and Osburn (1968) approached the definition of the universe of content in a unique way. They conceived of an exhaustive pool of all possible test items representing an instructional domain that defined a content area. As Osburn (1968) explained, in contrasting the method with latent trait analysis, "no amount of item analysis or factor analysis can provide a firm basis for generalization to a universe of content. The basis of generalization must be contained in the operational definition of the procedures used in generating and sampling items that go to make up the test [p. 96]."

Hively's invention, a technique called the *item form*, specifies the operational definitions of sets of items. This invention was prompted by the need to design tests for mathematics curriculum materials in the MINNEMAST (Minnesota Mathematics and Science Teaching Project) study at the University of Minnesota (Hively, Maxwell, Rabehl, Sension, & Lundin, 1973). The rationale for this approach is given in Rabehl (1971) and in an early unpublished paper by Hively (1966), quoted at length here in order to give an accurate account of the thinking behind it:

> For the purposes of evaluation and revision we would like to know the proportions of students, in a group exposed to a given unit of instruction, who have acquired various concepts and skills. . . . Two kinds of inferences are involved here: a statistical one, in which the proportion of students in the sample who answer an item correctly is taken as an estimate of the proportion of students in the entire . . . population who could answer *that item* correctly; and an intuitive one, in which we infer from a student's correct

response to a particular item that he does in fact 'have' a certain concept and could therefore respond correctly to *other* similar items. . . . A critic might object that in doing this we may merely be teaching rote answers to specific items and not the general concepts or skills behind them. The way to find out, of course, is to ask different questions involving the same concepts and skills. We now find ourselves making lists and cross indexes of equivalent items. A logical extension of this activity is to attempt to write the rules which generate *sets* of equivalent items representing clusters of related concepts and skills. These are called item forms [pp. 14–15].

Before we define and give examples of items forms, one additional rationale mentioned in the foregoing quotation, needs to be emphasized. A particular set of items is a basis for an inference about the student. We hope to infer the degree of knowledge or skill the student has. In order to achieve an unbiased estimate of achievement as the basis for such an inference, two conditions must be met: (*a*) the set of all possible items of a content–behavior type must be specified in advance, and (*b*) a given test must be a random sample of items from that total set (Osburn, 1968; Millman, 1974). The observed score on a domain-based test, then, is an unbiased estimate of and a sufficient statistic (Lord & Novick, 1968, p. 235) for the proportion of the entire domain that the student could be expected to achieve.

The concept of a test as a random sample of items is not unique to the criterion-referenced (CR) testing movement. Item sampling models in test theory (Lord, 1955; Lord & Novick, 1968, pp. 234–238) assume that *n* items in a test are a random sample of a population of items. The item-sampling model is contrasted with classical test theory, which assumes test forms that are strictly parallel—having equal means, standard deviations, and intercorrelations (Gulliksen, 1950, p. 173). The item sampling model makes no such assumptions—only that there is a random sample of items. As Lord and Novick have said (1968), "the model yields many important results not obtainable from the classical model [p. 234]." Item sampling, and the more complex stratified item-sampling theory, form the basis for some theories of test reliability (e.g., Tryon, 1957) and generalizability theory (Cronbach, Rajaratnam, & Gleser, 1963).

Item Forms

An *item form,* as explained by Osburn (1968), "has the following charac-teristics: (1) It generates items with a fixed syntactical structure; (2) it contains one or more variable elements; and (3) it defines a class of item sentences by specifying replacement sets for the variable elements [p. 97]." There are simple item forms, developed from existing items, and more formalized item forms such as those developed by Hively *et al.* (1973). A simple item form is kind of a skeleton of an item that provides blank spaces into which words or numbers are inserted to create one of a large number of items. Here is an example of a simple item form for introductory statistics that can potentially generate hundreds, perhaps thousands, of items.

Existing item
A random sample of 100 trucks weighed at a highway checkpoint had an average weight of 40,250 lbs. with a standard deviation of 2500 lbs. Find a 95% confidence interval for the true average gross weight of trucks passing this checkpoint accurate to at least one decimal place.

Simple item form
Given a random sample of *(N)* *(objects)* with an average *(dimension or feature)* of *(M)*, with a standard deviation of *(SD)*. Find a *(95%, 99%)* confidence interval for the true average *(dimension or feature)* of the *(objects)* accurate to at least one decimal place.

Replacement sets
N is the number of objects, an integer greater than 30 (because we are referring to the large-sample confidence interval estimation, Freund, 1960, pp. 217). The mean and standard deviation can be any integer or decimal number (accurate to two decimal places). Objects and dimensions or features can be the weight, height, temperature, or any other physical or psychological–educational measurement made on humans, animals, or things.

Scoring
The student is expected to use the formula that gives the interval as the mean plus or minus 1.96 (for 95%; 2.58 for 99%) times the *SD* divided by the square root of the *N*.

Hively and his colleagues (Hively *et al.*, 1973) reported working for several years on a format to display item forms adequately. An example of the current format for item forms is given in Figure 7.1. Each of the elements in this figure will now be explained in order to give the reader a full appreciation for the elegance and potential complexity of well-derived item forms. A more complete explanation with more examples is provided by Hively *et al.* (1973).

Figure 7.1 shows an item form for the concept of the relative weights of objects that vary randomly in size. The item form begins in the top left hand corner with an identifying number, a title, and a brief overall description of the task. In this case, the general description explains that the objects to be used may be indistinguishable by hefting but easily distinguished by an equal-arm balance.

Next, the "Stimulus and Response Characteristics" of the items are described in relation to the cell matrix that follows. It is explained that the objects to be examined will vary in both weight and size. Pairs of objects will be used, and three size relations will be used, defined in terms of the left and right objects as they are placed in front of the students. Thus, the cell matrix defines nine pairs of objects that will be used. As the reader can appreciate by now, this type of item form really specifies the task so that there is no confusion as to how testing will proceed, and yet the variety of individual items produced will measure a number of facets of the child's understanding of the concept that weight and mass are separate qualities of objects. In other words, the item form is specific without being trivial.

ITEM FORM 16.14[*]

Comparing two objects on equal-arm balance and choosing a symbol to complete a statement of the weight relation.

GENERAL DESCRIPTION

The child is asked to compare the weights of two objects that may be (1) indistinguishable by hefting but easily distinguishable on the balance, (2) indistinguishable even on the balance. In each of these situations, size varies as an irrelevant dimension. An equal-arm balance is available but instructions for its use are non-directive. The child is asked to select one of the three symbols ($>$, $<$, and $=$) and place it in the blank space provided between the two weight symbols.

STIMULUS AND RESPONSE CHARACTERISTICS

Constant for All Cells

The equal-arm balance is of similar construction to that used in MINNEMAST Unit 16, made of Tinkertoys, cardboard, string, a metal weight, and a foot ruler.

The objects are opaque, cylindrical bottles, identical except for weight (either 23 gm. or 25 gm.) and size (either $2'' \times \frac{5}{8}''$ or $2\frac{1}{2}'' \times 1\frac{3}{4}''$). Each is identified by a lower-case letter assigned at random.

The child is asked to complete a symbolic statement, corresponding to the weight relation, by choosing the correct relation symbol.

Distinguishing among Cells

Three weight relations (detectable by balance only, not by hefting or "feel") defined in terms of the location of the objects when placed in front of the child:

left $>$ right; left $<$ right; left $=$ right.

Three size relations:

left $>$ right; left $<$ right; left $=$ right.

CELL MATRIX

Size Relations	Weight Relations (Detectable by Balance Only)		
	$W_l > W_r$	$W_l < W_r$	$W_l = W_r$
$S_l > S_r$	(1)	(4)	(7)
$S_l < S_r$	(2)	(5)	(8)
$S_l = S_r$	(3)	(6)	(9)

[*] Originally developed by Wells Hively.

ITEM FORM SHELL

MATERIALS

Beam Balance
Objects l and r
from T.O. 16.14.0
Stimulus-Response sheet
(attached)
Pencil

DIRECTIONS TO E

Place materials in front of child. (Keep order of objects as given above.)

    Balance
← objects
☐ ← S-R sheet

    Subject

SCRIPT

Here are two objects. They have symbols attached to them. Compare them by weight and write one of these three signs (point) in the blank (point) to form the comparison sentence.

You may use this balance if you need to.

RECORDING

Attach Stimulus-Response sheet to this page. Describe what child did.

If balance was used, insert object symbols in schematic drawing of the balance given below, and mark the position of the plumb-line at the time of child's judgment.

DESCRIPTION OF MATERIALS

Pencil (T.O. 16.1.1)
Beam Balance (T.O. 16.13.1): Equal-arm beam balance made from tinker-toy materials as decribed in MINNEMAST Unit 16.

Set of Weight Comparison Objects (T.O. 16.14.0): Set of opaque plastic cylindrical bottles with firmly fitting lids. Two sizes of bottles have been chosen. The small bottle has a length of $2''$ and a diameter of $\frac{5}{8}''$. The large bottle has a length of $2\frac{1}{2}''$ and a diameter of $1\frac{3}{4}''$. Two weight values have been chosen so that the objects cannot typically be distinguished by hefting but can be distinguished on the balance. Each object is designated by a randomly chosen, lower-case letter.

Size	Weight	
	23 gm	25 gm
small	a	m k
large	b	o n

Stimulus-Response sheet (attached to item) (T.O. 16.14.1): a sheet of paper approximately $6'' \times 4''$ with the following display:

Write $>$, $<$, or $=$ in the blank

W_1 _____ W_r

where l and r are the appropriate subscripts (from Replacement Scheme).

REPLACEMENT SCHEME

(l,r) Objects		
Cell 1:	(o,a)	
Cell 2:	(m,b)	
Cell 3:	Choose	from R.S. 16:13
Cell 4:	(b,m)	
Cell 5:	(a,o)	
Cell 6:	Choose	from R.S. 16.14
Cell 7:	Choose	from R.S. 16.15
Cell 8:	Choose	from R.S. 16.16
Cell 9:	Choose	from R.S. 16.17

REPLACEMENTS SETS

R.S. 16.13	Ordered pairs	(m,a);	(o,b)
R.S. 16.14	Ordered pairs	(a,m);	(b,o)
R.S. 16.15	Ordered pairs	(b,a);	(o,m)
R.S. 16.16	Ordered pairs	(a,b);	(m,o)
R.S. 16.17	Ordered pairs	(m,k);	(o,n)

SCORING SPECIFICATIONS

A correct response is made by writing the correct symbol ($>$, $<$, or $=$) in the blank space to complete the comparison sentence. This should be $>$ in Cells 1, 2, and 3; $<$ in Cells 4, 5, and 6; $=$ in Cells 7, 8, and 9.

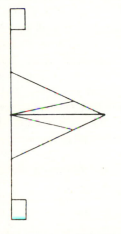

Figure 7.1. Example of a formalized item form. (From Hively et al., 1973.)

The "item form shell" section lists the materials to be used and offers directions to the examiner, including a script. Thus, it is revealed that this item form is an individually administered set of tasks, rather than a paper-and-pencil test or other kind of format. The "Recording" section tells the examiner what to write down and what to attend to when observing the child complete each task. The description of materials gives more details of the testing apparatus and supplies needed. The abbreviation "T.O.", under "Description of materials," refers to a separate list of test objects used by Hively *et al.* (1973). The T.O. inventory is separate from the item form and includes a listing of all materials, illustrations, objects, apparatus, etc. used in the entire curriculum, cross-referenced to different item forms if necessary.

Two important elements in the item form are the "Replacement scheme" and "Replacements sets." The replacement scheme and sets are the link between the actual objects used in the weighing task described in Figure 7.1 and the cell matrix. In simple terms, the replacement information simply tells the examiner which pairs of objects to present to the student. In general, the replacement sets define the characteristics of and the pattern for inserting the variable elements into the item form, in order to create a specific, individual item.

The final element in the item form is headed "scoring specifications." Hively *et al.* (1973, p. 31) suggest dichotomous scoring of items—correct versus incorrect—rather than a rating. They argue that this practice does two things: The scoring procedures (*a*) simplify the task so that we are estimating proportions of items a person can answer rather than a mean score on a scale of performance, and (*b*) define precisely what the examiner should do to judge correctness. Another important contribution of Hively *et al.* is the strategy of using actual student responses from field testings of items as a basis for defining the properties of correct responses.

Computerized Item Forms

Some item forms can be written in the form of a computer program. Most *computer-assisted instruction* (CAI) systems have the capability of producing item forms. The programming languages in CAI systems are called *author languages*. Some of the well-known author languages are COURSEWRITER, PLANIT and TUTOR.

An item form written in an author language is a series of computer commands that define the wording of the item form and the way the variable elements are chosen or computed. One of the great advantages of the computer generation of item forms is that even complex computations can be used to create numbers that are variable elements in story problems. For example, if story problems for navigation calculations were used, a computer could create a large number of correctly composed story problems without the item writer having to check all calculations for all items.

Millman and Outlaw (1978) and Millman (1980) have continued the work on item forms by using a small computer system to develop a special programming language that allows item forms to be computerized. Some of their item forms have been adapted to agricultural subject matter where the variable elements are not numbers but names of animals or concepts in veterinary practices. Braby and his colleagues at the Orlando Naval Training Center (Braby, Parrish, Guitard, & Aagard, 1978) have implemented item forms in a computer-aided system for writing programmed instruction for the teaching of symbol recognition.

Computers have been used for a number of years for assembling tests. Early efforts centered on the storage of item pools containing the complete wording of items. The second generation of systems included the ability to construct item forms. This was done in the mid-1960s in the drill-and-practice exercises created by the computer-assisted instruction project at Stanford University (Suppes, Jerman, & Groen, 1966).

Examples of areas in which computerized item forms have been created include the testing of spelling (Fremer & Anastasio, 1969), chemistry (Johnson, 1973), FORTRAN computer programming (Vickers, 1973), a wide variety of university courses (McClain, Wessels, & Sando, 1975), and others (e.g., Olympia, 1975).

Advantages of Item Forms

The advantages of using item forms have been suggested by the examples in this chapter, but they will be listed here for emphasis:

1. Item forms can save test-development time in the long-run if time is invested early, in the creating of the item form rather than in the writing of each individual item.

2. Item forms truly define domains that can be the basis of CR tests that are unambiguously interpretable as providing an unbiased estimate of the proportion of the total domain the student has mastered.

3. Computerized item forms, particularly in complex quantitative areas such as high-level statistical problems or cost accounting and budgeting, can benefit from the computer's calculation accuracy and power. Thus, quantitative story problems can be created in large numbers with great accuracy.

4. Computers can be programmed to compose and also print test forms randomly so that not only are items written, but test forms are prepared for

duplication, thus eliminating the need for clerical assistance in typing. If multiple-choice formats are used in the item form, the position of the correct answer can be randomly varied so that another clerical task can be eliminated.

Sources of Item Forms

At least four basic sources of item forms will be discussed in turn: (*a*) Existing item forms; (*b*) existing test items that can be elaborated into item forms; (*c*) any subject matter area in which there are coding systems, symbols, story problems, or calculations; and (*d*) task analyses or studies of hierarchical subject matter.

EXISTING ITEM FORMS

Using the references listed in this book and by contacting the computer specialists at a computer center, the reader should be able to access the item forms currently available in many of the scientific and quantitative areas in public schools, universities, and military training centers. These may be either direct sources of item forms or they may provide examples that can be adapted to fit the learning objectives of the reader's training program.

REVISE EXISTING TEST ITEMS

One of the best sources of item forms is a file of test questions used previously. Go through such a file and try to identify test items that can be made into item forms. This procedure may take some knowledge of the subject matter, but several clues should be obvious. First, if the question involves numbers that can obviously vary, as in story problems, the item will probably make a good item form. If the test question asks for the definition of a term or asks for the identification of an example of it, perhaps several terms can be substituted into the same item form. The latter is particularly likely in an area where there are a number of technical terms that the student sometimes confuses. In such a case, one can create multiple-choice questions that have much the same foils. For example, in a course on basic transistor theory, one could create an item form that would give the definition of a term like variable transistor, NPN transistor, PNP transistor, emitter resistor, dynamic bias, static bias, thermal runaway, and then alternate the use of these terms as wrong-answer foils.

Another possible source of item forms is diagrams of something like an electronic circuit that has variable elements that can create many identification problems. For example, in reference to a series of diagrams the question, "Which of the following circuits illustrates a push–pull amplifier?" would suggest a whole family of items in which drawings of a *push–pull amplifier,* a *common-base amplifier,* a *voltage regulator,* or a *phase splitter* are varied in systematic ways, by someone who is a subject matter expert in this area, to create foils.

Rabehl (1971) has developed ways to take existing items and transform them into item forms. Hively *et al.* (1973, p. 21) lists nine ways in which the characteristics of an item can be changed to produce item variations:

1. Directions may be written, spoken, nonverbal, or combined.
2. Responses may be written, spoken, behavioral, or combined.
3. Syntactic changes in the wording of items can create new versions.
4. Vocabulary may be varied from technical to nontechnical, and synonyms and paraphrase may be used.
5. Sequencing of the parts of the directions, the task, or the item can be rearranged.
6. Supplementary information can be supplied if a student responds to one part of the task, for example, as is done in medical simulation tests.
7. Numerical values can obviously be changed as mentioned earlier.
8. Materials can be used and/or varied to create requirements for the test item.
9. The student may be asked to either select or construct an answer or provide a product or a performance.

IDENTIFY ITEM FORMS FROM SUBJECT MATTER

Many item forms are suggested by many quantitative and factual areas of subject matter. For example, any subject matter involving a coding system, symbols, math problems, story problems, or calculations are obvious sources of item forms. Learning objectives, course materials, textbooks, charts, graphs, tables, and job aids such as reference or symbol lists can suggest item forms.

Discussions with subject matter experts can be conducted to ask questions such as "Are any calculation problems required on this job?" or "Do personnel ever use any reference manuals or tables to interpret codes or messages?"

Another subject matter area is that concerned with the identification of objects, drawings, and illustrations. For example, maps showing terrain can be systematically varied with details such as rivers and hills, leading to item forms that test the identification of those details. Identification of aircraft in flight could be tested by an item form in which the replacement elements are different types of planes seen from various views.

As will be seen even more clearly in Chapter 8, on the testing of concepts, another source of replacement elements for test items is composed of examples or nonexamples of a concept or principle. In many cases the learning objective for the student is to be able to correctly identify the proper application of a technique, method, formula, or procedure. The setting in which a technique is to be applied may be systematically varied to create item forms. For instance, dental students may be asked to identify the correct instances in which certain abrasives and polishing agents should be used. Abrasives vary in fineness and hardness, and therefore, their application varies. Abrasives and polishers include diamond chips, carbides, pumice, tripoli, etc. A large collection of items could be composed by varying the circumstances, the object to be polished, and the types of abrasives that might be available. Therefore, questions concerning the proper application of techniques used in many technical professions can be made into item forms.

One of the major benefits of using item forms in these cases is that an exhaustive list of all possible examples can be specified. If this is done, a test will not be inadvertently slanted toward certain peculiar applications, but rather will be an accurate representation of a very wide range of possible applications of a skill.

The prevalence of potential item forms is demonstrated by the following example. Reading the following description of a navigator's task, one can imagine at least one item form that can be created.

Navigators on ships perform calculations to find where they are in relation to landmarks. The navigator uses algebra, geometry and, often, trigonometry. One of four general methods of navigation is called piloting. Piloting is a means of navigating by watching for landmarks. Near land, the navigator might observe lighthouses and other landmarks to get their bearing or direction from the ship. He could measure two bearings during one observation. Each bearing line is then drawn as a straight line on a chart. When the navigator obtains two lines of position, the point at which they cross indicates the location of the ship. He plots the position on the chart and writes its latitude and longitude in a navigator's notebook. He also keeps a close check on the depth of the water by taking soundings with an instrument called a fathometer.

An item form for this example would involve plotting the two lines of position. A navigator's chart could be available to the student with landmarks noted. The landmarks could be variable elements in the item form. Then, the bearing or direction (in numerical value) of each landmark would be given. These clearly are variable elements in the item form. The student is requested to plot lines of position for two landmarks and to determine the position of the ship. This item form could presumably result in an infinite number of items.

Summary

There are a wide range of uses for item forms. Item forms can produce large numbers of similar items because they specify (a) a fixed format for a question, including actual wording; (b) one or more variable elements that can be replaced by words or numbers; and (c) the rules for replacing the variable elements.

Instead of writing each item, test developers can put their efforts into the initial specifications of the item form. Computers can be helpful in calculating some of the variable numbers in story problems and calculation questions. Computers can even help in the actual assembly and printing of tests, including the placement of the correct answer at a random position in the options for multiple-choice questions. Perhaps the greatest advantage of item forms, however, is that they define a *domain* of all the possible questions for a particular task. Domain definition allows CR tests to be developed that are unbiased estimates of the proportion of tasks a student is able to perform in a domain.

Sources of item forms include existing projects in computer-assisted testing and instruction in military training programs and universities. Also, existing test items can be examined to identify those that can be generalized into item forms. Any subject-matter area that contains symbols, coding systems, tables, calculations, or story problems will have item forms waiting to be discovered. Undoubtedly the reader who has just become familiar with the concept of item forms will see more and more places where they can be applied in education and training.

References

Bloom, B. S., Hastings, J. T., & Madaus, G. *Handbook on formative and summative evaluation of student learning*. New York: McGraw-Hill, 1971.

Braby, R., Parrish, W. F., Guitard, C. R., & Aagard, J. A. *Computer-aided authoring of programmed instruction for teaching symbol recognition*. (TAEG Report No. 58) Orlando, Florida: Training Analysis and Evaluation Group, 1978.

Cronbach, L. J., Rajaratnam, N., & Gleser, G. C. Theory of generalizability: A liberalization of reliability theory. *British Journal of Statistical Psychology*, 1963, *16*, 137–163.

Fremer, J., & Anastasio, E. J. Computer-assisted item writing—I (Spelling items). *Journal of Educational Measurement*, 1969, *6*, 69–74.

Freund, J. E. *Modern elementary statistics* (2nd Ed.). Englewood Cliffs, New Jersey: Prentice-Hall, 1960.

Gulliksen, H. *Theory of mental tests*. New York: Wiley, 1950.

Hively, W. *A test-item pool for MINNEMAST science unit 2.1: Measuring weight*. Unpublished paper, MINNEMAST Project, Univ. of Minnesota, 1966.

Hively, W. Introduction to domain-referenced testing. *Educational Technology*, 1974, *14* (6), 5–10.

Hively, W., Maxwell, G., Rabehl, G., Sension, D., & Lundin, S. *Domain-referenced curriculum evaluation: A technical handbook and a case study from the MINNEMAST project*. Los Angeles: Center for the Study of Evaluation, Univ. of California, 1973.

Hively, W., Patterson, H. L., & Page, S. A "universe-defined" system of arithmetic achievement tests. *Journal of Educational Measurement*, 1968, *5*, 275–290.

Hively, W. *Defining criterion behavior for programmed instruction in elementary mathematics*. Unpublished paper, Harvard Univ., 1963.

Johnson, K. J. Pitt's computer-generated chemistry exam. *Proceedings of the Conference on Computers in Undergraduate Curricula*, 1973, 199–204.

Lord, F. M. Sampling fluctuations resulting from the sample of test items. *Psychometrika*, 1955, *20*, 1–22.

Lord, F. M., & Novick, M. R. *Statistical theories of mental test scores*. Reading, Massachusetts: Addison-Wesley, 1968.

McClain, D. H., Wessels, S. W., & Sando, K. M. IPSIM—Additional system enhancements utilized in a chemistry application. *Proceedings of the Conference on Computers in Undergraduate Curricula*, 1975, 139–145.

Millman, J. Criterion-referenced measurement. In W. J. Popham (Ed.), *Evaluation in education: Current applications*. Berkeley, California: McCutchan Publishing Company, 1974.

Millman, J. Computer-based item generation. In R. A. Berk (Ed.), *Criterion-referenced measurement*. Baltimore, Maryland: Johns Hopkins Univ. Press, 1980.

Millman, J., & Outlaw, W. S. Testing by computer. *Association for Educational Data Systems (AEDS) Journal*, 1978, *11*, 57–72.

Olympia, P. L., Jr. Computer generation of truly repeatable examinations. *Educational Technology*, 1975, *14*(6), 53–55.

Osburn, H. G. Item sampling for achievement testing. *Educational and Psychological Measurement*, 1968, *28*, 95–104.

Rabehl, G. *The experimental analysis of educational objectives*. Unpublished doctoral dissertation, Univ. of Minnesota, 1971.

Suppes, P., Jerman, M., & Groen, G. J. Arithmetic drills and review on a computer-based teletype. *Arithmetic Teacher*, 1966, April, 303–308.

Tryon, R. C. Reliability and behavior domain validity: Reformulation and historical critique. *Psychological Bulletin*, 1957, *54*, 229–249.

Tyler, R. W. *Basic principles of curriculum and instruction*. Chicago, Illinois: Univ. of Chicago Press, 1950.

Vickers, F. D. Creative test generators. *Educational Technology*, 1973, *13*(3), 43–44.

Wright, B. D., & Stone, M. H. *Best test design*. Chicago, Illinois: Mesa Press, 1979.

8

The Mapping-Sentence Method

A key feature in the conceptualization of a criterion-referenced test, as described in Chapter 2, is the existence of the item domain. As stated earlier, the item domain and the instructional program should be logically related. In fact, Shoemaker (1975) maintains that there is one and only one item domain for an instructional program. The specifications of an item domain can be seen as the operational definition of the constructs and content in the instruction. The *mapping-sentence method* for specifying the constructs and content in instruction can be adapted from the theory of facet design.

In psychological and educational theories, constructs are believed to be useful entities that are represented in behaviors of persons. For example, *reading readiness* is a construct useful in examining reading behavior. Constructs become scientific, according to Foa (1965), when their measures are found to have empirical relationships with other observable variables predicted by a theory.

In fact, these principles are essentially those prescribed by Cronbach and Meehl (1955) in their classic definition of construct validity. Facet design theory appears to be one way in which a construct can be explicated in terms of measures in a precise and orderly manner.

The essence of facet design is that any construct can be described in terms of its components. Generally, facet design is a way of organizing and defining a

Table 8.1
Use of Guttman's Categorization Matrix: Samples of Cognitive Behavior[a]

	B.1 Figural	B.2 Numerical	B.3 Verbal
A.1 Rule Inferring	Geometric problems	Numerical progressions	Giving subordinates of two words (e.g., car: Ford)
A.2 Rule Applying	Matching cubes	Verbally formulated arithmetic problems	Giving kinds of categories (e.g., Robin: birds)
A.3 Achievement	Learning a symbolic language	Mathematics Physics Chemistry Statistics	History Literature

[a] Adapted from Guttman, 1969.

domain by specifying both the limits and ordering of components and other subparts. Further, facet design provides the structure and boundaries of the domain by specifying summary statements called mapping sentences that are similar to the item forms discussed in Chapter 7.

Historically, facet design has its roots in personality theory (see Foa, 1965 for a discussion of this background), but it was Guttman (1965, 1969) who proposed the application of facet design to achievement testing.

Guttman (1969) proposed a method for categorizing different kinds of subject matter and cognitive behavior. Table 8.1 applies Guttman's method for cognitive behaviors. All cognitive behavior can be viewed in one dimension as figural (B.1), numerical (B.2), or verbal (B.3), and in another dimension as rule-inferring (A.1), rule-applying (A.2), and achievement (A.3). For example, mathematics and physics are achievement and numerical, A.3–B.2; history is achievement and verbal, A.3–B.3.

Many cognitive tests of mental ability can be classified as rule-inferring or rule-applying. The categories of rule-inferring and rule-applying behaviors cutting across the figural, numerical, and verbal levels are similar to Guilford's Structure of the Intellect Model of Human Intelligence (Guilford, 1967). Thus, the context for facet design in achievement tests was set by Guttman in a type of hierarchical theory of learning. The theory posits that types of rule-applying and rule-inferring behavior lead to types of achievement, as a function of the mode of performance (numerical, figural, and verbal).

What Is Facet Design?

Guttman (1969) describes facet design as follows:

> First, a definitional system is specified for the universe of content and observations on it in the form of a mapping sentence. Second, specifications are made about the facets of the mapping sentence. . . . The definitions and specifications lead to a structural hypothesis which is tested by empirical data [p. 56].

Two aspects of the theory are (*a*) content and (*b*) statistical structure. Content deals with the specification of the domain via a summary statement called a *mapping sentence*. The mapping sentence is also the basis for predicting the statistical structure. Thus, theory is linked to empirical observation in a manner that is the essence of the construct validity approach to measurement.

The mapping sentence is the device for creating test items for an achievement domain. The process for creating a mapping sentence is called *structioning*. Each mapping sentence consists of fixed and variable parts. The fixed part of the mapping sentence is similar to an item form shell. Each of the variable elements are called *facets*. Facet elements are analogous to the replacement sets of item forms. The existence of a set of mapping sentences with all facets and facet elements constitutes a facet design. The facet design is the specification of the entire domain.

Guttman (1969, p. 54) provides an example, shown in Table 8.2, of a facet design that also illustrates his analysis of cognitive behavior as represented in Table 8.1. Table 8.2 shows a mapping sentence with four facets that have three,

Table 8.2
A Mapping Sentence

Facet 1

If Student X is given an item presented in $\left\{ \begin{array}{l} \text{figural} \\ \text{numerical} \\ \text{verbal} \end{array} \right\}$

Facet 2   **Facet 3**

language and requiring $\left\{ \begin{array}{l} \text{inference} \\ \text{application} \end{array} \right\}$ of a rule $\left\{ \begin{array}{l} \text{exactly like} \\ \text{similar to} \\ \text{unlike} \end{array} \right\}$

one taught within one of the student's courses, he or she is

Facet 4

likely to answer the item $\left\{ \begin{array}{l} \text{correctly.} \\ \text{incorrectly} \end{array} \right\}$

two, three, and two facet elements, respectively. Facet elements appear as the variable wordings of the sentence. The example serves to illustrate that rule-inferring or rule-applying behavior may serve to predict achievement. The third facet, in the mapping sentence of Table 8.2 suggests that rules should be classified according to their similarity to rule descriptions in instruction. The important point that Guttman makes is that attention needs to be paid to the relationship between the kind of achievement required in a course of study and the cognitive abilities needed to perform adequately. His analysis reveals, for example, that students with high levels of rule-inferring and rule-applying behavior in a numerical category, may be better performers in achievement of a numerical nature.

With the mapping sentence shown in Table 8.2 one could compose 36 different sentences, some of which could be true and some of which could be false.

For example we could compose the following statements for true–false questions:

1. If Student X is given an item presented in verbal language and requiring inference of a rule exactly like one taught within one of the student's courses, he or she is likely to answer the item incorrectly.
2. If Student X is given an item presented in numerical language requiring application of a rule similar to one taught within one of the student's courses, he or she is likely to answer the item correctly.

The format could be changed to multiple choice by holding constant the last three facets, rearranging the sentence, and letting the first facet (e.g., verbal, numerical, and figural) provide the correct answer and two foils. A completion format could be used, with one element removed from any of the 36 sentences. In this mode, the total number of completion items possible increases to 144, because with any of the 36 sentences, there are four facets and four possible completion items per sentence. The fourth facet in Table 8.2 could be expanded into four elements: high performance, moderate–high, moderate–low, and low. This would increase the number of sentences possible to 72. Obviously, the more elements and more facets in a mapping sentence, the more items possible. When structioning leads to the production of many mapping sentences, the domain may achieve significant size, ranging from several hundred sentences to even several thousand. Guttman (1969, p. 57) provides another example of a mapping sentence so complex that the number of possible sentences is over 25 million.

According to Engel and Martuza (1976), mapping sentences offer a number of unique benefits. First, items, stems, and foils can be created systematically. The foils can be logically selected from alternative elements of any facet. Since foil writing is a difficult aspect of item writing (Roid & Haladyna, 1980), and since foil writing is most subject to biases from item writers (Roid & Haladyna, 1978), it is easy to see why the systematic creation of foils through the use of an automated method is so attractive.

Second, there is contiguity among foils, some of which are closer to being correct than others. Therefore, the selection of a foil can provide diagnostic value. The student who chooses a less plausible foil has more to learn than the one who chooses a more plausible foil.

Third, there is a logical relationship between the content of the instruction and the test item. The mapping sentence becomes the basis for both instruction and testing.

Fourth, the creation of multiple, parallel forms is easier because items can be randomly generated for each test form without fear of biasing with respect to overall content or item difficulty and discrimination.

Fifth, computer generation of items is possible (Millman, 1980).

Sixth, facet designs can begin with instructional objectives that often form the basis for mapping sentences. Since much of educational curriculum planning includes instructional objectives, the translation of these objectives into mapping sentences, and the use of instructional objectives to identify the boundaries for the facet design can be easily accomplished.

The Engel and Martuza study (1976) experimented with item generation procedures and a modified facet design approach. The procedures permitted more item-writer freedom than originally intended in facet design, but provided a reasonable compromise between a rigorous and less rigorous application of the procedure. Phase 1 of the study was intended to develop a procedure for implementing facet design with a group of experienced item writers who were knowledgeable in a content area. Phase 2 included an empirical study of the properties of items so designed. Phase 2 also included a test of fit between the definition of the content and the actual test.

Engel and Martuza (1976) concluded that (*a*) the procedures they developed were systematic yet flexible enough to produce items in highly structured as well as loosely structured content areas, and that (*b*) the systematic development of foils was successful, permitting the diagnostic use of foils when selected by students.

The Engel and Martuza study provides sufficient detail for implementing facet design in a curriculum study and specifying how item writers can develop test items that lead to construct-valid interpretations.

As we have seen, facet design is uniquely tied to a theoretical analysis of content. As such, it is, perhaps, the only technology of test-item writing that leads directly to the establishment of valid interpretations of test responses. The foils it produces can be used diagnostically.

Limitations of Facet Design

The facet design approach does suffer from some limitations, as Martuza (1979) points out. Applying facet design to loosely structured material may be challenging for instructional developers. As with the linguistic approach to item writing, where the structure of prose is crucial, the person wishing to use facet design must be able to clearly understand the structure of the content in instructional material. Ideally, a content structure, such as the hierarchy of operations in arithmetic, should be based on a consensus among scholars in the field. Instructional material in the sciences may provide such structure, whereas humanities and even some of the social sciences may not. The clarity of the prose in instructional materials may also be important in making mapping sentences apparent.

A second limitation mentioned by Martuza is that one person's perception of the mapping sentences and facets of a content area may not necessarily agree with another's perceptions. Thus, there is the chance for endless mapping sentences, facets, and facet elements, with lack of agreement among developers being a major detriment to progress.

Another limitation we can add to those suggested by Martuza is that an enormous effort is put into mapping sentences and developing facets and elements. If the efforts lead to examples like those provided earlier, then our yield in numbers and quality of items will be meager. On the other hand, the one mapping sentence offered by Guttman (1969, p. 57) is quite productive in terms of numbers of items. Thus, it would seem, that more intensive efforts might lead to usable facet designs.

A final limitation of this method is the lack of empirical research at the time of this writing. Although the work of Engel and Martuza (1976) is important in demonstrating the feasibility of facet designs in test design, it is one of the very few research studies examining this theory. The early work of Guttman (1969) indicates a potential for an integrative theory of cognitive behavior that incorporates ideas of mental ability and achievement, yet there is surprisingly little effort to extend or develop this line of thinking. The recent work of Scandura (1977), as well as the work of Landa (1974), seems to be most closely related to the intent of facet design.

Although the attention given to facet design has been increasing, studies dealing with the properties of facet-based test items have not been extensive or numerous. This may be attributable to the great difficulty one faces in constructing mapping sentences to represent the aspects of content that need to be learned by students. Berk (1978), on the other hand, has shown that standard instructional objectives can be used to create the facet designs desirable for creating item domains.

The next section of this chapter provides a description of the procedures one follows in developing facet designs and ultimately writing questions. An example is provided at the end of this chapter displaying the entire process.

Creating Facet Designs

The specification of a content domain through facet design in the context of achievement testing is a process that requires considerable knowledge of content as well as of the process of instruction as it applies to this content. There are no hard and fast rules for developing mapping sentences. Engel and Martuza (1976) and Berk (1978) suggest that the instructional objective be used as the basis for a mapping sentence. They provide six steps for creating items from a facet design.

STEP 1. SELECTING AN INSTRUCTIONAL OBJECTIVE

The objective can be the basic building block of the mapping sentence. Within this objective one must identify important concepts that may be subject to identification as facets. For example, consider the following objective: The student will identify United States presidents when given a partial list of their accomplishments and political philosophies. *United States presidents* may represent one facet for which there will be many elements, and *accomplishments* and *philosophies* other facets. Given the great numbers of each of the three facets, the potential for many test items is great.

STEP 2. LIST INSTRUCTIONAL MATERIAL

Here some textual material is required to give the item writer some basis for amplifying the objective's instructional intent. Most instructional material is drawn from textbooks or training manuals that describe in greater detail, and in prose, the instructional intent.

STEP 3. DEVELOP AN AMPLIFIED OBJECTIVE

Amplified objectives were introduced by Popham (1978, pp. 129–131) in response to the vagueness and ambiguity that may be expressed in instructional objectives. Baker (1974) had also called for elaborations of objectives into domain specifications. An amplified objective provides a general description of the content to be specified, provides a sample item, and then describes the stimulus and response attributes of resulting items. For example, an objective may state that the student must apply principles of United States foreign policy to any simulated diplomatic situation. An amplified objective might state the form of the simulated situation, the name of the policy to be followed (e.g., the Monroe

Doctrine), and the standard form of the test question. Response attributes might indicate that four options are possible, that each foil will describe a logical foreign policy action. The list of foreign policies might also be given.

STEP 4. GENERATE A MAPPING SENTENCE

Simply stated, the amplified objective becomes the basis for the construction of a mapping sentence. Facets are identified and elements created that span the full range of possibilities for each facet.

STEP 5. GENERATE THE ITEM FACET STRUCTURE

As shown in Table 8.2, a mapping sentence and item facet structure is given. The explication of facets is critical both to completely mapping the domain and to providing enough alternatives to increase the number of possible sentences. Increasing the number of facets increases the number of sentences at an exponential rate; increasing the number of elements of a facet increases the number of sentences at a multiplicative rate. For example, a mapping sentence with a 3 × 2 × 3 (three facets, with three, two, and three elements respectively) yields 18 sentences. Adding a fourth facet of three levels increases the number of sentences to 54; adding three elements to the second facet produces 45 sentences. Adding facets yields a richer, more item-productive domain than adding elements to facets.

STEP 6. WRITE THE ITEM

This part could be the most computerized or clerical of the six steps. It simply involves the selection of a combination of conditions from each facet and the systematic variation of foils following the identification of the correct response.

As can be seen, the greatest effort goes into Steps 2, 3, 4, and 5. Step 6 (item generation) then follows in a virtually automated fashion. Thus, the item domain takes on the size needed for most testing needs within systematic instruction.

Runkel and McGrath (1972, p. 19) provide some rules that guide the item developer who uses facet design. These are summarized from Berk:

1. All properties or facets that have been chosen for a concept should be applicable to all objects being classified. Every facet should be applicable to all objects. Referring to the mapping sentence in Table 8.2, four facets exist to explicate Guttman's theory. Is this adequate? Do each of the facets cover all instructional settings and types of cognitive behavior? This kind of inquiry is a logical analysis of the mapping sentence for the criterion of inclusiveness. Any

exceptions should be noted, or the mapping sentence will be in jeopardy of being invalidated on these logical grounds.

2. Each facet should be divided into all possible elements. The essential question is: Are all elements given? For Guttman's example in Table 8.2, only high and low performances are listed for the fourth facet. Is this sufficient, or do we need three or more elements? In the third facet of Table 8.2, are the listed degrees of rule-similarity adequate? Again, an objective and logical analysis is required as the basis for an answer to each of these questions.

3. Elements should be mutually exclusive and should not overlap. Elements of one facet may not be elements of another facet also. If an object can be classified in more than one element of a facet, we must question the integrity of that facet. Drawing from the example in Table 8.2, if some problem could be classified as both verbal and figural, that facet would be subject to closer searching and possible revision or removal.

4. The relationships among facets should be logical and specific. If an order exists, this should be specified as well. The mapping sentence should be coherent, and the facets should be arranged in an orderly manner within the mapping sentence. The example we have been studying in Table 8.2 is quite good in terms of explicating Guttman's analysis of learning presented earlier in this chapter. All facets lead up to the last facet, that of student performance, which is the behavior to be predicted from knowledge about elements in the three previous facets. The logical relationships among facets, as well as among mapping sentences, can be viewed as the essence of formulating and explicating constructs, as part of the process needed in construct validation (Cronbach & Meehl, 1955).

5. The relationships among elements should also be logical and well described. Whenever possible, there should be an order to elements, where there are some surprising benefits. For example, the mapping sentence in Table 8.2 may lead to the establishment of multiple-choice items the options being the levels of performance in Facet 4, as predicted from knowledge of previous elements from Facets 1, 2, and 3. Students who select widely discrepant options and students who select options that are reasonably close exhibit two different levels of incorrect performance. The former type has a serious learning deficiency, while the latter may need only minimal corrective instruction. The ordering of elements, therefore, has much to do with providing diagnostic value in multiple-choice questions as well as providing good foils.

6. The facets should exhaust the supply of possible facets of a domain and represent the essence of the domain as governed by the intent of instruction. Whether or not the facets adequately map the domain is a question that is beyond the immediate mapping sentence [1978, p. 64].

In summary, an instructional domain consists of many mapping sentences, and each mapping sentence contains many facets and their respective elements.

The totality of the structioning process (the sum of all mapping sentences and their parts, the facets and elements) can be evaluated against standards imposed by examples of behavior for which the instruction is being designed. If there are situations or conditions that are not accounted by the facet design, then the adequacy of facets, elements, and mapping sentences is questionable, and more work is needed. We can conceive of mature and immature facet designs, the latter being precursors of the former, and instructional developers must constantly refine their designs to produce a better, more comprehensive, and appropriate facet design.

Once items have been generated, they may be subjected to scrutiny through empirical observation. Items should be administered to students in various stages of instruction, and item data should reveal patterns that are predictable from the foregoing analysis. As Berk (1978) submits, "A proposed testing procedure based on hierarchical assumptions of the facets, in particular, indicates a prediction about the content structure. It must be validated against a corresponding statistical structure [p. 66]." This type of statistical evidence was presented by Engel and Martuza (1976) who first applied a modified facet design strategy to a domain, and then checked for an empirical fit between the operational definition and the data. In the spirit of Berk's idea, Engel and Martuza evaluated the fit of the data to the structural model prescribed by the facet design. This study appears to be unique in investigating the statistical structure of a facet design. Both the methodology and the results are of interest.

Three teams were created, and each were given varying degrees of information regarding the creation and use of a facet design. Two instructional objectives formed the basis for the mapping sentences. The hypotheses of the study centered around two concerns: (*a*) that test items of equivalent difficulty would be written by team members if full information about facet design and item construction were given, and (*b*) that foils would have diagnostic value if full information, rather than only partial information, were given to item writers.

The results of the study indicated that within logically parallel item pairs, when information about the item facets was available to item writers, no differences existed between item difficulties, as predicted. When pairs of items were logically matched as a function of different teams, there were consistent differences in item difficulties, as predicted. The results also indicated that when item writers had different information or were given liberties in selecting their own wording, item difficulties varied predictably. Similar variation between item writers was found by Roid, Haladyna, Shaughnessy, and Finn (1979), and Roid, Haladyna, and Shaughnessy (1980). An analysis of foils and their diagnostic values suggested that foils constructed using the facet design method yielded psychologically sound interpretations with implications for remediation. Engel and Martuza (1976) concluded that "consistent selection of the distractor (foil) type would lead to a specific strategy for remediation [p. 26]." Thus, this study has shown the reasonableness of constructing items from mapping sentences, particularly those based on instructional objectives. Items were created that showed controllable difficulty and diagnostic power from foils that are not provided by many conventional multiple-choice testing formats.

Examples of Mapping Sentences as Part of a Facet Design

In this part of the chapter, we will present some mapping sentences and show how each can be used to develop test items. Then we will demonstrate a unique application of facet design—the measure of cognitive ability.

TRUE-FALSE TESTING

The simplest application of facet design theory and an easy way to develop test items is in true-false testing. A mapping sentence is constructed with facet and elements selected. Typically, facets are limited to two in number. More than two facets would result in a sentence that would be far too complex for the familiar true-false format. A good true-false item should contain a single idea.

All combinations of elements are used to produce sentences, some of which are true and some of which are false. These sentences comprise the test items that completely map all possibilities for a particular mapping sentence. A set of mapping sentences constitutes a domain. An example adapted from Berk (1978, pp. 63, 65), shown in Table 8.3, is a simple objective from which a total of 20 true-false items can be derived.

As we can see from Table 8.3, the production of the 20 items is completely automated. An item writer need only follow the rule to make it possible for every combination of elements to appear in the mapping sentence shell.

COMPLETION

A completion item format is as simple to use as true-false questioning. The main difference is that among sentences derived from a mapping sentence, true statements must be identified and placed in a separate category. These sentences constitute the pool of test items. For each of these, the element that distinguishes each sentence from any other must be removed, leaving the sentence in the form:

Algorithms are most appropriate for defining_____ domains.

In Chapter 6, we discussed algorithmic transformations based on sentence structures. Using that approach we would further revise the foregoing sample sentence so that it would appear as a question:

Table 8.3
The Development of True–False Questions from an Instructional Objective

---

Instructional objective: Given a type of domain strategy (e.g., item forms, algorithms, mapping sentences), the student will correctly identify the content domain that is appropriate.

Mapping sentence: " (Facet A) are most appropriate for defining (Facet B) domains."

Facet A has four elements:
1. Item transformations
2. Item forms
3. Algorithms
4. Mapping sentences

Facet B has five elements:
1. Reading
2. Language
3. Mathematics
4. Science
5. Social studies

Here are two of the 20 possible true–false items:

A_3B_3 *Algorithms* are most appropriate for defining *mathematics*. (False)
A_2B_5 *Item forms* are most appropriate for defining *social studies*. (False)

What kinds of domains are most appropriate for algorithms?

Or,

Algorithms are most appropriate for defining what kinds of domains?

MULTIPLE-CHOICE TESTING

The selected response format with four or more options requires that the student recognize the correct answer among a group of incorrect options. The writing of multiple-choice items based on instructional objectives is fraught with peril, as objectives allow much too much liberty in creating item stems and foils. Foil writing, as we have said, is the most difficult and important aspect of writing the multiple-choice item, and facet design theory makes foil writing both more automatic and more diagnostic.

A good example of a single mapping sentence developed from an instructional objective to create a large number of useful multiple-choice items, as provided by Engel and Martuza (1976), is shown in Table 8.4.

In Engel's example, the student must compute the relationship between two variables, and the mapping sentence identifies a total of ten facets, five of which enter into stem construction and five into foil construction. The selection of a foil, versus the selection of a correct option, takes on diagnostic value, because foils are systematically varied. Consequently, some foils are closer to being correct than others. This, in turn, dictates the direction and degree of remedial instruction on a student-to-student basis. In fact, the student's knowledge of results may be sufficient to provide the remedial instruction.

SKILL

A skill is distinguished from knowledge principally by its orientation toward a performance or a product. Assessment of knowledge is oriented toward an

Table 8.4
A Systematic Approach

Objectives
1. Given a set of ordered pairs of values on variable X and Y, correctly calculate r_{XY}.
2. Given statements about the Pearson r, point biserial, *phi*, and rank order (*rho*) correlation coefficients, the learner will identify those that accurately compare and contrast the various measures.

Mapping Sentence

Given a
- A. Presentation form
  1. table
  2. prose passage

in
- B. Content form
  1. verbatim
  2. concept

with
- C. A set of ordered pairs of values on variables
  1. 3 pairs
  2. 4 pairs
  3. 5 pairs
X

- D. Variable X
  1. one digit
  2. two digits
  3. three digits

and Y
- E. Variable Y
  1. one digit
  2. two digits
  3. three digits
,

the student will select the correct value of r_{XY} from a set of alternatives that vary with respect to

- F. Type of score
  1. deviation
  2. raw

- G. Multiplication of signed numbers
  1. correct
  2. incorrect
  $$- \times + = +$$
  $$+ \times - = +$$
  $$- \times - = -$$

- H. Division of SP (X, Y)
  1. no
  2. yes, that is, SP $(X, Y)/N$

- I. Square root of SS(X) SS(Y)
  1. yes
  2. no

- J. Type of unit
  1. no unit
  2. linear unit
  3. square unit

inference about information acquired. With knowledge, the inference is made on the basis of a paper and pencil test. Nonetheless, we can infer skill through paper-and-pencil performance as in the following example.

The student will correctly chart the shortest course on roads or highways between any two towns in any state given a road map. If the distance is great enought to justify an overnight stay, the student must identify a town in which to stay. The student must also identify places to stop for meals, picnics, and gas along the way.

The example requires a number of higher level thinking behaviors. The example also makes use of the kind of real-life behaviors that have embodied the competency-based education and testing movement that prevails in so many states (Spady, 1977).

Facet-design theory can be used to develop a mapping sentence for the generation of items for the measurement of this skill quite effectively, as shown in Table 8.5. The key to a successful mapping sentence is the generation of sufficient facets and sufficient elements for each facet. With larger numbers of facets and elements, the boundaries of the domain of items are extended and the domain becomes more comprehensive. The potential for useful items is greater, and students will not suffer from a lack of practice and test items during instruction.

The example in Table 8.5 is limited to 10 elements for the towns, making a possibility of 90 trips (e.g., Town 1 to Town 2, Town 2 to Town 1, . . . , Town 9 to Town 10, and Town 10 to Town 9). Two possibilities are the most scenic route, which is usually longer but more enjoyable, and the most direct route, for travelers who are eager to get there. Between any two towns, there will be other towns, gas stops, and the like, that comprise possible right answers for the condition that requires the student to select gas and roadside rests for car service and meals. When the distance is over a certain limit (an average day's drive,

Table 8.5
A Mapping Sentence for Measuring a Skill

Given a car that gets 30 mpg and two towns, one of which is a destination, the other a starting point
      {Given two towns (Town 1, . . ., Town 10)},
the student will identify the travel route that is the
      {1. shortest, most direct}
      {2. most scenic   }
route between the two towns and will identify places to stop for meals and gas and at least one
      {1. roadside rest.   }
      {2. park between   }
      {   the two towns.   }
If the distance is great enough to initiate an overnight stay, the student must identify the appropriate town in which to stay.

---

approximately 300 mi.), the student must identify a place about 300 mi. from point of departure for an overnight stay.

From this example, a number of multiple-choice items can be generated that can be used to assess a person's skill at trip planning. Since the performance is directly aimed at providing a written response, no inference is really necessary; the student can or cannot perform the trip planning, and a great many items for practice or testing are possible.

It should also be made clear that in most cases, we would probably use a format in which the student develops a written plan that we would evaluate using a checklist or a key. In this instance, for any given pair of towns, only one set of responses would be correct, if we are strict enough to limit gas stops to every 250 mi. and limit breakfast, lunch, and dinner hours (e.g., lunch 11:30 A.M.–1:30 P.M.). By carefully specifying departure and arrival times for the trip, we can clearly identify the correct answers and reduce uncertainty about the range of correct answers.

Mental Ability

It is possible to generate facet designs for mental ability. An example given by Guttman and Schlesinger (1967) involves analytic abilities relating to patterns of geometric figures. We modified these researchers' approach in an effort to illustrate how such a mapping sentence could be used to generate a universe of test items that measured these abilities.

The mapping sentence with its three facets and elements for each facet are shown in Table 8.6. As shown there, there are two shapes (Facet A), two sizes (Facet B), and four orientations (Facet C). The total number of combinations of the elements from each facet is $2 \times 2 \times 4 = 16$.

We generated some steps for constructing patterns that vary systematically in shape, size, and orientation in sets of four objects. The test exercise at the bottom of Table 8.6 calls for the removal of the fourth object, and the student must identify the missing object according to the pattern. The rules for generating items are as follows:

Step 1: Randomly select a facet to exclude.

Step 2: Randomly select a sequence of four objects that vary with respect to the other two facets.

Step 3: Place the existing sequence of four objects in boxes 1, 2, 3, and 4 as shown in Table 8.6.

Step 4: Randomly vary the two facets included in the sequence and place the resulting objects as foils a, b, c, and d.

Step 5: Replace the object in Box 4 with a question mark.

Table 8.6
A Diagram for Generating a Universe of Items to Test the
Recognition of a Sequence of Objects

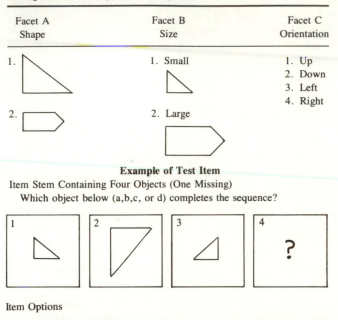

Facet A Shape	Facet B Size	Facet C Orientation
1.	1. Small	1. Up 2. Down 3. Left 4. Right
2.	2. Large	

Example of Test Item

Item Stem Containing Four Objects (One Missing)
   Which object below (a,b,c, or d) completes the sequence?

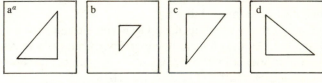

Item Options

a Correct answer.

This simple mapping sentence should serve to illustrate that identifying facets and developing relations among the facets is difficult but rewarding insofar as the procedure systematically creates items and foils for special abilities.

While Guilford's Structure of the Intellect model is a most complete study of the complex nature of intelligence, the tests of the aspects of that model come from a long history of factor analytic studies by French (1951) and subsequent studies by Guilford (1967). The tests and items of these tests were not necessarily theoretically developed, as is the case in facet design theory. Consequently, facet design theory has implications not only for achievement test construction but for ability testing as well. The major limitation of this approach for ability testing is obviously a lack of research and development that capitalizes on Guttman's work and extends it into an instructional system. Guttman's suggestions (Guttman,

1969) remain only skeletal with respect to such a rapprochement between intelligence and school achievement.

Summary

In this chapter, we have tried to describe the background for the development of facet design theory as a basis for defining the structure of content and for developing items that measure the learning of this content. As we have seen, facet design is a powerful concept that has theoretical significance in content analysis as well as in test-item writing. The most attractive feature of facet design is its ability to generate large numbers of items that conceptually exhaust the possibilities for items that map the entire domain of interest. One of the most limiting characteristics of facet design theory is the skill that is needed by the instructional developer to produce mapping sentences that adequately tap the domain. Martuza (1979) notes that different persons may produce different conceptions of domains, as expressed by different mapping sentences, facets, and elements.

The search for an ultimate design for a particular course of study, such as freshman algebra or American history, is therefore, quite frustrating when one uses facet design. On the other hand, scientific inquiry is fruitful when persons interested in the same objective reach agreement on the essence of a topic, subject matter, or content area. Facet design theory may provide a means for such discussions and resolutions regarding critical domains like reading, social studies, science, and mathematics, which comprise basic skills in public schools. In specialized, more specific applications, facet design theory provides a basis for sharing thinking about what is taught and what is tested.

A major problem with the application of facet design theory is the need for further development to promote this technology of test-item writing from an interesting idea to a practical methodology.

The work of Guttman and his colleagues (Guttman, 1965, 1969; Guttman & Schlesinger, 1967) has stimulated others (Engel & Martuza, 1976; Berk, 1978) into thoughtful and effective applications and research. Guttman's ideas about mental abilities and achievement also bear further examination. Facet design theory permits the systematic application of these ideas in much the manner that Guilford (1967) has outlined in his classic work on the nature of human intelligence and in accordance with his belief that intelligence is multifaceted.

References

Baker, E. L. Beyond objectives: Domain-referenced tests for evaluation and instructional improvement. *Educational Technology,* 1974, *14*(6), 10–16.

Berk, R. A. The application of structural facet theory to achievement test construction. *Educational Research Quarterly*, 1978, *3*(3), 62–72.

Cronbach, L. J., & Meehl, P. E. Construct validity in psychological tests. *Psychological Bulletin*, 1955, *52*, 281–302.

Engel, J. D., & Martuza, V. R. *A systematic approach to the construction of domain-referenced multiple-choice test items*. Paper presented at the meetings of the American Psychological Association, Washington, D.C., September 1976.

Foa, U. G. New developments in facet design and analysis. *Psychological Review*, 1965, *72*, 272–274.

French, J. L. The description of aptitude and achievement tests in terms of potential factors. *Psychometric Monographs*, 1951, *5*.

Guilford, J. P. *The nature of human intelligence*. New York: McGraw-Hill, 1967.

Guttman, L. The structure of interrelations among intelligence tests. *Proceedings of the 1964 Invitational Conference on Testing Problems*. Princeton, New Jersey. Educational Testing Service, 1965.

Guttman, L. Integration of test design and analysis. *Proceedings of the 1969 Invitational Conference on Testing Problems*. Princeton, New Jersey: Educational Testing Service, 1969.

Guttman, L., & Schlesinger, I. M. Systematic construction of distractors for ability and achievement test items. *Educational and Psychological Measurement*, 1967, *27*, 569–580.

Landa, L. N. *Algorithmization in learning and instruction*. F. F. Kopstein (Ed.), V. Bennett (Trans.) Englewood Cliffs, New Jersey: Educational Technology Publications, 1974.

Martuza, V. *Domain definition/item generation for criterion-referenced tests: A review and directions for future research*. Paper presented at the annual meeting of the Eastern Educational Research Association, Kiawah Island, South Carolina, February 1979.

Millman, J. Computer-based item generation. In R. A. Berk (Ed.), *Criterion-referenced measurement*. Baltimore, Maryland: Johns Hopkins Univ. Press, 1980.

Popham, W. J. *Criterion-referenced measurement*. Englewood Cliffs, New Jersey: Prentice-Hall, 1978.

Roid, G. H., & Haladyna, T. M. A comparison of objective-based and modified-Bormuth item writing techniques. *Educational and psychological measurement*, 1978, *35*, 19–28.

Roid, G. H., & Haladyna, T. M. *Handbook on item writing for criterion-referenced testing*. San Diego, California: Navy Personnel Research and Development Center, 1979.

Roid, G. H., & Haladyna, T. M. The emergence of a technology of test item writing. *Review of educational research*, 1980, *50*, 293–314.

Roid, G. H., Haladyna, T. M., & Shaughnessy, J. *A comparison of item-writing methods for criterion-referenced testing*. Paper presented at the annual meeting of the National Council on Measurement in Education, Boston, April 1980.

Roid, G. H., Haladyna, T. M., Shaughnessy, J., & Finn, P. *Item writing for domain-referenced tests of prose learning*. Paper presented at the annual meeting of the American Educational Research Association, San Francisco, 1979.

Runkel, P. J., & McGrath, J. E. *Research on human behavior: A systematic guide to method*. New York: Holt 1972.

Scandura, J. M. *Problem solving: A structural/process approach with educational implications*. New York: Academic Press, 1977.

Shoemaker, D. M. Toward a framework for achievement testing. *Review of Educational Research*, 1975, *45*, 127–148.

Spady, W. G. Competency-based education: A bandwagon in search of a definition. *Educational Researcher*, 1977, *6*(1), 9–14.

9

Test Items for Concepts

Frequently, when educators discuss testing, they refer to the desire to go "beyond facts." Books have been written about testing for higher level thinking (Miller, Haladyna, & Williams, 1978). Popular critics of educational practices in the United States have even commented on the level of questions used by teachers (Holt, 1964). Workshop materials for teachers and university professors frequently outline procedures, that may include videotaping and practice, designed to encourage the asking of questions that really make students think. Chapters 9, 10, and 11 will be concerned with the measurement of some aspects of higher levels of thinking.

Concept learning is contrasted with the learning of principles or procedures and with other cognitive functions such as the application of learned material. Most educational programs have objectives that require the learning of concepts. Fortunately for the test developer, there has been considerable research and development on concept learning. Some areas of research have concentrated on perceptual patterns and other visual "concepts," that have not as yet been shown to apply directly to school learning (Carroll, 1963). Other areas of research on concept learning have focused on the conditions of learning (Gagné, 1965, 1970), or the learning effects of conceptual questions (Andre, 1979). There are fewer complete approaches to the writing of actual test items. The method for developing test items for concept learning to be presented here is the most complete approach currently available for the analysis and domain-based testing of concepts. This method was developed by Tiemann and Markle (1978a), and more details and examples of their method can be obtained from their original work, which is highly recommended.

The method of Tiemann and Markle is a synthesis and an inventive addition to the important work on conceptual learning in schools (e.g., Gagné, 1965; Anderson, 1972; Merrill, 1971; Mechner, 1965). One of the basic assumptions of this work is that the full understanding of a concept cannot be taught or tested by a single item. As Mechner (1965) has said, "one single experiment or observation is not enough for the formation of a concept, for two reasons: (a) it is not possible to generalize from one instance, and (b) in order to form a discrimination, the student needs at least one instance and one noninstance of the concept in question [p. 480]." The importance of instances (examples) in the teaching and testing of concepts has been stressed by several investigators (e.g., Anderson, 1972, p. 152; Merrill, Reigeluth, & Faust, 1979, p. 182). Gagné (1970) has particularly deplored the "single item used in traditional achievement testing" because it "constitutes an uncontrolled, ambiguous measure which can only in rare instances be shown to be related directly to the learning outcome of interest [p. 372]." In explaining this, Gagné (1971, p. 367) gives the example of teaching the concept of a certain shade of tan, called "bilpad." If the student is presented with one shade of tan along with three other shades of red, green, and blue, and asked "Which is a bilpad?" sufficient measurement will not have been made. It would be important, at least, to test discrimination between several shades of tan.

Anderson (1972, p. 152) has emphasized that a student's verbatim recall of the definition of a concept cannot be considered an indication of comprehension. The acceptable method of teaching and testing concepts from definitions is to provide the student with a paraphrase of the definition. The student is asked either to identify the paraphrased definition after being given the name of the concept or to provide or select the name of the concept after being given the paraphrased definition. Because students may simply repeat the verbatim definition from instruction, a selected response mode is recommended in which the item presents the name of the concept with alternative, paraphrased definitions. The student's selection of a paraphrased version of the definition indicates a deeper comprehension than is indicated by his or her selection of the definition in the exact form in which it was first studied.

There is some evidence that the use of both definitions and examples of concepts in instruction provides the best learning by students. Johnson and Stratton (1966) used dictionary-type definitions, short stories, synonyms of concepts, and classifications of examples and nonexamples and found that instruction containing a mixture of these methods was more effective than any of the methods used separately.

The methods developed by Tiemann and Markle (1978a, 1978b) in concept testing can result in the specification of domains of examples and nonexamples of concepts. The method provides a systematic way for both teaching and testing the student's real understanding of concepts. The method is replicable and based on rules so that a public description of the method of test construction can be provided. This is because the method is based on lists of all the possible examples and nonexamples of each concept and uses tests composed of samples from each list. Becoming skilled in the method of concept analysis will provide a highly useful tool to the test-item writer.

In order to present the method in rather complete form, it will be necessary to discuss

1. The definition of identities and concepts
2. Critical and variable attributes of concepts
3. Testing for generalization and discrimination
4. Listing and sampling examples and nonexamples
5. Advanced methods of testing coordinate concepts and principles

The foregoing list suggests five steps in understanding the Tiemann and Markle method of writing items for concept testing. Each of these steps will be discussed in turn.

Differentiating Identities and Concepts

A *concept* represents a class of things, objects, events, ideas, or relations, to each member of which we give the same label. All of the members of the class vary among themselves, and yet we group them all together, give them the same label, and respond to them by describing them by the same word or phrase. For example, when we see a four-legged domestic animal that barks, we think to ourselves, "There is a dog." When we teach a child about dogs, we want to show them lots of examples of members of the class *dog*—we show them large dogs, small dogs, hairy dogs, and hairless dogs. All of these dogs vary among themselves, but we group them together and call them by the same name.

If we are teaching the concept of "homonym," we explain that it involves words with the same pronunciation but different origins and meanings. We give examples such as *weak* and *week,* or *mail* and *male.* We emphasize that words can be of the same spelling (seal, 'the animal' and seal, 'to shut') and that they may exist not only in pairs but in larger numbers (*to, two, too*).

An identity has only one member, no matter how complicated it may be, or all its members are exactly alike. For example, an *IBM 360, Model 50,* is an identity; "computer," "data processing system," and "terminal" are concepts. Following are several examples of distinctions between concepts and identities.

Concept	Identity
transistor	General Electric PNP transistor
punctuation mark	comma
blood vessel	aorta
polishing agent	pumice
chemical element	chlorine

That the world of instruction and teaching abounds with concepts is evidenced by the lists in Table 9.1 given by Markle and Tiemann (1970) and by Mechner (1965).

Attributes of Concepts

In order to analyze a concept we need to identify its *attributes*. The characteristics that all the members of a class have are called *critical attributes*. Table 9.2 presents an analysis of the concept "chair." The critical attributes are three in number. A chair must be a one-person seat, must have a back, and must allow for an appropriate sitting position. The attribute of a one-person seat is critical to the concept of "chair" because if an object holds two people, it will be a sofa,

Table 9.1

Examples of Concepts in a Wide Range of Subject Matters

Subject matter	Concept
Literature	Soliloquy
Grammar	Antonym
Speech and theatre	Theatre of the Absurd
Political science	Political power
History	Mercantilism
Sociology	Subculture
Physical education	Fly foul ball
French	Doubt
German	Diphthong
Spanish	Superlative
Music	Early Mozart
Medicine	Infarction
Psychology	Behavioral contingency
Mathematics	Set
Biology	Angiosperm
Physics	Free vector
Geography	Floodplain
Art	Perspective

Table 9.2
Analysis of the Concept of Chair[a]

Critical Attributes (CAs)

1. One-person seat
2. Supports the back
3. Appropriate sitting position

Rational set of nonexamples	Description of nonexamples
Lacks CA 1; has CAs 2 and 3	Two-person sofa
Lacks CA 2; has CAs 1 and 3	Small stool
Lacks CA 3; has CAs 1 and 2	Canvas/frame beach lounger

Variable Attributes (VAs)

4. Construction material
   (a) wood   (b) metal   (c) plastic   (d) upholstery   (e) combinations
5. Arms
   (a) present   (b) absent
6. Rocker
   (a) yes   (b) no
7. Number of legs
   (a) none   (b) one   (c) two   (d) three   (e) four
8. Size of back
   (a) high   (b) medium   (c) low

Examples for a complete test of generalization

Rational set of varied examples	Description of examples
4a, 5a, 6a, 7a, 8a	A wooden rocker (no legs) with arms and high back
4e, 5a, 6b, 7b, 8a	An upholstered oval (egg) chair with arms and high back swiveling on one metal pedestal leg
4b, 5b, 6b, 7c, 8b	An armless metal kitchen chair with two spring-arch platform legs and medium-sized back
4c, 5a, 6b, 7d, 8c	A plastic designer chair with low back, arms, and three arch legs
4d, 5a, 6b, 7e, 8b	An upholstered easy chair with four legs, medium back, and arms

[a] Adapted from P. W. Tiemann and S. M. Markle. *Analyzing instructional content: A guide to instruction and evaluation.* Copyright 1978 by Stipes Pub. Reprinted by permission.

loveseat, bench, or other nonexample. By changing each one of the critical attributes in turn, you can create nonexamples. If we took a tall, wooden chair and removed the back, we might create something that looked like a stool and not a chair. When people really understand a concept, they use these critical attributes in their minds even if they are not aware of them.

Characteristics of class members that vary among members are called *variable attributes*. These attributes are irrelevant to the concept and hence are sometimes called *irrelevant attributes*. For example, it is irrelevant whether a chair is made out of metal or wood or whether it is upholstered. As shown in Table 9.2, construction material, presence of arms, rockers, number of legs, and sizes of the sides and back are all variable attributes of the concept of "chair." These variable attributes help to provide a wealth of examples of members of the class of objects in the concept "chair." By investing some time in listing the critical and variable attributes of a concept, the instructor or test developer can provide a wealth of examples and nonexamples for both teaching and testing a concept.

Some of the critical and variable attributes of the concept "fly foul ball" in baseball are listed below to provide another example (Markle & Tiemann, 1970).

Critical attributes
1. The ball must have an initial direction of motion that will cause it to fall out of bounds. (A player's attempt to field the ball that deflects it "fair" must not alter the umpire's judgment.)
2. The bat must make contact with a pitched ball. (Contact with that bat is critical in defining a foul tip.)
3. The ball must not be caught on the fly. (If the ball is caught, it is an out rather than a foul ball.)

Variable attributes
1. Distance the ball travels (fly foul ball can pop up from a bunt or be a long fly ball).
2. Direction of flight of the ball (toward the outfield or toward the rear screen behind the catcher).
3. Type of movement of bat (a swing, a bunt, or an accidental striking of the ball).

Testing for Generalization and Discrimination

A valid test of conceptual understanding must discriminate between those who really understand and do not understand a given concept. To recognize real understanding takes two kinds of testing: generalization and discrimination.

Generalization is the ability to call new, true examples by a concept's name or label. For example, if a child is learning about dogs and has seen the family dachshund and Grandma's chihuahua, a true test of generalization would be his or her calling the neighbor's English sheepdog a *dog*. If we were teaching the concept of the "vacuum tube" in basic electronic parts, we would want the student to recognize all examples—from the smallest, two-pin vacuum tube to the largest, shielded one. Thus, generalization shows whether the student understands the full domain—all possible members—of the class of objects. *When testing for generalization, one must use examples that were not used in teaching.* Otherwise you are simply testing rote memory.

Table 9.2 shows good examples of a rational set of varied examples used for testing generalization of the concept "chair." The third panel of Table 9.2 lists such things as a wooden rocker with arms and a tall back; an upholstered, egg-shaped chair; an armless, metal kitchen chair; a plastic, designer chair; and an upholstered, easy chair. All these examples are different with respect to the dimensions of the variable attributes of the concept. In other words, *variable attributes provide the clue to testing for generalization*. By writing a long list of examples that differ from the variable attributes, you can assemble examples both for teaching and for testing. Again, the two sets must be different. Repetition of a teaching example in a test will test only memory, not concept generalization. Some of the best examples are "far-out examples"—those that are dramatically different from other members of the class.

Discrimination is the ability to call an object by a different name if it is a nonmember of a class of objects even though it shares some properties of the general concept. For instance, a cat is a domestic animal that has four legs, but it is not a dog. A child needs to learn that a cat is similar but different from a dog and has another name, *cat*. A trainee in basic electronics will see some solid state electronic parts and must learn to tell the difference between transistors, resistors, diodes, coils, and other parts. Some of these parts may look very similar to each other, but there are critical attributes, labeling numbers, or other cues that the student must learn to be able to discriminate.

When testing for discrimination, we use what are called *close-in nonexamples* (Markle & Tiemann, 1970). A close-in nonexample is very similar to one of the objects that belongs in the concept but is missing *one* of the critical attributes. Table 9.2 shows close-in nonexamples for the concept "chair." A two-person sofa has a back and allows an appropriate sitting position but is missing the critical attribute of being a one-person seat. A small stool can allow a standard sitting position, and it is for one person, but it is missing a back. A canvas-framed beach lounger is for one person and has a back, but it requires the person to lie directly on the sand. Close-in nonexamples are excellent teaching and testing devices for discovering whether a student really understands a concept. A good test of understanding includes both examples to test generalization and nonexamples to test discrimination. Such a test can be created by systematically varying each of the critical and variable attributes.

Following are listed some items that include both a concept and either an example or a nonexample of the concept. The examples (E) and nonexamples (N) are labeled as to whether they would test generalization (G) or discrimination (D)

Concept	Examples or nonexamples
1. car	a Stutz-Bearcat (E,G)
2. chemical element	gallium (E,G)
3. message code	semaphore (E,G)
4. a basic cooking spice	allspice (N,D)
5. team sport	singles racquetball (N,D)
6. metal alloy	iron (N,D)

Listing and Sampling Examples and Nonexamples

Once a concept has been identified and its critical and variable attributes have been named, the next task is to develop lists of examples and nonexamples. Both examples and nonexamples can be divided into two kinds: those that will be used for teaching and those that will be used for testing. Table 9.3 from Tiemann and Markle (1978b) shows an analysis of the grammatical concept of "antonym," which has three critical and three variable attributes. Notice that Table 9.3 contains four lists: teaching examples, teaching nonexamples, testing examples, and testing nonexamples. Next to each entry on these lists are letter–number codes that represent the variable or critical attributes present or lacking in the particular example or nonexample, these codes show how the examples were created. Of course, these lists are not exhaustive.

Recall that a good criterion-referenced test should use a random sample or stratified sample of items from a domain or universe of items. *The domain for testing a concept like "antonym," as shown in Table 9.3, is the list of all possible testing examples and nonexamples for a given item format.* For example, the item below could be used:

What is the best antonym for hot?
  a. cold
  b. icily
  c. non-hot
  d. freezing

In this item, we have tried to include the one correct example plus three close-in nonexamples. Option (b), *icily,* differs only in the critical attribute that is not the same part of speech as *hot.* Option (c) is the opposite of *hot,* but it violates the third critical attribute listed in Table 9.3 by being only a variation of the given word. Option (d), *freezing,* also is not the same part of speech as *hot.* Therefore, in the test item shown above, we have tested generalization, because presumably we did not use the antonym for hot in teaching. Second, we have tested discrimination by using three close-in nonexamples.

Advanced Methods of Concept Testing

For a complex concept, Tiemann and Markle recommend that one curriculum decision may be to reserve some portion of the concept domain for an advanced course. If some discriminations are very subtle, it would seem fair to the student in a beginning course to exclude these discriminations from a CR test. Again, it should be emphasized that both generalization and discrimination should always be tested with new examples and nonexamples. To quote Markle and Tiemann (1970): "Conceptual learning is therefore easily discriminated from

Table 9.3

Example of a Concept Analysis Used to Develop Domain-Referenced Tests of Concept Learning[a]

Grammar Concept: Antonym

A word which:

Critical Attributes

1. has a meaning opposite to the meaning of some other (given) word
2. is the same part of speech as the given word
3. is a new word, not a variation of the given word

Variable Attributes

4. may be drawn from various parts of speech:

  (a) nouns   (c) pronouns   (e) adjectives

  (b) verbs   (d) adverbs   (f) prepositions

5. relative syllabic length of two words may be:

    (a) equal

    (b) unequal

6. opposition of meaning may exist:

    (a) across some continuum

    (b) in a dichotomous sense

Teaching Examples		*Teaching Nonexamples*	
1. bad; good	4e,5a,6a	1. vain, greedy	lacks only 1
2. danger, safety	4a,5a,6a	2. reason; motive	lacks only 1
3. live; die	4b,5a,6b	3. we; us	lacks only 1
4. he; she	4c,5a,6b	4. above; upon	lacks only 1
5. rapidly; slowly	4d,5b,6a	5. merrily; sad	lacks only 2
6. in; out	4f,5a,6b	6. happy; unhappy	lacks only 3
		7. capable; incapable	lacks only 3
		8. disputable; agree	lacks only 2

Testing Examples		*Testing Nonexamples*	
1. hot; cold	4e,5a,6a	1. imaginary; fanciful	lacks only 1
2. loss; gain	4a,5a,6a	2. chair; couch	lacks only 1
3. elevate; lower	4b,5b,6a	3. behind; next to	lacks only 1
4. you; me	4c,5a,6b	4. gloom; bright	lacks only 2
5. gaily; sadly	4d,5a,6a	5. violent; non-violent	lacks only 3
6. over; under	4f,5a,6b	6. valid; invalid	lacks only 3
		7. weak; forcibly	lacks only 2

Sample Test Item

Which of the following pairs of words are antonyms?

    (a) imaginary—fanciful   *Correct Answer:* b

    (b) elevate—lower

    (c) valid—invalid

    (d) weak—forcibly

[a] From P. W. Tiemann and S. M. Markle *Analyzing instructional content: A guide to instruction and evaluation.* Copyright 1978 by Stipes Pub. Reprinted by permission.

rote learning in which, by definition, the stimulus used in instruction is presented again to measure the learner's acquisition [p. 54]." Andre (1979, pp. 293–302) provides an excellent review of the problems involved in ensuring that questions assess more than verbatim recall.

COORDINATE CONCEPTS

In an extension of their earlier work, Tiemann, Kroeker, and Markle (1977) have extended the use of concept testing to include what they call coordinate concepts. These are concepts that to a new student are so similar in meaning that they seem to overlap. Concepts are said to be coordinated when a nonexample of one is an example of the other. Two simple coordinate concepts are "dog" and "cat"; these concepts have several attributes in common and, if we were testing a toddler, we could use examples of one concept as nonexamples of the other.

Another set of coordinate concepts are the four psychological concepts of "positive reinforcement," "negative reinforcement," "positive punishment," and "negative punishment." Positive reinforcement involves giving a subject an attractive stimulus following the subject's response; positive punishment involves giving an adversive stimulus. In negative reinforcement, we remove an uncomfortable stimulus; in negative punishment, we remove an attractive stimulus. These four concepts can easily be confused and examples can be interchanged. There are many examples of coordinate concepts in teaching, because most courses involve the learning of many concepts at the same time.

Table 9.4
Variable Attributes of Four Coordinate Concepts
of Reinforcement and Punishment

---

1. Age relationship between agent and recipient
   (a) both adult
   (b) both child
   (c) adult and child
   (d) other (e.g., person and animal)

2. Role relationship between agent and recipient
   (a) one a socially defined authority figure
   (b) family
   (c) none

3. Status relationship between agent and recipient
   (a) agent and recipient equal
   (b) agent and recipient unequal
   (c) indeterminate

4. Nature of the event
   (a) physical–tangible
   (b) verbal–social

In their analysis of the four coordinate concepts of reinforcement and punishment, Tiemann, Kroeker, and Markle defined the variable attributes as shown in Table 9.4. As can be seen, this listing of the variable attribute dimensions immediately suggests variations in possible test questions. The details of how a test is composed as a domain-based measure of concept learning for these coordinated concepts are presented in Table 9.5. Here the treatment exercises (teaching) and the posttest are shown as a composition of carefully sampled variations on the four variable attributes. The letters *a, b, c,* and *d* from the attribute list of Table 9.4 are entered in Table 9.5 to show the sampling of variable attributes. The four concepts are represented by symbols such as $_+S^+$, addition of a positive stimulus, or $_-S^-$, removal of a negative stimulus.

PRINCIPLES

Principles are statements or rules that show the relationship between concepts. They may be laws of physics, such as, "For every action there is an equal and opposite reaction." The student needs first to learn the concepts "action" and "opposite reaction." Then by understanding the concepts' interrelationship, the student can understand the principle. Thus concept learning is at the base of the learning of principles. Another principle, mentioned in Chapter 4, was the Premack principle: "For any pair of responses, the high probability one will reinforce the low probability one." Building domain-based tests of learning for this principle involves listing examples and nonexamples of high and low probability behaviors, which are concepts in the principle.

There are a number of other sources of information about the testing of principles. Anderson (1972, pp. 155–159) discusses the testing of principles and makes an important distinction between concepts that are superordinate terms and those that are not. Superordinate terms are concept names that describe a class of members that have labels that do not repeat the concept name. The term *tool* is a superordinate term that can be replaced by a particular (wrench, saw, hammer). In the principle, "Water heated to its boiling point turns to steam," there are two concepts that are *not* superordinate terms, *water* and *steam.* To give instances of water, we would have to describe well water, river water, muddy water, heavy water, and so forth, repeating the concept name. Steam is even more difficult to describe in terms other than the words steam or *water vapor*—even though there are many examples of steam, in the kitchen and in industry. Anderson feels that concepts that are not superordinate terms cannot be assessed by written tests using the method of examples and nonexamples because students could respond via rote memory if the concept name were repeated in a written item. This is a type of item-writing fault.

Anderson (1972) uses the idea of superordinate terms to suggest a method for assessing principles. He lists three steps in the generation of test questions:

Table 9.5
A Test Design for the Coordinate Concepts of Punishment and Reinforcement[a]

		Attribute		Dimensions	
	Concept	(1)	(2)	(3)	(4)
Treatment exercises					
First[b]	$_+S^+$	b	c	a	b
	$_-S^+$	b	c	a	b
	$_-S^-$	b	c	a	a
	$_+S^-$	b	c	a	a
Second[c]	$_-S^+$	d	c	c	a
	$_+S^-$	d	c	c	a
	$_-S^-$	d	c	c	a
	$_+S^+$	d	c	c	a
Third	$_+S^+$	a	b	a	b
	$_-S^+$	a	b	a	a
	$_-S^-$	a	b	a	b
	$_+S^-$	a	b	a	b
Fourth	$_-S^-$	c	a	b	b
	$_+S^-$	c	a	b	b
	$_+S^+$	c	a	b	b
	$_-S^+$	c	a	b	b
Classification posttest[d,e]					
Item No.					
2	$_+S^+$	b	c	a	b
8	$_+S^+$	c	b	b	a
16	$_+S^+$	c	a	b	a
17	$_+S^+$	a	c	b	b
19	$_+S^+$	c	a	b	b
22	$_+S^+$	d	b	c	a
3	$_-S^-$	a	a	b	a
5	$_-S^-$	c	b	b	b
6	$_-S^-$	c	a	b	b
11	$_-S^-$	d	a	b	a
18	$_-S^-$	d	c	c	a
23	$_-S^-$	b	c	a	b
1	$_+S^-$	d	b	b	a
4	$_+S^-$	d	c	c	a
10	$_+S^-$	c	b	b	b
13	$_+S^-$	a	a	b	a
15	$_+S^-$	a	b	a	b
20	$_+S^-$	d	c	b	a
7	$_-S^+$	c	b	b	a

(*continued*)

Table 9.5 (*Continued*)

		Attribute		Dimensions	
	Concept	(1)	(2)	(3)	(4)
9	_S⁺	a	a	c	a
12	_S⁺	b	c	a	b
14	_S⁺	c	b	b	a
21	_S⁺	d	b	b	b
24	_S⁺	c	a	b	a

^{a}Attribute numbers are given in parentheses. A list of attributes and their dimensions are shown in Table 9.4.

^{b}Dimensions of variable attributes *divergent* across coordinate concept examples (with one instance of each concept in each exercise).

^{c}Dimensions of variable attributes *matched* across coordinate concepts (each a nonexample of the others).

^{d}Dimensions varied across the range of possibilities for each attribute within each concept set.

^{e}Each of the 24 examples used here was "new," that is, specifically reserved for the post-test and *not* previously encountered by the students during instruction.

> (1) Replace every superordinate term in the principle statement with an appropriate particular term. (2) Substitute synonyms for every remaining substantive word. When the preceding instruction illustrates the principle with an example, another proviso is necessary. (3) The test instance should have no substantive words in common with illustrative instances [Anderson, 1972, p. 155].

Merrill, Reigeluth, and Faust (1979) in discussing the design of objectives, tests, and instruction for the learning of principles stress the need for examples. They state:

> One of the most frequent problems of much instruction . . . is the lack of a sufficient number of instances. Somehow the notion seems to have been adopted that instances are fine for grade school students, but that adult students should be able to grasp abstract ideas without any illustrative material. This problem is characterized as generality-rich but example-poor instruction [1979, pp. 187–188].

Summary

A number of educational researchers have called for the use of tests filled with multiple examples and nonexamples of concepts in order to truly assess conceptual learning. Tiemann and Markle (1978b) have concluded that "For us, domain-referenced testing is essential to answer the question: Are the students learning what we want them to learn? [p. 1]." The lists of examples and nonexamples of a concept, generated from an analysis of the attributes of a concept, define the item domains. Tests of concepts that go beyond the comprehension of the definition of the concept are composed of samples of examples and nonexamples from domains.

As one becomes familiar with identifying concepts and analyzing them into their attributes, it becomes clear that a powerful method for concept testing is available. Just the idea of using examples and nonexamples is a very important tool in both teaching and testing. Sorting out the examples and nonexamples used in the teaching materials versus those used in the test is a very important procedure, if you are truly measuring concepts rather than recall. Studying this chapter and then examining the writings and materials of Tiemann and Markle will provide the test-item writer with an effective tool.

The method of concept testing explained in this chapter allows for pure CR tests to be developed. Concept analysis and the listing of examples and nonexamples provides a precise description of the domain across which testing of a concept will be sampled. Each test becomes a random sample of the examples and nonexamples for a concept. Such a test will provide an accurate estimate of the student's mastery of a concept. Moreover, this test item writing method can be precisely described so that another person, given the concept analysis information, should be able to duplicate an original test closely. Clearly, most other CR tests include the testing of several concepts, but in such tests, examples and nonexamples may not be randomly sampled for each concept.

One of the important promises of the type of explicit item writing described in this chapter is the furtherance of a science of learning. Andre (1979), Anderson (1977), and others have attempted to build models of how concepts, principles, and prose material are processed and stored in human memory. This kind of theory building requires an accurate description of the test-item tasks required of the student during learning experiments. Theory explication also requires a precise statement of the relationship between the instructional materials and test items. Entirely different kinds of human memory are apparently operating when the mind processes a paraphrased concept and when it processes a verbatim repetition of a statement that appears in the instructional material. Similarly, the processing of examples and nonexamples is different depending on whether they are unique and newly encountered in the testing situation or simply repetitions of instructional examples.

References

Anderson, R. C. How to construct achievement tests to assess comprehension. *Review of Educational Research*, 1972, *42*, 145–170.
Anderson, R. C. The notion of schemata and the educational enterprise. In R. C. Anderson, R. J.

Spiro, & W. E. Montague (Eds.) *Schooling and the acquisition of knowledge.* Hillsdale, New Jersey: Lawrence Erlbaum Associates, 1977.

Andre, T. Does answering higher-level questions while reading facilitate productive learning? *Review of Educational Research,* 1979, *49,* 280–318.

Carroll, J. B. A model for school learning. *Teachers College Record,* 1963, *64,* 723–733.

Gagné, R. M. The analysis of instructional objectives for the design of instruction. In R. Glaser (Ed.), *Teaching machines and programmed instruction II: Data and directions.* Washington, D.C.: National Education Association, Department of Audio-Visual Instruction, 1965.

Gagné, R. M. Instructional variables and learning outcomes. In M. C. Wittrock & D. Wiley (Eds.), *The evaluation of instruction: Issues and problems.* New York: Holt, 1970.

Gagné, R. M. *Defining objectives for six types of learning.* Washington, D.C.: American Educational Research Association, 1971.

Holt, J. *How children fail.* New York: Pittman Publishing, 1964.

Johnson, D. M., & Stratton, R. P. Evaluation of five methods of teaching concepts. *Journal of Educational Psychology,* 1966, *57,* 48–53.

Markle, S. M., & Tiemann, P. W. *Really understanding concepts.* Champaign, Illinois: Stipes Publishing Company, 1970.

Mechner, F. Science education and behavioral technology. In Glaser, R. (Ed.), *Teaching machines and programmed learning, II.* Washington, D.C.: National Educational Association, 1965.

Merrill, M. D. Necessary psychological conditions for defining instructional outcomes. *Educational Technology,* 1971, *11*(8), 34–39.

Merrill, M. D., Reigeluth, C. M., & Faust, G. W. The instructional quality profile: A curriculum evaluation and design tool. In H. F. O'Neil, Jr. (Ed.), *Procedures for instructional systems development.* New York: Academic Press, 1979.

Miller, H. G., Williams, R. G., & Haladyna, T. M. *Beyond facts: Objective ways to measure thinking.* Englewood Cliffs, New Jersey: Educational Technology, 1978.

Tiemann, P. W., & Markle, S. M. *Analyzing instructional content: A guide to instruction and evaluation.* Champaign, Illinois: Stipes Publishing Company, 1978. (a)

Tiemann, P. W., & Markle, S. M. *Domain-referenced testing in conceptual learning.* Paper presented at the meetings of the American Educational Research Association, Toronto, March 1978. (b)

Tiemann, P., Kroeker, L. P., & Markle, S. M. *Teaching verbally-mediated coordinate concepts in an on-going college course.* Paper presented at the meetings of the American Educational Research Association, New York, April 1977.

10

Logical Operations for Generating Intended Questions (LOGIQ): A Typology for Higher Level Test Items

REED G. WILLIAMS
THOMAS M. HALADYNA

Individuals reading this chapter have taken tests numbering in the hundreds. Many of these tests contained items unrelated to the important concepts taught and learned. Further, items often did not test the most appropriate use of such concepts (typically, use in higher level thinking processes).

The failure of tests to reflect primary instructional goals is not intentional. Even when test items result from long and painstaking item-writing efforts, they frequently do not match the instructor's personal convictions about what should be and are the important outcomes of instruction.

This chapter provides the test developer with a set of conceptual tools for transforming instructional content into test items that require appropriate higher level use of the content. A method is presented for classifying tasks according to type of thinking based on observable characteristics of the tasks themselves rather than on an abstract description of the thought processes required. Also presented is a set of six steps for taking the content of books, lectures, or other materials and creating test items of each type in the classification system.

The Classification System

One common problem in matching test items to instructional intent is the difficulty of distinguishing among test items that represent different types of intellectual processes or uses of content. Semb and Spencer (1976) provided 17 liberal arts instructors with operational definitions of both recall questions and thought level questions and asked the instructors to classify their test items accordingly. The instructors reported that an average of 31% of their items measured higher level thinking rather than recall. Inspection of the items by trained evaluators, however, revealed that less than 9% of the items were thought level questions.

Bloom and his associates (1956) created a taxonomy of educational objectives for the cognitive domain to help instructors, instructional designers, and researchers distinguish among tasks representing various levels of thinking. The taxonomy is undoubtedly one of the most important contributions to educational practice in recent times. It was enthusiastically received and has been widely used ever since its publication. However, it has weaknesses as a tool for helping instructors reliably translate their intuitively held educational goals into matching test items.

First, the categories of Bloom's taxonomy are defined in terms of the unobservable intellectual processes required of learners rather than in terms of the observable characteristics of tasks presented to learners or test takers. A typology with categories defined in terms of concrete characteristics of tasks should lead to better interrater agreement in classifying test items. Seddon (1978) reports that researchers have had considerable difficulty in classifying items according to Bloom's taxonomy. Percentages of agreement were shown to vary considerably around a median agreement of 35.5%.

Studies of the statistical properties of the taxonomy (e.g., Kropp & Stoker, 1966; Madaus, Woods, & Nuttall, 1973; Miller, Snowman, & O'Hara, 1979) have raised questions about the existence of some of the levels. Moderate support was generated for lower levels, but unusual patterns were exhibited at the higher levels. The results of the Miller, Snowman, and O'Hara study led them to conclude that the patterns suggested only two factors, fluid and crystallized intelligence.

Second, Bloom's taxonomy lends itself primarily to retrospective analysis of test items. Once a test item is constructed you can use the taxonomy to classify it. However, Bloom's taxonomy provides the test developer little guidance regarding the process of selecting content and transforming that content into test items that measure various types of thinking.

The classification system used in this chapter is designed to overcome these deficiencies in Bloom's taxonomy. The system represents a refinement of work reported earlier (Miller & Williams, 1973; Williams, 1973; Miller, Williams, & Haladyna, 1978) and is intended to help in the formulation and refinement of both behavioral objectives and test items.

The basic premise of this classification system (or typology) is that any instructional objective, test item, or other environmental demand on an individual can be classified according to (*a*) the information or content to be used, and (*b*) the use to be made of such material (the intellectual operation or task to be performed). For testing purposes, a third dimension is added, (*c*) response mode. The classification system is illustrated in Figure 10.1. Each partition of the cube in Figure 10.1 represents a classification category into which objectives or test items can be placed. Each category dimension will be discussed in turn.

CONTENT DIMENSION

Content is subdivided into the following types: facts, concepts, and principles.

Facts are associations between names, other symbols, objects, and locations. ''Springfield is the capitol of Illinois'' is an example of a fact. Other examples include learning the names of individuals, dates of significant events, and spelling of words. Some test items based on knowledge of facts include (*a*) *name the nerves of the central nervous sytem*, (*b*) *identify the symbol for potassium*, (*c*) *name the author of the Declaration of Trieste*, (*d*) *identify the person in this picture*.

Concepts define classes of objects or events that are grouped together by virtue of sharing common defining attributes as was discussed in Chapter 9. Concepts can be *conjunctive* (all defining attributes must be present), *disjunctive* (one subset or another subset of attributes must be present), or *relational* (the attributes must exist in some specific relationship to each other). Items testing concepts might require students to (*a*) identify examples from works by romantic poets, (*b*) name members of the brachiopod family, or (*c*) distinguish gases from liquids.

Principles are statements of relationship among objects or events. Principles can be communicated in the form of *if–then* statements. Some examples of principles are (*a*) hot air rises, cold air sinks; (*b*) for every action there is an equal and opposite reaction; (*c*) *i* before *e* except after *c* or when sounded like *a* as in *neighbor* or *weigh*.

Procedures, a subset of principles, include physical as well as mental activities. With a slight but important modification, we will use the definition of procedures provided by Anderson and Liu (1980). *Procedures* can be defined as sequences of mental and physical activities used to solve problems, gather information, or achieve some defined goal. In the case of our third example of a principle, the associated procedure would involve actually spelling a previously unseen word with an *ie* or *ei* letter constellation. Anderson and Liu (1980) identify two types of procedures: those in which a sequence of activities are performed *in a specified* order regardless of the outcome of any one step (*linear procedures*), and those that are followed by activities that are dependent on the outcomes of a prior activity (*branching procedures*). Branching procedures re-

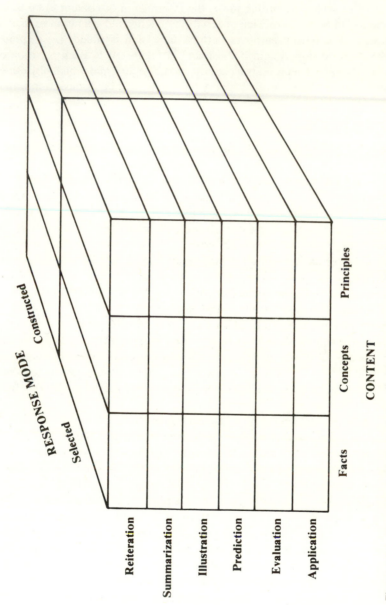

Figure 10.1. Diagram of the typology for classifying objectives and test items by content, task and response mode.

quire decision making during the chain of events; linear procedures require only the initial decision to use the procedure.

As you read further, you will see that procedures can as easily be defined as the application of principles. We have chosen to describe procedures here for two reasons. First, use of procedures is quite common. Second and most important, it is possible to develop test items that involve reiterating or illustrating the use of procedures as well as actually applying the procedures.

TASK DIMENSION

Intellectual operation or *task* refer to the way in which content is *used*. The principle, ''A stitch in time saves nine'' can be used in various ways. It may be recited verbatim (reiteration). It may be restated in different words (summarization). Individuals may be asked to provide or identify examples of the rule in use (illustration). The rule or principle may be used to anticipate the consequences of certain acts, for example, one may observe that failing to sew up small rips in clothing leads to larger tears (prediction). Or a principle or procedure may be employed to make a judgment, for example, one may decide to sew the rip up now rather than wait (evaluation). The rule or principle may also be used in arranging conditions and initiating procedures to produce a desired outcome (application).

For purposes of the typology presented in this chapter, the intellectual operations and their respective definitions are as follows:

Reiteration is a task that requires an individual to recognize or produce information in essentially the same form as that in which it was originally received. Examples of reiteration are recalling names, facts, and principles; locating places and things on previously seen maps and models; reproducing maps, diagrams and formulae; restating material verbatim. Reiteration can be employed with all three types of content, as the following sample items show:
Facts. State the sum of 4 + 6. (The student has already learned this problem.)
Concepts. Give four defining attributes of mammals. (Again, the student has learned these attributes.)
Principles. State a principle that governs the prediction of rain. (The student has been taught "When dew is on the grass, rain will not come to pass.")

Summarization requires an individual to report the substance of a message accurately as opposed to recalling the message verbatim. In summarizing, information irrelevant to a current goal or situation may be omitted while especially relevant information is highlighted. All three types of content can be summarized:
Facts. Summarize the events leading up to the Boston Tea Party.
Concepts. Describe in your own words the distinguishing characteristics of infants with phenylketonuria.
Principles. Describe in your own words the effects of a continuous schedule of reinforcement on learning rate (acquisition) and on resistance to extinction.

Illustration requires the student to demonstrate understanding by recognizing or providing previously unseen or unused examples of a concept or principle. Only two types of content can be used in illustration:

Concepts. State which of the following are examples of romantic poetry. (The student is given several lines from each of a number of previously unencountered works.)

Principles. (*a*) Name the principle used by the defensive coach in the following play. (The student is given a description of an athletic contest in which a change in offensive strategy by one coach is countered by a change in defensive strategy by the other.) (*b*) Name one principle of foreign policy on which the following action could be based. (The student is given a description of an international event and the official action of the U.S. government.)

Prediction Confronts an individual with a previously unencountered situation and asks him or her to employ a rule to predict (*a*) changes in the situation at a later time, or (*b*) changes in related situations. Like illustration, prediction can be based only on concepts and principles.

Concepts. Given the following account of the findings of history and physical examinations, describe the findings you would expect in concurrent x-ray investigations and laboratory studies. (The account the student is provided describes a classic cardiovascular problem.)

Principles. (*a*) Given the following long-term environmental changes, forecast the relative chances of survival for the two species named. (The student is given specified changes and the names of two species that differ in genetic endowment). (*b*) Describe how consumer behavior will be altered by the following changes in Federal Reserve Banking policies. (Specified actions of the Bank are described.)

Evaluation involves the use of criteria in making a decision or selection. It consists of careful analysis of a problem or situation to determine factors to be considered in making the decision and the careful weighting of each factor.

Evaluation is based on the use of principles, as it normally involves anticipating the consequences of an act and then judging the acceptability of those consequences on the basis of appropriate standards. This process holds even when historical precedent is the apparent basis for a decision because such precedent is normally based on the anticipated consequences of an act.

Evaluation items may require the test-taker to complete an entire process of evaluation or any of the following component parts: (*a*) selection of criteria, (*b*) operationalizing of criteria, (*c*) using given criteria to make a judgment, or (*d*) determining what criteria were used in making a judgment. One example of an evaluation item follows:

Principles. What factors should be considered in deciding the degree of emphasis to be placed on nuclear generation of energy for the next ten years? (The question asks for discussion of appropriate criteria to be used in making the decision.)

Application is the reverse of prediction. Here the individual is given a desired outcome and a description of the initial state or situation and is asked to arrange the conditions necessary to achieve the desired outcome. Application involves using other types of behavior (summarization, prediction, etc.) in sequences and includes those activities commonly referred to as problem solving and creative thinking. Application is normally based on use of principles. One major characteristic that differentiates application (and evaluation) from illustration and prediction is the requirement that the examinee *formulate* possible courses of action rather than just choose among options provided.

Principles. Given the following description (of environmental conditions such as degree days, amount of direct and indirect radiation, latitude, etc.), develop plans for a fuel-efficient home.

RESPONSE MODE DIMENSION

In addition to content and task, a third dimension, response mode, is considered in our typology. *Response mode* has two categories that were discussed in Chapter 4, *selected* response and *constructed* response. Examples of selected

Table 10.1
Behavioral Typology of Objectives, Test Items, and Environmental Demands[a]

Content	Response mode: Selected	Response mode: Constructed	Example objectives
Reiteration Facts, verbal descriptions of: concepts principles procedures events objects	Given a cue and a set of alternatives, select the exact replica of information previously learned.	Given a cue, construct an exact replica of information previously learned.	Given the previously studied diagram of body compartments and a list of words identifying each compartment, label each compartment with the appropriate identifying word. Name the ganglionic blocking agents commonly used as peripheral vasodilators. *Other examples:* Recalling normal values, synonyms, definitions of terms; defining attributes of concepts, poetry, drama; names of people.
Summarization Facts, verbal descriptions of: concepts principles procedures events objects	Given a paraphrased description, select the correct name for the fact, concept, principle, procedure, or event from a set of alternatives. Given the name, select the correct paraphrased descrip-	Given a paraphrased description, write the correct name for the fact, concept, principle, procedure or event. Given the name, write a paraphrased description of	Given paraphrased descriptions of optical measurement instruments, select from a list the correct name of each instrument. Describe in your own words the four major morphologic patterns

(continued)

Table 10.1 (*Continued*)

Content	Response mode: Selected	Response mode: Constructed	Example objectives
	tion of a fact, concept, principle, procedure, or event.	the fact, concept, procedure, or event.	of irreversible cell injury or death.
			Other examples: Summarizing events, theories, substance of articles.
Illustration Concepts Principles Procedures	Given the name, select a previously unused example of the concept, principle, or procedure from a set of alternatives.	Given the name, describe a previously unused example of the concept, principle, or procedure.	Give an example, not provided during instruction, of each of the antagonisms listed below: chemical antagonism physiological antagonism pharmacological antagonism noncompetitive (nonspecific) antagonism
	Given a previously unused example of a concept, principle, or procedure, select the correct name from a set of alternatives.	Given a previously unused example of a concept, principle, or procedure, name it.	Given any electron microscope slide of an injured or dead cell, locate the following major ultra-structural changes: swelling of mitochondria thickening of plasma membrane distortion of microvilli
			Other examples: Identifying patterns of events. Identifying patterns in data.

(*continued*)

Table 10.1 (*Continued*)

Content	Response mode: Selected	Response mode: Constructed	Example objectives
Prediction			
Concepts	Given some of the defining characteristics of an object, select other expected characteristics from a list.	Given some of the defining characteristics of an object, list other expected characteristics.	Given a case history and physical exam findings, predict what findings you would expect on a radiograph.
Principles	Given a previously unused description of a situation or event with the antecedent conditions of a relationship embedded, select from alternatives the most likely consequences.	Given a previously unused description of a situation or event with the antecedent conditions of a relationship embedded, describe the most likely consequences.	Given biographical information about residents of a precinct, descriptions of successful and unsuccessful candidates in the precinct in prior elections, and descriptions of candidates currently running for office, name the candidate most likely to win the election.
	Given a previously unused description of outcomes (consequences), select from alternatives the ordered set of antecedent conditions that would achieve those outcomes.		Given a medical sign or symptom and a list of all sites where a lesion might exist, name the sites of lesions that would produce that sign or symptom and give a sound physiological explanation as to how a lesion in each site could cause the resultant symptom.
Procedures	Given a previously unused description	Given a previously unused description	Given the description of a

(*continued*)

Table 10.1 (*Continued*)

Content	Response mode: Selected	Response mode: Constructed	Example objectives
	of a situation in which a procedure is applied, select from alternatives the most likely outcome.	of a situation in which a procedure is applied, describe the most likely outcome.	hypotensive patient, predict the actions of therapeutic doses of norepinephrine on cardic output.
	Given a previously unused description of outcomes (consequences), select from alternatives the ordered set of procedures that would achieve those outcomes.		*Other examples:* Predicting correct spelling of previously unseen words through knowledge of rules. Predicting amount of time necessary to accomplish anything, given knowledge of conditions.
Application Concepts Principles		Given a previously unused case or problem and a desired outcome, arrange the antecedent conditions necessary to achieve that outcome. (Less preferred alternative: describe the antecedent conditions necessary to achieve that outcome.)	Given results from a history, physical, and a laboratory workup for a patient with any of the listed diseases or disorders (diagnosis unknown to the student); Order or describe appropriate preventive measures and/or therapeutic regimens for preventing or altering the disease.

(continued)

Table 10.1 (*Continued*)

Content	Response mode: Selected	Response mode: Constructed	Example objectives
Procedures		Given a previously unused case or problem and a desired outcome, perform the procedures necessary to achieve that outcome. (Less preferred alternative: describe the steps in using procedures necessary to achieve that outcome.)	Given any patient's symptom, describe the procedure necessary to determine if the symptom is an adverse reaction due to drug–drug interaction rather than a disease manifestation.
			Other examples: Arranging effective marketing procedures. Building a better mousetrap.
Evaluation Principles Procedures		Given a description of a situation that calls for a judgment or decision, name the most desirable action and describe the criteria or values on which your decision was based.	You want to measure the level of a constituent (X) of cerebrospinal fluid and have decided that a spectrophotometer is the instrument of choice in this particular case. You must carefully select a technique to make a quantitative measurement. • List possible experimental techniques that you could undertake to resolve the problem.

(*continued*)

Table 10.1 (*Continued*)

Content	Response mode: Selected	Response mode: Constructed	Example objectives
			• Describe the most appropriate technique, and describe the criteria on which your decision was based.
			Other examples: Judging quality of products. Judging communications in terms of accuracy, internal consistency, etc.

 a Adapted from Williams, 1977.

response items described in Chapter 4 were matching, and true–false items. In constructed response, the individual is required to determine available choices as part of the selection process. All open-ended evaluation procedures (e.g., essay tests, performance tests) are included in the constructed response mode.

As a means of integrating the three dimensions of the typology and helping users to construct test items that fit each category, a set of generic behavioral objectives similar to Hively's (1974) item forms has been constructed. These statements describe the situation to which the learner or examinee must respond, the information and tools made available to him or her, and the type of learner-examinee behavior that will demonstrate competence. The generic objectives are presented in Table 10.1.

Casting the typology in the form of behavioral definitions was seen as a convenient way to guide test developers in recognizing and measuring thought processes commonly used in the nonschool environment but slighted on most tests. The behavioral definitions should play a useful role in guiding the actual item production process by indicating the information that should be provided and the nature of the response to be required.

Inspection of Table 10.1 reveals that in a particular test mode, some categories such as reiteration are represented by one behavioral definition while others are represented by more than one definition (e.g., prediction using principles), indicating that these categories may be tested in more than one way. Some cells in the matrix are empty (e.g., application in the selected response mode), indicating that the particular task or operation cannot be tested in the response mode specified by that column. All empty cells are prediction, application and evaluation cells. Specifically the empty cells are a function of the presence or absence of test item alternatives from which to choose. Whenever item alternatives are *present* (selected response mode), the examinee is able to work any problem that nominally appears to be an application problem through use of the ability to *predict*. The examinee reviews the desired outcome specified in the stem and the action plans specified by the response options. The examinee can then make a prediction of the outcome for each course of action and select the action most likely to produce the desired outcome. What makes application unique is the need to *formulate* possible courses of action and to then choose among them. Selected response items do not lend themselves to measuring application. Evaluation cannot be measured through use of selected response items, as the process of analysis must be that of the examinee.

An Evaluation of the Typology

One criterion for evaluating any typology is the degree to which the typology categories are clearly defined so that individuals can accurately classify objectives or test items. In a study by Williams (1977), 13 instructional designers were asked to classify 18 objectives according to the typology. Nine of the objectives were selected by the author to fit the various categories. Nine were chosen by an individual not familiar with the typology as objectives representing the spectrum of thinking.

In sorting the nine objectives selected to fit the categories, the instructional designers made only 15 classification errors in 117 decisions. For the objectives selected to represent the spectrum of thinking, 53 of 117 decisions deviated from those of the author. However, 33 of the 53 "incorrect" decisions were attributable to unclearly stated objectives or to objectives containing too little information for adequate classification. Adding a total of 5 words to 3 objectives, 21 errors of classifications could have been avoided. These changes were suggested by the category definitions themselves.

Finally, the study indicated that raters were easily able to fit all objectives selected as representing the range of intellectual behaviors into categories of the typology. Certainly more research is desirable to establish the validity of the typology more positively. Nonetheless this initial study was most encouraging.

The next section describes a series of steps which, when used in conjunction with the typology, should make the construction of appropriate test items an easier and more dependable process.

Guidelines for Transforming Instructional Content into Appropriate Test Items

The frequent overemphasis on testing knowledge of facts occurs because the most "natural" strategy for seeking information to be tested and creating an item results in an item that demands only recall of the information. Facts are the most discrete bits of information in a textbook. As a result, they are most easily identified as content for test items. Only a very deliberate strategy will ensure representative sampling of concepts and principles in addition to facts.

Once representative sampling of content is achieved, the item writer faces a similar challenge to ensure adequate sampling of tasks. A nondeliberate approach will result in a large majority of items that test the ability to reiterate or summarize, whereas the natural environment is more likely to demand predicting and applying.

What is needed is an algorithm that gives the item writer more conscious control over the item-writing process. The desired control is established by making the item writer aware of common types of content and of alternative tasks posed by the natural environment and by providing a series of steps for creating items that represent all combinations of content and task. The typology describes common tasks that represent a large percentage of the normal uses of information. The following steps provide the guidance required to assure creation of items that measure an examinee's ability to perform *predetermined* intellectual tasks.

STEP 1. SELECT THE INFORMATION TO BE TESTED (THOUGHT UNIT)[1]

Selecting the information to be tested is the most appropriate entry point in the item creation process. Thus the entry point is not different from the one naturally used by most people.

In preparing to create test items, first review the source of information that serves as the basis for the test. The conventional sources are books, lecture notes, films, videotapes, and audiotapes. Conceivably, other sources might be used. In the case of aptitude tests, the stimulus for creation of test items might be an analysis of normal daily activities of the target population. In other cases, pre-

---

[1]If you have created instructional objectives for your course and you are comfortable with them, you will find that you have already completed much of the work described in Steps 1–3. If not. the product of Steps 1–3 can easily be transformed into instructional objectives.

viously created test items may serve as the source of information that stimulates development of a new test item. However, stimuli for the majority of test items created are most often found in the more conventional information sources listed first. The remainder of this discussion will focus on these conventional sources, but the procedures can be extrapolated to the less conventional sources.

In reviewing conventional sources of information, you will identify certain segments as containing key facts, concepts, or principles. Often a subtitle, heading, or underlined phrase or word will serve as the trigger to identification of a key idea. Sometimes a statement embedded in the text will be the trigger. The topic sentence in the paragraph is often the best source.

In each instance, the information source serves as a stimulus that calls to the surface your intuitively held objectives for teaching this material or your beliefs about which information is most important. In most cases, you will discover that the information identified as important is so identified because it has important *uses* in the nonschool environment.

STEP 2. CONDENSE

At this point some statement has caught your attention and has signaled the existence of a key idea worthy of testing. The second step involves selecting and integrating other information related to this key idea from the information source (and, in some cases, from other information sources).

First you may wish to underline related sentences that add information of substance and to identify the relationship with arrows or marginal notes. However, your final objective for this step is to summarize all the important information in a brief written statement or statements. In the case of *facts,* the product of this step is simply a list of the associated characteristics (age, size, color, etc.) of the identified entity (specific person, place or thing, e.g., "Springfield" in our earlier example). In the case of a *concept,* the written statement will list the defining characteristics possessed by all members of the class of objects represented by the concept. Again, using an earlier example from Chapter 9, the statement will list the characteristics that must be present if an object is properly to be called a *chair.* When the key idea is a principle, the written summary can often be stated in the form of an *if–then* statement. (If, in the game of bridge, you and your partner together have 26 points, then you should be able to bid and make game.)

Although the logic of the material to some extent dictates what material is included and excluded in a thought unit, there is also a degree of arbitrariness that reflects the preferences of the item writer. One item writer might group the information from four pages of material into one thought unit, but another item writer might subdivide that material into two or more thought units. This decision will be a function of the item writer's perceptions about the importance of the material and his or her ideas about how to use the material in creating test items. It is in this way that the item writer's ideas and those of the author of the information come together.

The item writer must be very selective in picking key ideas to serve as the basis for test items. There is never enough time to test every key idea (fact, concept, principle). Choose only the ones that are used frequently, have many uses in the natural environment, or are important for some other reason.

STEP 3. SELECT THE TASK

The final step before actually constructing the test item is to determine how you want examinees to *use* the information summarized in Step 2. Will the test item require the individual to simply reiterate or summarize the information? Or, if the information is a concept or principle, should examinees be required to (*a*) recognize a previously unseen example or application of the concept or principle, (*b*) use the concept or principle to predict the outcome of some sequence of events, or (*c*) arrange conditions necessary to cause a prespecified outcome through use of a relevant principle? You may choose to have examinees analyze a situation, select criteria, and make a decision. If you want examinees to use the information in more than one way, create a number of items requiring different uses of the same facts, concepts, or principles.

To be logically valid the test item should require the examinee to use the information in a manner that approaches the way that content is and will be used in practice once the individual finishes the course of instruction. In reviewing banks of multiple-choice items for measurement courses, it becomes evident that some thought units or ideas have been regularly tested in an appropriate manner while others have not. For example, students in measurement courses have been frequently required to compute and use item difficulty and discrimination to troubleshoot items. On the other hand, when students have been learning about test validation they may be required only to reiterate or summarize the definition. There have been few items requiring examinees to plan strategies for test validation. Such items would be a better test of "working knowledge."

The behavioral typology as shown in Table 10.1 is intended to help you recognize typical alternate uses of key content and therefore to aid you in determining how you would like an examinee to *use* a particular *thought unit* to demonstrate appropriate working knowledge. In most cases you will find a satisfactory match between one of the specified tasks and the thought unit you have identified. In some cases you may choose to develop a variation of one of the specified tasks. In both cases the typology should be of help by aiding you in conceptualizing the types of tasks.

While test items can be created by linking *concepts* or *principles* with any one of the tasks (reiteration, summarization, illustration, prediction, evaluation, application), *facts* can only be tested by creating items that call for reiteration or, in some cases, summarization. Facts do not lend themselves to other uses. Previously unseen examples of facts are not logically possible. Likewise, specific facts alone do not allow for prediction or application. Prediction and application are possible only when one can generalize from one situation to another. Generalization occurs only when using concepts and principles. Table 10.1 reflects these limits.

STEP 4. WRITE THE ITEM STEM

Regardless of test modes, items designed to measure behaviors other than reiteration and summarization normally have item stems composed of two elements. First, a portion of the stem sets the scene or describes a situation for the examinee. This description contains information about persons, places, things, historical events, or anticipated future events, as necessary. In cases testing illustration, prediction, evaluation, and application, one of the most important abilities to be tested is the ability to identify events or patterns that represent concepts or principles when those events are embedded in a context including many irrelevant features. The description, therefore, should include such irrelevant information. In the case of application items, the situation description should also tell the examinee what tools are and are not available for use in solving the problem or accomplishing the task.

To economize on examinee time and thus allow for broader domain sampling, test item developers often create one situation description (case) followed by a series of items utilizing that description. This is sound practice when employed with three to six items per case. Larger numbers of items normally require long case descriptions and force much rereading, thus decreasing the number of key ideas tested. In Table 10.1, the portion of each behavioral definition that specifies the givens should serve as a reasonable guide to the creation of an appropriate case description of an item.

The key to creating an item at the illustration level or above is to ensure that examinees cannot answer the item by memory alone. To prevent this, it is critical to create a case description not used in the textbook or as a classroom example. For the same reasons, it is critical to use a paraphrased definition in summarization items.

A second portion of the stem describes for the examinee the nature of the performance required to demonstrate competence. This portion typically takes the form of a question to be answered or a statement to be completed. Regardless of form, this portion of the stem directs the student to do what is specified in the *action* portion of the appropriate behavioral definition from Table 10.1.

In reiteration items, examinees are normally given a name and asked to select or construct a verbatim definition, description, or rendering (poetry). In other cases, they are provided a definition, description, or rendering and asked to produce the correct name. Summarization items are different only in that examinees are given or are asked to construct or select a paraphrased version of the definition, description or rendering.

In illustration, examinees are either given previously unseen examples of concepts or principles and asked to name them, or they are given the name and asked to construct or select a new example. In prediction, examinees are given a situation and asked to describe the likely outcome, or they are asked to choose from among possible outcomes based on their knowledge of the appropriate rules or generalizations.

Evaluation items require examinees to analyze a situation, choose appropriate criteria, and make a decision related to that situation. In application, an examinee is given a description of a set of circumstances and a desired outcome and is told to describe or demonstrate the set of actions required to produce the desired outcome.

As mentioned earlier, we believe evaluation and application to be truly testable only by use of the production test mode. Although not a true test of application, the third prediction level generic objective under the selected-response mode in Table 10.1 may provide an indicator of *application* level ability when the compromise of using selected- rather than constructed-response mode is required to allow for objective scoring. (Compare the third prediction level objective to the first application objective in Table 10.1). However, we feel this action is a major compromise and the results are that the item is a very imprecise indicator of application. The ability specified in this objective is necessary for one to perform at the application level but is not sufficient to ensure successful performance at that level.

One final consideration in preparing item stems is the need to ensure that the task required by the item stem matches as closely as possible an important task required of examinees outside the school and test environment. Compromises are sometimes necessary on account of practical constraints, but they should not be made as a result of lack of careful consideration, in deference to tradition, or both. Two forms of incompatibility frequently occur. In the first, the task required by the test is unnatural because the test specifies alternatives to choose from whereas the natural environment does not. In the second, the test prohibits use of job aids (textbooks, other people, calculators), where the natural environment would allow use of these.

The portion of the stem that directs the behavior of the examinee is the most critical portion of the item. If the stem clearly specifies the task, the item will be a good measure of the examinee's ability in that task-content domain. If the instructions are not clear, some students who have achieved the desired outcome may answer incorrectly because they misinterpret the item stem. This is true with all items. It is most critical with constructed-response, items however, because the absence of specified alternative answers eliminates one additional source of information that helps to clarify the intention of the item writer for the examinee. The writer's intentions are most clearly conveyed when constructed-response items are very pointed (e.g., *Give three reasons why . . .*) and the test is composed of items that require a number of short answers rather than a few very long answers.

Consistent use of selected terms to elicit specified intellectual operations (tasks) helps to clarify the writer's intentions. Where appropriate, specification of the concepts or principles to be used in addressing the problem is also helpful. Beyond that, the rules of clear communication prevail.

The most useful prospective test of item clarity is to ask colleagues to review the item, answer it, and provide you with comments. The best source of data for improving clarity is provided by having members of the target population think out loud as they take the test.

STEP 5. WRITE THE ANSWER

Good testing practices require one to construct the correct answer for an item for both constructed- and selected-response items. For constructed-response items, the correct answer serves as the model against which student answers are compared. In selected-response items the correct answer is one of the options presented to students.

For purposes of constructing the correct answer, items created using the typology can be subdivided into two groups: those requiring reiteration or summarization and those requiring illustration, prediction, evaluation, or application. For items intended to measure reiteration and summarization, the summary prepared during Step 2 will serve as the basis for the correct answer. In fact, having completed Step 2 means that 90% of the work of creating a correct answer is behind. The main work to follow will be the shortening and rephrasing of information included in the Step 2 summary. The key is to provide the shortest possible adequate answer to the question posed. Above all, the correct answer in selected-response items should not be longer than the distractors written in Step 6. Likewise, it should not be distinguishable in other non-content related ways that may allow the examinee to answer correctly without having actual mastery of the content and process. Besides length, examinees look for a difference in the quality of writing, thinking that the correct answer may have been taken from the book and therefore will be more polished.

To ensure that summarization items truly measure summarizing ability, it is necessary to avoid wording the answer in selected-response items in a way that resembles wording in the text or lectures. The message should be the same, but the wording of the answer should be quite different from that in the text.

Answers to selected-response items calling for illustration or prediction are generally of two types: (*a*) those requiring selection of an example or expected outcome, and (*b*) those requiring selection of an example or outcome *plus* recognition of the grounds for the selection. In the case of illustration, a statement of the grounds would be a listing of the critical attributes that qualify objects or events as members of the class or examples of the principle or procedure. In the case of prediction, the defense would include a listing of situational characteristics that make a particular rule apply and, perhaps, naming of the rule in addition to selecting the most likely outcome. One caution is needed. Including the grounds for selection of each alternative sometimes provides a clue that enables the examinee to answer the item correctly without mastery of the content and process.

Again, the key to writing items that measure prediction is to use example situations to which the examinee has not been previously exposed. If, under these circumstances, the examinee can recognize that the antecedent conditions are present and can use the rule to anticipate later consequences, we can be sure that the individual has both learned the rule and how to use it.

As for evaluation and application items, we have already made the case that these higher level processes can be measured adequately only through use of constructed-response items. Evaluation behavior is an analytic process. The only true test of this behavior requires the examinee to go through the process in such a way that the examiner can observe and judge the process itself. This requires observation of the behavior or of a written record that captures the behavior for later review. Judgments are based on determining adequacy of the process through using criteria rather than determining whether the examinee selects the same answer as did the item writer.

As for application, the focus is again on observing and determining the adequacy of a process. Examinees are required to organize and use their knowledge and skills to cause a prespecified outcome. The process itself is judged through use of criteria appropriate to the discipline and circumstances. The process includes generating alternatives as well as choosing among them. Selected-response items provide the alternatives to the examinee. Also, selected-response items are judged by determining whether examinees choose the same answer as the item writer or validation sample did. Good answers to application questions are often novel. The circumstances thus demand a constructed-response item with relevant criteria for judging the student answers.

STEP 6. WRITE THE FOILS

By far the most difficult part of selected-response item writing is the construction of foils. Foils are designed to attract examinees who lack understanding of the content or who are unable to use the material in the desired way. Therefore, foils must be plausible responses for those examinees whose mastery of the content is incomplete. At the same time, foils should *not* trick knowledgeable examinees into incorrect answers.

The best way to create foils is to anticipate (predict) the kinds of misunderstandings or errors in knowledge that examinees are likely to experience. Then create a foil that will be attractive to those who demonstrate each type of error in understanding. This is not only the best type of foil to create from the point of being attractive alternatives, but it is the most educationally sound because it helps to diagnose the problems examinees are having.

One good strategy for determining appropriate foils is to create the stem and first administer the items to students in short-answer, essay format. The incorrect answers provided by students can easily be converted into foils for multiple-choice items, as was discussed in Chapter 6.

In the case of reiteration and summarization items, the best foils will likely leave out important components of the answer (definition, description of a situation, etc.) or will add components that are often present but not required. In other cases, the foils may be definitions of closely related terms or descriptions of similar events.

In the case of illustration, either the name is given and examinees pick out the example that goes with the name, or an example is given and examinees have to name it. In the first case, the best foils are examples that possess some but not all of the critical attributes that define the concept or demonstrate the applicability of the principle. In the latter case, the best foils are names of closely related concepts or principles. Sometimes test developers try to confuse the examinee by using similar words, but this approach verges on creating trick items that are of little utility in helping to diagnose knowledge–process deficiencies in examinees.

In the case of prediction items, examinees are either given a description of a situation establishing that some of the defining characteristics of a class of objects or events are present and are asked to predict what other characteristics should be present or they are given a description of a situation to which a principle or procedure applies and asked to predict the consequences based on knowledge of the procedure or rule. In both cases, the key to effective foils is the creation of choices that are plausible by virtue of describing characteristics or actions that may be associated in real life but are not linked to each other by the rule or concept serving as the basis of the item. Of course, this procedure is appropriate only when the item allows the knowledgeable student to correctly identify the concept, rule, or procedure to be applied.

A Case Study in Item Development

As a means for showing how the classification system and item-writing methodology described in this chapter are used in the development of items that are useful for instructional testing, a hypothetical case study is presented here.

A BASIC SCIENCE UNIT: THE MOLECULE AND THE BIOSPHERE[2]

This unit from the science curriculum was planned for seventh grade students. It emphasizes a better understanding of the environment, the issues facing citizens in that regard, and possible solutions to various environmental problems. The main objectives of the unit are to

1. Make students aware of their environment and these issues
2. Help them think about problems they will face in the future and have them work on tentative solutions
3. Develop a positive attitude toward these issues

A science curriculum committee developed a list of issues and problems to be solved that bear on the environment of the region where the town is located. Instructors reviewed the chapter and developed a set of teaching objectives. These objectives were correlated to the goals of the unit and were used as the basis for a set of corresponding test items. Items were carefully developed to represent various combinations of content and operations as defined in the classification system in this chapter. The planners of instruction believed that concepts and principles were the most important content, but all operations except reiteration were included. Seven items are traced in their development to illustrate how the classification system is used to develop achievement tests. These items, their operation type, content area, and test mode are given in Table 10.2.

Item 1 in Table 10.2 deals with summarization of a concept, and a multiple-choice item is used. Essentially, the objective calls for the definition of a number of terms that represent essential concepts in ecology. The curriculum committee felt these were essential terms that must be understood before more complex ideas could be introduced. Each item was written to elicit a response that would define the concept. All correct answers are *not* verbatim-type responses found in the book or in other available sources but actually paraphrased definitions that were not used.

Item 2 deals with summarization of a principle—that there is an interdependent relationship among three types of living organisms: plant eaters, animal eaters, and decomposers. Although the principle is rather complex, the question asks specifically for the relationship between the first two and for some mention of how decomposers help. Ultimately, the unit leads students to understand problems of depletion of natural wildlife due to overhunting, defoliation of the forest, and infestations of certain species of animals.

Item 3 deals with the identification or naming of examples of concepts. The multiple-choice item gives four new examples, one of which is a consumer. Item 4

---

[2]This case study describes an instructional unit modeled after one developed by Navarra, Zafforoni, and Garone (1965).

Table 10.2
Example Test Items for a Hypothetical Seventh Grade Ecology Unit[a]

Operation	Content	Response mode	Item
1. Summarization	Concept	Selected	What is the lithosphere? *a.* a portion of the biosphere *b.* any part of the earth not covered by water *c.* the upper part of the earth covered by water *d.* any part of the earth covered by water
2. Summarization	Principles	Constructed	Describe in your own words, the relationships among plant-eaters and animal-eaters. Include the role of the decomposer in your answer.
3. Illustration	Concepts	Selected	Which of the following are consumers according to the definition in your text? *a.* arthropods *b.* chickens *c.* eels *d.* weeds
4. Illustration	Principles	Constructed	Give an example of how plants depend on decomposers.
5. Prediction	Concepts	Constructed	If one animal eats smaller animals, what will the animal be likely to do if smaller animals are not available?
6. Prediction	Principles	Selected	If the host of a parasite dies, the parasite will likely *a.* die. *b.* move to a similar host. *c.* become a host to another animal. *d.* become a decomposer.
7. Evaluation	Principle	Constructed	If animals drink from a calcium-free stream, will this be good for the calcium cycle? Explain.

[a] Some of the material in this table was suggested by portions of Navarra, Zafforoni, and Garone (1965).

is similar to Item 3 in terms of operation, but a principle is being tested, and the student must give his or her own example of the principle. This activity is considerably harder than an item where four examples are given and the student must choose the one that illustrates the principle.

Item 5 involves prediction, and the content is a concept. Earlier in this chapter, we stated that the prediction of a concept involves giving the student some characteristics of the concept and asking him or her to identify other characteristics. The concept is that of the behavioral characteristics of larger animals who are first-order consumers that prey on smaller animals nearby. The item elicits a response to the question, what would a larger animal do if smaller animals were not available? A student who is well-versed in the concept must anticipate other characteristics that have not been formally presented. In other words, the student is expected to go beyond, to generalize to a larger set of characteristics. This item is considerably more difficult than others presented.

Item 6, a selected-response item, calls for prediction using a principle. The principle is simple, dealing with the habits of parasites. If the source of food is discontinued, the animal adapts or dies. It is assumed that the consequence of a host dying has not been taught. The student must anticipate the consequences based on all the reading about the behavior of parasites. Although the chapter on which the text is based does not state that a parasite typically searches for another host or dies, a principle given earlier applies (that a first-order consumer typically adapts to changes in the environment or dies). In this instance, adaptation is unlikely and dying is a more likely consequence for the parasite than finding another host.

Item 7 deals with the evaluation of a principle using the constructed-response mode. As noted earlier, evaluation may require any of three different kinds of behaviors, and this question deals with using a criterion to make a decision. The student must determine whether or not a calcium-free stream seriously affects a calcium cycle.

Up to this point, the test-item examples in Table 10.2 have dealt with operations that are unitary. Application, you will recall, is one operation that is complex and often involves several other types of operation.

Application in this unit was focused on concepts and principles again, with each item requiring a constructed response that centered around a community or regional environmental problem that involved wildlife management, industrial development, and land use. Since each student will serve in various life roles— such as policymaker, organizer, a member of the informed public—each will have a need to understand the basic issues and creatively solve problems that arise.

The student activities and application test items used centered around real-life problems. Each group of students dealt with a single issue, performing a study of the issue, identifying the problems, planning for the solution of the problems, suggesting tentative solutions, selecting a solution, and describing a program of action to resolve the issue. Issues included water resources in the region, rodent infestation in the forest, whether or not to build a dam on a local river to generate hydroelectric power, and turning farmland into five-acre parcels for homes.

Each of these activities and the resultant products constitutes an application item that involves complex chaining of the operations across the content areas of concepts and principles.

Summary

We have presented a classification system that is seen as useful for categorizing objectives and test items as well as for planning and guiding the production of test items. The main features of the typology are: (*a*) content, (*b*) task, and (*c*) test mode. The crucial aspects of the content dimension are facts, concepts, and principles; the task dimension includes reiteration, summarization, illustration, prediction, evaluation, and application. The two test modes are recognition and production.

Generic objectives were developed for each category. These provide the structural form for objectives that are appropriate for each content and task category. Practical guidelines were presented for preparing items, using a six-step procedure. Many of these steps become covert and abbreviated when the item writer is experienced in the use of the system. Having instructional objectives replaces much of the work in Steps 1–3. Finally, some examples were presented in the framework of a hypothetical science unit in a seventh grade science class.

The classification system has its roots in earlier work (Miller and Williams, 1973; Williams, 1977; Miller, Williams, and Haladyna, 1978) and the related work of Merrill and his colleagues (Merrill, Reigeluth, & Faust, 1979; Wulfeck, Ellis, Merrill, Richards, & Wood, 1978) on the development of the Instructional Quality Inventory (presented in Chapter 11), and there are common elements in these systems. Specifically, the content dimension of facts, concepts, and principles can be found in both systems.

Research done to date on this classification system, though limited, has been promising. Certainly more research is needed if this classification system and item-writing approach is to have broad appeal and if it is to be helpful to instructional developers.

References

Anderson, L. W., & Liu, J. M. *The applicability of three systematic approaches to item writing to the assessment of different types of instructional objectives.* Presented at the meeting of the American Educational Research Association, Boston, April, 1980.

Bloom, B. S., Engelhart, M. D., Furst, E. J., Hill, W. H. and Krathwohl, D. R. *Taxonomy of educational objectives: The cognitive domain.* New York: Longmans, Green, 1956.

Hively, W. Introduction to domain-referenced testing. *Educational Technology,* 1974, *14,* 5–10.

Kropp, R. P., & Stoker, H. W. *The construction and validation of tests of the cognitive processes as described in the taxonomy of educational objectives.* Cooperative Research Project No. 2177. Tallahassee: Univ. of Florida, 1966.

Madaus, G. F., Woods, F., & Nuttall, R. L. A causal model analysis of Bloom's taxonomy. *American Educational Research Journal,* 1973, *10,* 253–262.

Merrill, M. D., Reigeluth, C. M., & Faust, G. W. The instructional quality profile: A curriculum evaluation and design tool. In H. F. O'Neil, Jr. (Ed.), *Procedures for instructional systems development*. New York: Academic Press, 1979.

Miller, H. G., & Williams, R. G. Constructing higher level multiple choice questions covering factual content. *Educational Technology,* 1973, *13*(5), 39–42.

Miller, H. G., Williams, R. G., & Haladyna, T. M. *Beyond facts: Objective ways to measure thinking*. Englewood Cliffs, New Jersey: Educational Technology Publications, 1978.

Miller, W. G., Snowman, J., & O'Hara, T. Application of alternative statistical techniques to examine the hierarchical ordering in Bloom's taxonomy. *American Educational Research Journal,* 1979, *16*, 241–248.

Navarra, J. G., Zafforoni, J., & Garone, J. E. *Today's basic science: The molecule and the biosphere*. New York: Harper & Row, 1965.

Seddon, G. M. The properties of Bloom's taxonomy of educational objectives for the cognitive domain. *Review of Educational Research,* 1978, *48*, 303–323.

Semb, G., & Spencer, R. Beyond the level of recall: An analysis of higher-order educational tasks. *Proceedings: Third National Conference on Behavior Research and Technology in Higher Education,* Atlanta, 1976. (Available from James A. Johnston, Psychology Department, Univ. of Florida, Gainesville, Florida 32511.)

Williams, R. G. A behavior typology of educational objectives for the cognitive domain. *Educational Technology,* 1977, *17*(6), 39–46.

Wulfeck, W., Ellis, J. A., Merrill, M. D., Richards, R. E., & Wood, N. D. *The instructional quality inventory: Vol. I, Introduction and overview*. San Diego, California: Navy Personnel Research and Development Center, 1978.

11

The Instructional Quality Inventory

Instructional Systems Development (ISD) is a model for systematic instruction that is widely applied in military training (O'Neil, 1979). Typically, the sequence of development includes five steps. The first is the job or task analysis leading to the specification of objectives. The second is the design of instruction including the development of criterion-referenced tests to measure student progress relevant to the objectives. The third step is the design of new instruction or the adaptation of old instruction that is relevant to the objectives. The fourth is the implementation of training programs. In the fifth and last step, evaluation and feedback are used to modify course objectives, instruction, or testing.

It is widely recognized that the combined training programs of the United States military constitute the largest training effort in the world. It is interesting, therefore, to note that the military is deeply committed to instruction based on objectives (U.S. Training and Doctrine Command, 1975) and CR testing (Swezey & Pearlstein, 1975; Ellis & Wulfeck, 1980). The military approach is consistent with the view of researchers such as Shoemaker (1975) who have analyzed systematic instruction. Shoemaker describes an algorithmic relationship that should exist among the components of (*a*) objectives, (*b*) instruction, and (*c*) testing. The Instructional Quality Inventory (IQI) is an attempt to systematically keep the three components (objectives, instruction, and testing) in concert throughout the instructional process.

The IQI is a method of logical analysis that incorporates principles of learning and instruction. The intent of the IQI is to improve the time efficiency and effectiveness of instruction. The IQI can also be seen as an aid to validating an instructional program, particularly in the sense of content validity or relevance to job performance.

Some of the underlying concepts of the IQI were developed under contract to the U.S. Navy by Courseware, Inc. (Merrill, Wood, Richards, & Schmidt, 1977). The Navy Personnel Research and Development Center then made significant revisions to the initial version. Further revisions and additions were made to the IQI, resulting in the current version, which is the topic of this chapter (Wulfeck, Ellis, Merrill, Richards, & Wood, 1978; Ellis & Wulfeck, 1978; Ellis, Wulfeck, & Fredericks, 1979; Fredericks, 1980). Related conceptual issues have also been discussed by Merrill, Reigeluth, and Faust (1979).

One way to view the IQI is as an aid to ISD. The ISD is the overall model for instruction and the IQI is the evaluation arm of the ISD. From another perspective, the IQI is a means for systematically studying the structure and content of instructional intent, as stated through objectives. Also, the IQI provides a conceptual framework and checkpoints for evaluating the correspondence between the intent of instruction and the results obtained from tests.

The presentation of the IQI in this chapter is based on the IQI user's manual (Ellis *et al.*, 1979). The reader is referred to this and its companion volumes for more comprehensive presentation of the IQI and examples of its application.

A Qualifying Note

The IQI was initially designed to be used with the ISD model and job training. However, we believe that the IQI is a useful device for examining any subject matter content, objectives, and test items to determine if there is a logical correspondence among each of these.

A qualification of our use of the ISD model and the IQI is that we conceive of three products of instructional development: objectives, instructional presentations, and tests. The IQI is product oriented, and the areas of interest are the cognitive and psychomotor domains.

Another qualification of our use of the IQI stems from the fact that the inventory is based on the premise that the test designer is working from an adequate description of the content domain. That is, the designer assumes that the domain specification is adequate, and that it comes from a good task analysis or that content specialists are in agreement. As discussed in Chapter 2, there remains a basic difference between objective-based and domain-based methods of test development. The IQI, as an objective-based method, takes a different approach to domain specification than an item form does. The universe of potential test items that match an objective must define the domain for that objective. The IQI provides guidelines for assessing the match between items and objectives and, thus, is a precondition for, but does not guarantee, the creation of item domains.

Finally, the IQI in and of itself was not designed originally as a method for writing test items, but it is an aid. What the IQI is particularly useful for is leading the item writer from instructional intent to the identification of the kind of test item that is appropriate.

The Classification System

The classification system of the IQI has two major dimensions, the content and the task, as shown in Figure 11.1.

The *task* is what the student must actually do. *Content* is what the student must learn—specifically, the type of information the student must learn. We can develop a task-by-content matrix with any of the three products of instruction (objectives, instructional presentations or tests). Each of these will be treated in detail and examples will be provided to give a more complete picture of the IQI and its workings.

TASK

Students can either *remember* information or they can *use* information. These behaviors comprise two major levels of the task dimension. For example, we can have the student remember four types of unsafe driving practices. Alternatively, the student may be asked to use knowledge of unsafe driving practices to avoid accidents, based on this knowledge. The latter example is clearly a use of information to achieve an end. While we may deem the use of information more important—and it is—we generally agree that knowledge, or the possession of information, is a enabling condition for performing a skill.

An important distinction must be made between two types of tasks, one without aid and one with aid. Without aid, a student must remember what must be used and then use it. With aid, the student is provided with what must be remembered and then gets to use it. For example, a student may be asked to dissassemble and reassemble a clock without the use of a set of instructions. In another instance, a student may assemble the clock with the use of instructions.

CONTENT

The second dimension of the IQI has five levels, comparable in design to those levels found in the typology of higher level thinking presented in the previous chapter.

Content

Task	FACT– Recall or recognize names, parts, dates, places, etc.	CATEGORY– Remember characteristics or classify objects, events or ideas according to characteristics	PROCEDURE– Sequence of steps remembered or used in a single situation or on a single piece of equipment	RULE– Remember or use a sequence of steps, that apply across situations or across equipments	PRINCIPLE– Remember, interpret, or predict why or how things happen, or cause-effect relationships
REMEMBER–Recall or recognize facts, concept definitions; steps, procedures, or rules; statements of principle					
USE, UNAIDED–Tasks that require classifying, performing a procedure, using a rule, explaining or predicting, with no aids except memory.					
USE, AIDED–Same as use, unaided, except job aids are available.					

Figure 11.1 The Content-by-Task Matrix of the Instructional Quality Inventory.

The five types of content are: facts, categories, procedures, rules, and principles.

Facts are associations between names, objects, figures, symbols, locations, concepts, etc. The fact level of content is analogous to the first level of Bloom's taxonomy—knowledge. Some examples include:

1. Naming the stages of transition of a cyclone
2. Listing the states alphabetically
3. Identifying the name of an element when given a chemical code
4. Recalling a foreign word for an English equivalent
5. Providing a name for a description of a person

It should be noted that all of these behaviors can be reproduced identically in a factual way. As we have noted in the previous chapter, prior learning and the nature of instruction have everything to do with designating the type of learning that prevails. For example, many kinds of higher level behaviors are actually at the recall level, if identical cues have been provided during instruction. Recalling a foreign word is factual when the student has memorized the equivalents. If students are confronted with words for which they have no equivalent, they must engage in another form of thinking that is not factual. Thus, the instructor must be alert to both the intended type of content and the actual type of content encountered.

Categories are classes of objects or events that are defined by a set of attributes. Terms we use to define categories are *concept analysis, definition,* and *summarizing,* the latter term being drawn from the typology discussed in the previous chapter. As you can see, the typology of higher level thinking discussed in Chapter 10 and the IQI are similar up to this point, but serious differences develop at the next levels.

Some examples of categories include:

1. Identifying examples of mollusks (that have not been previously presented)
2. Identifying electrocardiogram results that indicate heart disease
3. Classifying previously unstudied minerals by their attributes

Procedures, which comprise a third type of content, are series of steps or operations that one performs in a single context. For example, the person may assemble a working model of a pendulum or describe the steps that one follows to travel from one place to another. In every subject matter, there is a set of procedures that must be followed to achieve an end. It should be noted that these procedures may be either remembered or used depending on the level of the task dimension.

Rules, the fourth type of content, are very much like procedures, the major exception being that when a rule is used, the object of application is broader than a single sequence. Therefore, this fourth type of content is broader in application and has greater generality. For example:

1. Calculate the navigational distance between any two points when given the exact latitude and longitude.
2. Identify the steps one would follow to repair any engine that consumes an inordinate amount of oil.
3. Describe the sequence of events one follows in planning any three-day backpacking trip.

Principles comprise the fifth of the five content types and include any behavior that involves explanations or predictions. Specifically, we are interested in cause–effect relations. This category is identical in intent to the one called "prediction" in the typology discussed in the preceding chapter. Some examples are:

1. Describe the effects of anemia on the body defense system.
2. Identify the consequences of intermittent reinforcement versus the consequences of reinforcements in planned intervals.

IQI Procedures

There are a series of steps to follow in the IQI to ensure that the three products of the ISD are coordinated and focused toward the same instructional intent. Brief descriptions of these steps follow:

1. *Objective Adequacy:* Objectives are examined to see if they follow or meet three specific criteria (described in the next section).
2. *Test Consistency and Adequacy:* Test items are judged consistent with the instructional intent and adequate with respect to characteristics of good item writing, as reviewed in Chapters 4 and 5.
3. *Presentation Consistency:* Instructional presentations are examined for consistency with the objectives and test items.
4. *Presentation Adequacy:* Several criteria are used to determine whether instructional presentations are suitable and effective in meeting desired ends (see Ellis *et al.*, 1979 for more details).

In the balance of this chapter, we will focus on the first two steps, as they are most germane to the technology of test-item writing. The interested reader will want to read Chapters 4 and 5 in Ellis *et al.* (1979) for more information on presentation consistency and adequacy. These authors' manual also provides references that cover this approach to instructional evaluation in greater detail. Also, the reader is referred to an excellent review of a process related to the IQI in Merrill *et al.* (1979).

Objective Adequacy

As we have noted, the instructional objective is the initial, formal statement of instructional intent. Typically, the objective states what the student must do, that is, under what conditions the behavior is performed to exhibit evidence of achievement. The objective, it has been argued (Baker, 1974; Popham, 1976) has not met all expectations originally proposed for developing items, and studies have shown that the use of objectives may lead to uncontrolled item-writer bias (Roid & Haladyna, 1978).

On the other hand, objectives may be redefined, as we have seen, by using any of the item-writing technologies or amplified objectives. The first step in the IQI is to examine the objective with respect to three criteria. An objective that meets these criteria is viewed as suitable for the development of items representing that objective. Unsuitable objectives must be reanalyzed, rejected, or improved. This initial step in the IQI has much the same function that the mapping sentence has in facet design theory: to place the instructional intent in clear perspective. In facet design theory, we try to modify the objective appropriately; with the IQI, we examine the objective.

IS THE OBJECTIVE CORRECTLY STATED?

The first criterion is concerned with the content of the objective. Mager (1962) was among the first to describe the role and structure of objectives. The traditional three conditions of any objective comprise the structure of an "adequate" objective:

1. Does the objective indicate what the student must do to demonstrate achievement represented by the objective?
2. Are the conditions for performance specified?
3. Is there a specific standard of performance that must be met?

In addition, an objective may be inadequate if measurement or instruction are made difficult or unclear by the wording of the objective. These weaknesses are more fundamental in nature and must require a study of the rationale for including that objective in the plan for instruction. For example, if an objective is stated so that the student must solve a previously unsolved problem, what method of instruction and testing would be appropriate? With every objective, the intent of instruction, the presentation of instruction, and the observation of behavior (testing) must be thought of as one central activity with three aspects, or perspectives.

DOES THE OBJECTIVE FIT THE TASK–CONTENT MATRIX?

All objectives, if they are adequate, may be classified using the task–content matrix. If we are not clear as to what the student must do to demonstrate that he or she has learned, then that objective will probably not help us in designing either instruction or test items.

The task–content matrix of the IQI is one of several attempts to classify all

objectives by means of a typology that reflects various levels of cognitive behavior. The cognitive taxonomy of Bloom and his colleagures (Bloom *et al.*,
1956) and the one introduced in the preceding chapter (Miller *et al.*, 1978) are
examples of alternative approaches to classifying objectives and test items. If an
objective is found to be unclassifiable by any such classification system, the
taxonomy or typology becomes open to criticism as not being comprehensive.
Which of the alternative systems of classification is best is an empirical question
that requires comparative study of any and all approaches to classifying cognitive
behaviors.

IS THE INSTRUCTIONAL INTENT OF THE OBJECTIVE ADEQUATELY EXPRESSED?

This judgment is most difficult, and it requires a logical analysis by the
content specialist or instructional designer. The object of the analysis is the
search for the reason for including the objective in the instructional plan and its
relation to end-of-instruction behavior. In a training program, knowledge and
skills are viewed as outputs—they are what each student must do to be successful. In educational programs, these outputs can be viewed as building blocks for
general fields of study that comprise specific subject matter; for example, a
course in American Diplomatic History contributes to a growing understanding
of American history in general and of the forces that created and maintain our
nation. Unfortunately, as Guttman (1969) observes, there is, as yet, no well
established theory of content structure that is readily applicable to this problem.

Test-Item Consistency

Following the careful examination of the instructional objective, we turn to
the examination of the item, the essential building block of any test. Two central
concerns are *consistency* and *adequacy*.

Test-item consistency calls for the analysis of the logical relationship between the objective and the test item. This is the very essence of Chapter 12: the
logical review of items. Although the authors of the IQI do not prescribe all of
the procedures discussed in Chapter 12, they do give some advice regarding
test-item consistency.

ACTION VERBS

The action verb in the objective must be logically consistent with action in
the test question. Along this line, one can arrange verbs into a matrix to suggest
the type of test question. For example, five common verbs we find in objectives

are: *identify, name, order, describe,* and *construct.* These may be arranged by test format:

Behavior verb	Test format	Part of cognitive domain
identify	multiple choice	knowledge
name	completion	knowledge
order	performance	skill
describe	essay	knowledge
construct	product	skill

The table presented is only suggestive and illustrative. The word *identify* implies choosing among a set or series of possibilities, as is done in the multiple choice format. *Name* implies the providing of a correct response, as in a completion item. *Describe* involves a verbal (oral or written) behavior representing knowledge. *Order* and *Construct* are used to convey the idea that a skill is demonstrated either through performance or through a product. Verbs can be tested against a criterion such as the following: If the verb suggests a clear-cut item format, the verb is useful in an objective.

CONDITIONS

The conditions under which the behavior is being observed in the testing condition should resemble those conditions described in the objective as well as the conditions under which the student will perform after instruction or training. The conditions expressed in the objectives must agree with the conditions required in testing as well as with postinstruction behavior. Instructors may argue that a transfer-of-training effect would require that conditions be changed, but unless transfer is specifically stated in the objective as an intent of instruction, it should not constitute part of the instructional program or the testing program. Examples of consistent and inconsistent test items appear in Table 11.1.

STANDARDS

There has been much criticism of standards in testing (Glass, 1978; Burton, 1978). Standards have been imposed on test performance in numerous situations, for example, systematic instruction, competency testing, and licensure at state and national levels for various professions and occupations. In the IQI some of these issues are discussed, such as the adequacy of standards for expressing the real requirements of a job or cognitive task.

As Millman (1973), Meskauskas (1976), and others have pointed out, the problem of standard setting is both difficult and complex. Shepard (1976) further points out that extensive social and political considerations, including much common sense, are involved in standard setting.

Table 11.1
Examples of Consistent and Inconsistent Test Items

Objective:
   Given the necessary tools and an operator's manual, the student will set up and operate a double-acting reciprocating pump, in five minutes and according to the manual specifications.

Inconsistent test item:
   "List the steps of procedure for starting, operating, and stopping a double-acting reciprocating pump."
   This test item is inconsistent because its *task–content* is *remember–procedure* instead of *use–aided–procedure*. Note also that the action the student is asked to perform in the test is not the action required in the objective.

Consistent test item:
   "Use the operator's manual and necessary tools to set up and operate a double-acting reciprocating pump. You will pass this test if you complete this task within 5 minutes, in accordance with the manual specifications."
   This test item is consistent with the objective. Notice, however, that if either the conditions or grading standards had been left out, the item would have been inconsistent.

FORMAT

The format of the objective should agree with the format of the test item with respect to the task–content matrix. This is a most difficult situation to compromise. If the objective falls in the category of remember-rule, the test item must elicit remember-rule behaviors. Wulfeck *et al.* (1978) made the point that selected-response items are not acceptable for the remember-level if they fail to reflect "typical job performance requirements [p. 9]."

This is one of the IQI's most unique characteristics. For the most part, item developers have been disposed to use the multiple-choice format regardless of the words of the instructional objective. The rationale for this common practice is probably provided by statements like those of Nunnally (1967) who, like many other test specialists, suggests that multiple-choice testing is not only more efficient but more "valid" in the sense that a domain of behaviors can be more adequately sampled when using multiple-choice items.

It must be remembered that the IQI is set in a context of military training where the outcomes of the programs are mainly in the areas of skill. Consequently, objectives and test items must be identified in terms of student behavior, and job performance requirements. Thus, the familiar multiple-choice item does not serve so prominent a role in this system as it does in criterion-referenced testing in academic settings.

Test-Item Adequacy

The many guidelines for test-item adequacy have been reviewed mainly in Chapters 4 and 5. As the reader can see, these guidelines constitute what Cron-

bach (1971, p. 509) called "distillations of wisdom" from measurement prac-
titioners. In the IQI manual (Ellis *et al.*, 1979, pp. 55–77), the user is
cautioned to determine whether the test items are clear, unambiguous, well-
constructed (as described in Chapters 4 and 5, pp. 49–87 of the present book), free
of hints that inappropriately give away the answer, made up of options in the
multiple-choice format that reflect common errors, and representative of the
required behavior.

Ellis and Wulfeck (1980) also recommend that the user of the IQI system
consult sources such as Anderson (1972) for design of paraphrase items, Markle
and Tiemann for testing concepts (see Chapter 9 of the present book), and Durnin
and Scandura (1973) for testing the understanding of rules. Expanded information on such item-writing methods is available in an IQI handbook on item
writing (Ellis & Wulfeck, 1981).

Summary

The Instructional Quality Inventory is a system of guidelines for evaluating
the consistency and adequacy of objectives, instructional materials, and test
items. It was developed for military training to provide guidance to instructional
developers and instructors who lack formal schooling in teaching and testing, and
yet, it has much to offer to instructional designers and test developers at all
levels. The IQI is a subsystem of the Instructional Systems Development (ISD)
model, which has been adopted by all branches of the U.S. military as the
approved method of developing training courses.

The ISD and the IQI rest on a broad research base distilled from the many
years of work on a variety of instructional design and measurement issues such as
behavioral objectives, adjunct questions, type of feedback in instruction, advance organizers, information mapping, concept learning, programmed instruction, criterion-referenced testing, task analysis, conditions of learning and others
(Merrill & Boutwell, 1973). Empirical studies on the IQI are those by the
developers of the technique (Merrill, Wood, Baker, Ellis, & Wulfeck, 1977;
Merrill & Wood, 1977; Wood, Ellis, & Wulfeck, 1978).

The major strength of the IQI system in relation to the technology of item
writing is in its ability to prepare the item writer to understand the context in
which items will be used, as well as to evaluate their consistency and adequacy.
The IQI uses a typology in the form of a task–content matrix that is a unique way
of classifying educational objectives and test items. The logical structure of the
IQI provides a means of linking instructional intent, the instructional presentation, and testing. Since this linking is the hallmark of systematic instruction, as
discussed in Chapter 2, it seems that the IQI makes a major contribution here
with respect to preparing the item writer to select or produce useful items.

One concern about the IQI task–content matrix, as with any taxonomy or typology of educational objectives, is that research must continue to examine, refine, and validate such classification systems. Validation by experts outside of the military-training community will be the important next step in establishing the generalizability of the IQI system to other settings. With the cognitive taxonomy of Bloom and his colleagues, research reviewed by Seddon (1978) has indicated that the taxonomy has not lead to the establishment of validity of measures intended to represent various levels of that taxonomy. The typology described by Miller *et al.* (1978; also, see Chapter 10) also needs further research, although one study (Williams, 1977) does provide a glimpse of hope for the validity of that typology for classifying objectives and items.

Ellis and Wulfeck (1980) have described two main criteria for evaluating the adequacy of typologies or category systems for objectives or items—reliability and usefulness of the prescriptions provided for testing and instruction. Data from workshop evaluations (Wood *et al.*, 1978) indicated that the IQI matrix allowed users to reliably classify objectives or items with agreement in the range of 80% to 100%. With respect to the second criteria, the IQI is unique among typologies in providing a wealth of guidelines for such things as selection of item formats and consistency–adequacy ratings.

Perhaps a practical limitation of the IQI system is not with its methodology but with the dissemination of knowledge about how to use the system. By their nature, military reports and publications are less widely obtained by educators and psychologists around the world, and, hence the diffusion of the technique is slower than that of other methods available through commercial publishers or journals. However, for the test developer who takes the time to obtain the reports, and perhaps attend a training workshop on the technique, there is a potential gold mine of valuable practical advice available for the taking.

When the IQI is expanded to include a handbook on item writing (Wulfeck & Ellis, 1981), it will more directly address some of the issues discussed in earlier chapters of this book. In fact, a portion of a related manuscript by the authors (Roid & Haladyna, 1980) will form a part of that expanded handbook.

As noted earlier, the technologies of item writing are just beginning to emerge, and all suffer under the scrutiny of the critical eye of the researcher in educational psychology who wishes to see empirical evidence and logical argument for the value of such new techniques. Each item-writing technology will require extensive tryout, revision, research, and implementation on a wider scale across more subject matters. Clearly, the IQI is one of the more well-developed approaches to content specification and CR testing, but due to its broad scope, it will require wider use before it can be validated in education and training outside of the military.

References

Anderson, R. C. How to construct achievement tests to assess comprehension. *Review of Educational Research*, 1972, *42*, 145–170.

Baker, E. L., Beyond objectives: Domain-referenced tests for evaluation and instructional improvement. *Educational Technology*, 1974, *14*(6), 10-16.

Bloom, B. S., Engelhart, M. D., Furst, E. J., Hill, W. H., & Krathwohl, D. R. *Taxonomy of educational objectives*. New York: Longmans, Green, 1956.

Burton, N. W. Societal Standards. *Journal of Educational Measurement*, 1978, *15*(4), 263-271.

Cronbach, L. J. Test validation. In R. L. Thorndike (Ed.), *Educational measurement* (2nd ed.). Washington: American Council on Education, 1971.

Durnin, J. H., & Scandura, J. M. An algorithmic approach to assessing behavior potential: Comparison with item forms and hierarchical technologies. *Journal of Educational Psychology*, 1973, *64*, 262-272.

Ellis, J. A., & Wulfeck, W. H. *The Instructional Quality Inventory: Vol. IV, Job Performance Aid*. San Diego, California: Navy Personnel Research and Development Center (NPRDC), Special Report 79-5, 1978. (Available from Defense Technical Information Center (DTIC) document Number AD A083928).

Ellis, J. A., & Wulfeck, W. H. *Assuring objective-test consistency: A systematic procedure for constructing criterion-referenced tests*. San Diego, California: NPRDC, Special Report 80-15, 1980.

Ellis, J. A., Wulfeck, W. H., & Fredericks, P. S. *The instructional quality inventory: Vol. II, User's manual*. San Diego: NPRDC, Special Report 79-24, 1979. (DTIC #AD A085678).

Fredericks, P. S. *The instructional quality inventory: Vol. II, Training workbook*. San Diego, California: NPRDC, Special Report 80-25, 1980. (DTIC #AD A092804)

Glass, G. V. Standards and criteria. *Journal of Educational Measurement*, 1978, *15*(4), 237-261.

Guttman, L. Integration of test design and analysis. *Proceedings of the 1969 Invitational Conference on Testing Problems*. Princeton, N.J.: Educational Testing Service, 1969.

Mager, R. F. *Preparing instructional objectives*. Palo Alto, California: Fearon Publishers, 1962.

Merrill, M. D., & Boutwell, R. C. Instructional development methodology and research. In F. N. Kerlinger (Ed.), *Review of research in education*. Itasca, Illinois: F. E. Peacock, 1973.

Merrill, M. D., Reigeluth, C. M., & Faust, G. W. The instructional quality profile: A curriculum evaluation and design tool. In H. F. O'Neil, Jr. (Ed.), *Procedures for instructional systems development*. New York: Academic Press, 1979, 165-204.

Merrill, M. D., & Wood, N. D. *Validation of the instructional strategy diagnostic profile: Empirical studies*. San Diego, California: NPRDC, Technical Report 77-25, 1977. (DTIC #AD A042334)

Merrill, M. D., Wood, N. D., Baker, M. S., Ellis, J. A., & Wulfeck, W. H. *Empirical validation of selected Instructional Strategy Diagnostic Profile prescriptions*. San Diego, California: NPRDC, Technical Report 77-43, 1977. (DTIC #AD A045309)

Merrill, M. D., Wood, N. D., Richards, R. E., & Schmidt, R. V. *The Instructional Strategy Diagnostic Profile training manual*. San Diego, California: NPRDC, Special Report 77-14, 1977.

Meskauskas, J. A. Evaluation models for criterion-referenced tests: Views regarding mastery and standard-setting. *Review of Educational Research*, 1976, *46*, 133-158.

Miller, H. G., Williams, R. G., & Haladyna, T. M. *Beyond facts: Objective ways to measure thinking*. Englewood Cliffs, N.J.: Educational Technology, 1978.

Millman, J. Passing scores and test lengths for domain-referenced tests. *Review of Educational Research*, 1973, *43*, 205-216.

Nunnally, J. *Psychometric theory*. New York: McGraw-Hill, 1967.

O'Neil, H. F., Jr. (Ed.) *Issues in instructional systems development*. New York: Academic Press, 1979.

Popham, W. J. *Expanding the technical base of criterion-referenced test development*. Paper presented at the annual meeting of the American Educational Research Association, San Francisco, April 1976.

Roid, G. H., & Haladyna, T. M. A comparison of objective-based and modified-Bormuth item writing techniques. *Educational and Psychological Measurement*, 1978, Vol. 35, 19–28.

Roid, G., & Haladyna, T. *Handbook of item writing for criterion-referenced tests*. San Diego, California: NPRDC, Technical Note 80-8, 1980.

Seddon, G. M. The properties of Bloom's taxonomy of educational objectives for the cognitive domain. *Review of Educational Research*, 1978, *48*, 303–323.

Shepard, L. Setting standards and living with them. *Florida Journal of Educational Research*, 1976, *18*, 28–32.

Shoemaker, D. M. Toward a framework for achievement testing. *Review of Educational Research*, 1975, *45*, 127–148.

Swezey, R. W., & Pearlstein, R. B. *Guidebook for developing criterion-referenced tests*. Arlington, Virginia: U.S. Army Research Institute for the Behavioral and Social Sciences, 1975.

U.S. Army Training and Doctrine Command. *Interservice procedures for instructional systems development* (TRADOC Pamphlet 350-30) Ft. Benning, Georgia, 1975.

Williams, R. G. A behavioral typology of educational objectives for the cognitive domain. *Educational Technology*, 1977, *17*(6), 39–46.

Wood, N. D., Ellis, J. A., & Wulfeck, W. H. *Instructional Strategy Diagnostic Profile training manual: Workshop evaluation*. San Diego, California: NPRDC, Special Report 78-17, 1978.

Wulfeck, W. H., & Ellis, J. A. *Handbook for criterion-referenced testing in Navy schools*. San Diego, California: NPRDC, 1981.

Wulfeck, W. H., Ellis, J. A., Merrill, M. D., Richards, R. E., & Wood, N. D. *The instructional quality inventory: Vol. I, Introduction and overview*. San Diego, California: Navy Personnel Research and Development Center, 1978.

IV

REVIEW OF TEST ITEMS

12

Logical Review of
Criterion-Referenced Test Items

Every test item is in some way like a little test (Thorndike, 1967). There-fore, every item is subject to certain forms of analysis to determine its adequacy. Traditionally, this analysis was limited to estimating each item's difficulty and discrimination. Both of these types of analysis required responses to items by students for which the items were intended. These analyses, albeit statistical, were preceded by judgments regarding content coverage. Any item that adequately represented a part of that curriculum and that passed the test of item analysis was retained, while other items were revised or discarded. It is easy to show that highly discriminating items contribute to test reliability (Guilford, 1965; Nunnally, 1967). Thus test developers were prone to select items that had high discrimination indexes.

With the advent of criterion-referenced testing came a change in emphasis from earlier practices in test development to a set of procedures, described in Chapter 3, in which the specification of content domain is done carefully and completely and in which test items are logically related to instructional intent. As a consequence of this different emphasis in the design of tests, two types of item review have emerged: logical and empirical. Logical review refers to the logical relatedness of items to their instructional intent. Empirical review refers to pat-terns of students' responses that are viewed as desirable.

Logical review methods are presented for assessing test *consistency* and

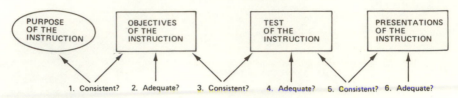

Figure 12.1 The Instructional Quality rating method. (From O'Neil, 1979.)

adequacy. These two dimensions of tests have surfaced as important qualities of tests used in instruction, as suggested by the multiyear effort of the team of researchers who developed the Instructional Quality Inventory and related systems (Ellis, Wulfeck, & Fredericks, 1979; Merrill, Reigeluth, & Faust, 1979), described in detail in Chapter 11.

The overall strategy of the Instructional Quality rating method can be reviewed by examining Figure 12.1. The important principle underlying systematic instruction is that there is a consistency among instructional intent, instructional methods, and tests. The first part of the logical review of CR test items, therefore, focuses on an examination of the consistency of the items and statements of instructional intent, which may be either objectives or domain specifications (Priestly & Nassif, 1979). Also, the consistency among items, instructional materials, and strategies is examined. Consistency is essentially an indication of the content validity of a CR test in the setting of an instructional system. Some of the methodology developed to assess item-objective congruence is also relevant here (e.g., Rovinelli & Hambleton, 1977).

The second focus of logical review is the format, quality of wording, and other factors that can be seen by an experienced item writer as contributing to test adequacy. A comprehensive listing of practical guidelines for writing clear and reliable test items, particularly for the knowledge domains, is provided in Chapter 4. The present chapter will elaborate on some of the principles of test-item adequacy but with major emphasis on the principles and methods of test-item consistency, for both knowledge and skills.

Logical Review of Knowledge Items

There are two very different conditions under which logical review of knowledge items will take place: (*a*) in the case where domain specifications are completely operationally defined and (*b*) when some subjectivity in the composition of the domain still remains.

In the instance where a domain specification completely maps the domain of test items, the problem of item-objective consistency is solved. In other words, if a domain specification completely defines all of the items that are possible, then no logical review by subject matter experts is necessary for *individual* items. This state of affairs is realized when one employs the methods described in Chapters 6 through 9.

Rather than examine items, subject matter experts should examine the *domain specifications* of the item-writing algorithms, item forms, facet designs, or concept analyses themselves for consistency and adequacy. Logical review in these cases would be at the level of the item-writing rules or specifications provided to item writers. The requirement for logical review, even in the case of complete or partial domain specification, points out the fact that operational definitions of items by themselves do not necessarily result in an accurate or valid test. The appropriateness of the algorithm or item-writing rules should still be screened by experts even when an empirical review is conducted as explained in Chapter 13.

The major thesis of this book is that domain specification is a goal to be attempted regardless of whether a complete operational definition can be made. A desirable goal would be to work toward a better and better description of the total range of items that represents the domain of instructional intent. This goal is based on the fact that a better interpretation of a CR test score can be made when the score is an estimate of the proportion of tasks in a domain that the student can accomplish (Hambleton *et al.,* 1978, p. 40). Practically speaking, it is clear that in many subject-matter areas, item formats cannot be completely specified to the point where computerization of item writing would be possible. Therefore, the remainder of this section of this chapter will examine recommended procedures for the logical review of items that may be expected to vary in their congruence with the instructional intent of a program.

TEST ADEQUACY

Some aspects of the way an item is written will signal a common flaw on inspection by an experienced item writer. Multiple-choice items may have lengthy alternatives instead of concentrating most of the information in the stem. A negatively stated stem may be misinterpreted by the student. Alternatives may not be grammatically parallel, plausible, or clearly indicative of one correct answer. One alternative may be longer than all the others, providing a clue to the correct answer. A number of excellent guidelines for the test editor are discussed in Chapter 4 and in Conoley and O'Neil (1979). These guidelines are based on the idea that an objectively scored item should be unambiguous to the knowledgeable student and result in a predictable guessing pattern for a group of less knowledgeable students. For a test composed of four-option multiple-choice items, a random guessing percentage of 25% (e.g., 25 out of 100 items correct by chance) is obtained from a sample of uninstructed students. The more an item deviates from this ideal, the more ''flawed'' it is likely to be.

The guessing pattern of an item may be partially determined by inspection or may require field testing. A number of item flaws are detectable only by field testing, and these are discussed in Chapter 13. For example, some multiple-choice test items, when field tested on a wide-ranging sample of students, may show an unpredicted pattern of incorrect responses among high-ability students. Such items may have two correct answers that are discovered only by the very bright student who interprets the items in a subtle and different way than was intended by the item writer.

In examining the adequacy of constructed-response items such as appear on essay tests, the test editor may attend to what Merrill, Reigeluth, and Faust (1979, p. 178) have called the ''input–output'' form of the item. The test item provides the student with information about the scope of the problem to be addressed, the expected length of the answer, and virtually an implied checklist of the elements that will form an acceptable response. This information is the input that allows the knowledgeable student to begin with a clear concept of the task. The input should also be clear to a subject matter expert who reads the item during an editing session.

The item also asks the student to provide some information, in the form of a constructed answer. This is the output from the item. A well written item should result in a predictable response from the knowledgeable student, with the addition of a creative and imaginative element. The experienced essay writer may be able to identify the presence of such clarifying phrases as ''give two examples of'' or ''list at least three people for whom this was true.'' The best strategy for examining the adequacy of constructed-response questions may be to have expert colleagues respond to them so that a consensus ''model answer'' can be identified. The more disparity there is in achieving a model answer, the more flawed the item would presumably be.

TEST CONSISTENCY

Three major concerns in rating test consistency are whether (a) a collection of items is representative of the domain, (b) items are consistent with objectives, and (c) items are consistent with the instructional presentation.

Representativeness of Domain Sampling

In the case of items that are created from an item form or where the domain specification is completely operationally defined, random sampling of items will accomplish representativeness of domain sampling. However, if there is some degree of subjectivity in the definition of the domain, it may be necessary to check the item pool in terms of its complete coverage of the domain. Once this coverage has been examined by subject matter experts and is judged as adequate, sampling can again be used.

One of the clearest statements and examples of the power of item sampling is given by Lord and Novick (1968, p. 234). These authors describe a spelling test in which spelling ability is defined as the proportion of words from a particular dictionary that a student is able to spell correctly. A random sample of N words is drawn from the dictionary and read to the student, who then writes out the spelling of each word. The student's score is the proportion of the N items correctly spelled. As Lord and Novick explain (1968), "Clearly this proportion is an unbiased estimator of his spelling ability.. ... As a matter of fact, in the situation defined, it is a sufficient statistic for estimating the examinee's spelling ability.... It is true that more efficient spelling tests can be built by stratified sampling from a dictionary [p. 234]."

To ensure adequate representation of all aspects of a domain, you may want to employ a stratified random sampling plan of the kind that Millman (1974) recommends. To illustrate, let us assume there are six learning objectives and approximately 200 items, as illustrated in Figure 12.2. To construct a 35-item CR test we would randomly draw a predetermined percentage of items from each "region" of the domain. For Objective 1, we would randomly select about six items; for Objective 5, two items. In this manner, we guarantee that all six objectives will be represented on the CR test in some fair way. A more detailed plan for this level of approach to assessment is given by Haladyna (in press).

A rigorous test of the representation of a set of items would be the procedure recommended by Cronbach (1971, p. 456). This would involve an experimental design in which two groups of skilled item writers and subject matter experts would work separately to create two versions of the same CR test. They would be asked to construct domain specifications, item-writing rules, and empirical and logical methods of item review. The two versions of the CR test could be tried out in a field test in which the same students were given both tests. The relationship between the two tests would be a rigorous measure of the accuracy of the domain-sampling method used.

Item–Objective Consistency

A number of different procedures are possible for examining the judgments of experts as to the consistency between items and objectives.

Learning objectives	Representative CR test items	Percentage of domain	1	2	3	4	5	6
1	35	17.5	6 items	8 items	12 items	5 items	2 items	2 items
2	40	20.0						
3	50	25.0						
4	32	16.0						
5	21	10.5						
6	22	11.0						
	200	100.0		35-item CR test				

Figure 12.2 Sampling plan for items representing six learning objectives.

The IQI, as described in Chapter 11 and the article by Merrill *et al.* (1979), both provide guidelines for assessing the consistency between items and objectives. From the domain-based perspective of this book, one can translate the phrase "item–objective consistency" into the more general phrase "item–instructional intent consistency." The latter would include a consideration of the consistency between an item form or some other domain specification and the intent of the instruction. In discussing the IQI and the work of Merrill *et al.* (1979), the term objective will be used to signify any domain specification. This is possible because an item form, for example, is a structure that represents actual items, perhaps hundreds, all of which are parallel.

As described in Chapter 11, the two characteristics of objectives that are considered essential for use in classifying objectives and test items are content type and task level. The IQI classification table is then used to assess the consistency between items and objectives. An objective and a test item are considered logically consistent if they both can be classified as having the same type of content (e.g., fact, concept, procedure, principle) and the same task level (e.g., remember, use). More details on the procedures for classifying items are contained in the original references.

Another procedure that provides a very comprehensive index of congruence when several subject matter experts are available for reviewing items has been proposed by Rovinelli and Hambleton (1977) and has been shown to be reliable. The method involves having subject matter experts rate each item, using a numerical rating scale.

Descriptions of the three possible ratings are as follows:

$+1$ = definite feeling that an item is a measure of an objective
O = uncertainty as to whether an item is a measure of an objective
-1 = definite feeling that an item is not a measure of an objective

For example, we might have four subject matter experts rating 50 items designed for five learning objectives. Each of the four experts would rate all 50 items first on Objective 1, then on Objective 2, etc. Perfect item–objective congruence should be found when all judges give a $+1$ rating to an item for Objective 1 and a -1 rating to the same item for all other objectives. We would have the poorest fit of an item to an objective if an item were consistently judged -1 in respect to an objective that it was originally intended to measure and $+1$ in respect to all other objectives presented that it was *not* intended to measure. Clearly, a rating of zero is poorer than a $+1$, but better than a -1. In other words, it is better for an expert to be undecided about an item than it is for him or her to feel that it is definitely not a measure of the objective.

Although the phrases objective congruence and item–objective consistency have been used in this discussion, it should be kept in mind that the same procedure could be used to examine the item form in respect to domain congruence. That is, judges could examine item-writing rules or algorithms for their match to the instructional intent of an instructional system. When several sets of rules or item forms were present, the same method of rating could be used.

The next section of this chapter will be devoted to explaining the actual computation of an index of item-objective congruence. Keep in mind that the same procedure could be used to study rule–domain congruence.

Computation of an Index of Item–Objective Consistency

Suppose we have 4 expert judges rating 5 objectives, each of which has 10 items. This can be depicted by the drawing shown in Figure 12.3. Each of the smaller cubes shown in Figure 12.3 will be filled with a rating. That is, each expert rates each item for each objective.

An example of a nearly perfect pattern of ratings is shown in Figure 12.4, which gives the ratings for Item 1. In this case, Item 1 was intended to measure Objective 1. As can be seen from Figure 12.4, all four experts rated Item 1 as +1 for Objective 1. Also, nearly all other ratings were −1, except for two cases where experts were undecided and gave a zero rating.

Now in order to compute an index of item–objective consistency, a formula will be introduced and explained. The formula as developed by Rovinelli and Hambleton (1977) is an index that ranges from −1.0 to +1.0. A +1.0 reflects perfect item–objective consistency; a −1.0 reflects lack of consistency between an item and any of the objectives. The formula uses the following quantities:

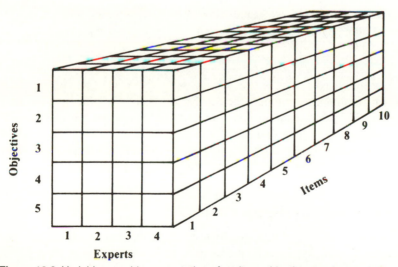

Figure 12.3 Variables used in computation of an item–objective consistency index.

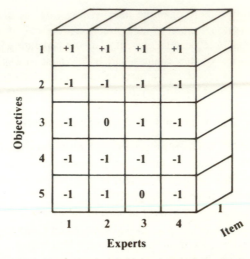

Figure 12.4 Example of a nearly perfect pattern of ratings.

N = number of objectives
n = number of subject matter experts
S_1 = sum across all experts' ratings for one objective and one item (in the foregoing example, this would be a sum of 4 ratings)
S_2 = sum of ratings across all experts for all objectives for one item (in Figure 12.4, this would be a sum of 20 ratings)

Given these definitions, we can now examine the computing formula that is the index of item–objective consistency (*IOC*) for one item–objective pair:

$$IOC = \frac{(N-1)S_1 - S_2 + S_1}{2(N-1)n}$$

Using this formula, we multiply the number of objectives minus 1 (*N*-1) by the first sum (S_1), subtract the second sum (S_2), and again add the first sum. The resulting quantity is then divided by the product of two times the number of objectives minus 1 (*N*-1) times the number of experts (*n*). A numerical example of this formula as applied to Item 1 for Objective 1 and Item 1 for Objective 3 is given in Figure 12.5.

Item-Instructional Presentation Consistency

One of the aspects of high-quality tests employed in instructional systems is the degree to which they are consistent with the instructional materials and strategies. An example of this was described in Chapter 9 on concept-based

Objective 1–Item 1	Objective 3–Item 1

$$N = 5$$
$$n = 4$$
$$S_1 = +4$$
$$S_2 = (+4 - 14) = -10$$
$$IOC = \frac{(4)4 - (-10) + 4}{2(4)4}$$
$$= \frac{30}{32}$$
$$= +.94$$

$$N = 5$$
$$n = 4$$
$$S_1 = -3$$
$$S_2 = -10$$
$$IOC = \frac{(4)(-3) - (-10) - 3}{2(4)4}$$
$$= \frac{-5}{32}$$
$$= -.16$$

Figure 12.5 Numerical examples of the *IOC* formula.

testing. Certain examples and nonexamples used in instruction are purposely not used in the tests. This allows the tests to truly assess comprehension and generalization. With the domain-based method of concept testing, examples and nonexamples can be sampled for both instruction and testing. Such sampling creates a strong relationship between tests and the instruction. This sampling is designed to ensure that the student really understands the concept through an adequate coverage of *close-in nonexamples* (Markle & Tiemann, 1970) in the instruction. Then, systematic sampling of examples to create items ensures that assessment really uncovers any misconceptions of the students or any lack of ability to generalize from material learned. This is test design at its best.

On another level of consideration, the instructional materials and strategies need to be classifiable. Merrill and Boutwell (1973) have provided a means of classifying instruction into what they call *primary presentation forms*. There are four primary presentation forms in most cognitive subject matter, as shown in Figure 12.6. For example, concepts and principles can be presented by defining them (generality) or allowing the student to induce them from examples (instance). Both forms of presentation can be accomplished by either showing or telling the student, or asking the student to demonstrate or answer a question. When the student is asked a question, the process of answering is a form of practice in dealing with a generality or instance.

The four primary presentation forms can be identified in various segments of the instructional materials. If the materials have been designed with this

	Tell the Student	Question the Student
Presentation of Generalities	Generality	Generality Practice
Presentation of Instances	Instance	Instance Practice

Figure 12.6 The four primary presentation forms.

system of presentation forms, there will be recommended forms in position for each task level (e.g., remember or use) in the instruction. Merrill, Reigeluth, and Faust (1979, p. 184) provide more details of how the presentation forms are matched to task levels. Once this kind of classification of the instructional presentation has been accomplished, test items are classified in the same way. Then, matches and mismatches between the forms of the instruction and the test items will be revealed. Depending on the discrepancy, either the instruction or the test items (or item forms) will need revision to achieve the most effective instructional strategy.

Logical Review of Skill Items

The two types of logical review for rating scales, observations, and checklists are: (a) expert judgments of adequacy and (b) expert ratings of consistency between measures and task analyses, objectives, or specifications.

ADEQUACY OF SKILL MEASURES

Instructional personnel with backgrounds in testing can examine drafts of rating scales and observation systems to identify possible common flaws that may be present. For example, the adequacy of behavioral anchoring of a rating scale can frequently be determined by inspection—are concrete examples of people's behavior given at the various points of a descriptive rating scale? The guidelines provided in Chapter 5 on skill measurement can be applied to the inspection of skill items.

ITEM-OBJECTIVE CONSISTENCY FOR SKILLS

Using the procedure and formula described in the preceding section of this chapter, one can have expert judges rate the congruence between skill items and the instructional intent of a training program. In addition, the representativeness of the selection of skill items can be judged by asking questions such as, "Are the skills being assessed under all ranges of possible times and conditions under which the skill should occur?" and "Are any parts of the skill crucial but absent from the assessment?" Also, sampling plans, as were discussed earlier, can be employed.

LOGICAL REVIEW WITH TASK ANALYSIS

In the background of skill assessment has been the initial job analysis or task analysis conducted before the learning objectives or domain specifications were written. These task analyses may have been based on empirical studies of critical incidents, time–motion studies of job behaviors, or interviews and observations of experts on the job. Job analyses and task analyses should be used to note the frequency of occurrence of elements that appear on rating scales, checklists, and observation schedules. A group of independent job experts could be employed to double-check the relationship between the original job analysis studies and the final criterion-referenced skill measurements. Except in the case of rating scales, this screening by subject matter experts should be more easily conducted than the statistical study of item–objective congruence used for items in the knowledge domain. In the case of rating scales, the choice of behaviors to rate or the descriptors used in defining points along a numerical scale could be evaluated by a team of subject matter experts.

Summary

There are several sources of information for the logical review of CR test items. Two major factors in item quality have been suggested: *adequacy* and *consistency*. Adequacy can be assessed by applying the commonly listed guidelines for good item writing. In the knowledge domain, experts can be used to rate test consistency where a precise domain specification is not completed. If an operationally defined domain specification is employed, the problem of item–objective congruence has been solved, but domains or item-writing rules should be reviewed by experts. Also, the problem of representativeness of items on a test is solved when domains are specified, because random sampling and sampling plans ensure good content coverage.

Two choices have been suggested for assessing the consistency of items and objectives (or domain specifications): the IQI and a numerical rating method. The numerical index of item–objective consistency (Rovinelli & Hambleton, 1977) involves a team of experts who rate the match between items and objectives on a scale of -1, 0, or $+1$. A formula provided in this chapter produces a numerical index that ranges from $+1.0$ to -1.0 for each item–objective pair. It will be necessary to become familiar with the distribution of index values for a particular knowledge or skill domain in order to set a criterion for what constitutes a good level of consistency. This may be in the range of $+.70$ to $+.80$, for example.

In the case of the logical review for items to assess skills, data from initial job analysis or task analysis studies can be used in addition to the ratings of expert judges. Experts can review critical incidents, time–motion studies and the like, to double-check the selection of skill items for a test.

References

Conoley, J. C., & O'Neil, H. F., Jr. A primer for developing test items. In H. F. O'Neil, Jr. (Ed.), *Procedures for instructional systems development.* New York: Academic Press, 1979.

Cronbach, L. J. Test validation. In R. L. Thorndike (Ed.), *Educational measurement* (2nd ed.). Washington: American Council on Education, 1971.

Ellis, J. A., & Wulfeck, W. H., & Fredericks, P. S. *The instructional quality inventory. Vol. II, user's guide.* San Diego, California: Navy Personnel Research and Development Center, 1979.

Guilford, J. P. *Fundamental statistics in psychology and education.* New York: McGraw-Hill, 1965.

Haladyna, T. A comparison of two approaches to criterion-referenced instructional program assessment. *Educational Leadership,* in press.

Hambleton, R. K., Swaminathan, H., Algina, J., & Coulson, D. B. Criterion-referenced testing and measurement: A review of technical issues and developments. *Review of Educational Research, 1978, 48,* 1–47.

Lord, F. M., & Novick, M. R. *Statistical theories of mental test scores.* Reading, Massachusetts: Addison-Wesley, 1968.

Markle, S. M., & Tiemann, P. W. *Really understanding concepts.* Champaign, Illinois: Stipes Publishing Company, 1970.

Merrill, M. D., & Boutwell, R. C. Instructional development methodology and research. In F. N. Kerlinger (Ed.), *Review of research in education.* Itasca, Illinois: Peacock Publishers, 1973.

Merrill, M. D., Reigeluth, C. M., & Faust, G. W. The instructional quality profile: A curriculum evaluation and design tool. In H. F. O'Neil, Jr. (Ed.), *Procedures for instructional systems development.* New York: Academic Press, 1979.

Millman, J. Sampling plans for domain-referenced tests. *Educational Technology, 1974, 14*(6), 17–21.

Nunnally, J. *Psychometric theory.* New York: McGraw-Hill, 1967.

O'Neil, Jr., H. F. (Ed.), *Procedures for instructional systems development.* New York: Academic Press, 1979.

Priestly, M., & Nassif, P. M. From here to validity: Developing a conceptual framework for test item generation in criterion-referenced measurement. *Educational Technology, 1979, 19*(2), 27–32.

Rovinelli, R. J., & Hambleton, R. K. On the use of content specialists in the assessment of criterion-referenced test item validity. *Dutch Journal for Educational Research, 1977, 2,* 49–60.

Thorndike, R. L. The analysis and selection of test items. In D. N. Jackson & S. Messick (Eds.), *Problems in human assessment.* New York: McGraw-Hill, 1967.

13

The Empirical Review of
Test Items

In this chapter, we will discuss methods and problems in item analysis as they apply to criterion-referenced (CR) testing. We will introduce a new test-item concept and review research that bears on this new concept. Then, in an effort to give the reader a fuller understanding of the role that this test-item concept plays in the empirical review of items, we will introduce and illustrate measures of the concept.

Item Analysis

The traditional study of test items has had a long history. Perhaps the most apt statement about the role of item analysis came from Thorndike (1949), who stated that the study of test items is desirable to produce effective tests, since tests depend on the characteristics of test items. Thorndike held that test items may be added or removed from tests based on item characteristics.

In a modern context, the central goal of item analysis is not to select items but to review the quality of items in domains. Deficiencies in the quality of items have traditionally been viewed in two ways. Items may be inherently too difficult or too easy for the population for which they were intended, or they may not be suitably related to the trait that the test is intended to measure. These two ways of looking at item deficiency represent two types of item concepts, difficulty and discrimination.

ITEM DIFFICULTY

Any test item's difficulty can be calculated by noting the proportion of subjects in a representative sample that give correct responses. The statistic that reflects this finding, frequently expressed in decimal form, is often called the "p-value," which is directly translatable into the probability of a correct response. If 100 students try an item and 75 get the item correct, the p-value is .75, and the probability that any student will get the item correct is also .75.

Item difficulty is one of the simplest of concepts yet one of the most difficult to measure. If one could simply administer items to 100 students after instruction has been given to them and count the number of correct responses, item difficulty would be quite simple to compute. However, the major problem with item difficulty is the nature of the sample on which the item difficulty estimate is based. If the item is given to students following instruction, the item appears to be easy in most instances. A p-value might be .75 or higher, indicating an easy item. On the other hand, if one gave that same item to students before instruction, the p-value might be lower than .40. Which p-value is appropriate? Or is it better to take the mean of these two p-values? The problem of sampling in the estimation of difficulty has led to dissatisfaction with the traditional notion of "difficulty." Difficulty, as you can see, is a relative matter.

Item response theory was introduced as an alternative to classical test theory for solving the problem of estimating difficulty and other item parameters (Lord & Novick, 1968). Item response theory is often referred to as "latent trait theory" or "item characteristic curve theory." All of these terms capture the essence of the theory: that item difficulty and other item characteristics can be estimated without referring to or being affected by the sample of students responding to the items. A number of models have been built from item response theory, ranging from the rather simple Rasch model (Rasch, 1966, 1980; Wright, 1977; Wright & Stone, 1979) to the more complex models of Lord and Novick (1968; Lord, 1980). Baker (1977) provides one of the best accounts of the features of item response theory as it pertains to item analysis, but he also expresses concern for the applicability of item response theory to the problems of instructionally based testing.

Slinde and Linn (1978), using noninstructionally based items, found some difficulty with the simplest of the item response theories, the one-parameter or Rasch model. Gustaffson (1979), however, is critical of Slinde and Linn's methods and interpretations, pointing out that in some cases we expect too much of the model, particularly when the student sample is low-achieving. Subsequently, Slinde and Linn (1979) continued studies of the Rasch model, using data that departed less from the model, and found that the model was fairly robust and more adequate than their earlier paper had suggested. Wainer and Wright (1980) have further examined the robustness of the Rasch model. With instructionally based tests, Haladyna and Roid (1979) found that Rasch item difficulty estimates fluctuated slightly when calculated on varying samples of instructed and uninstructed students, but that reasonably good estimates were obtained when the sample used to estimate difficulty was carefully drawn. Thus the suggestion to average the difficulty estimates taken from samples of students before and after instruction appears to be most reasonable. In any event, with instructionally based tests, care should be taken to note the type of sample used to estimate the difficulty when using item response theory.

ITEM DISCRIMINATION

Each and every item is a kind of test. Every item can be related to the total test score. This correlation between item and test performance is the discrimination index, which can range from -1.00 to $+1.00$. Any negative index indicates that students who get high scores tend to get the item wrong whereas students with low test scores tend to get the item right. A discrimination index of zero would indicate no pattern. At a minimum, an item should differentiate between levels of achievement. If items fail to discriminate, they need to be examined carefully for sources of invalidity revised and field-tested again.

The traditional view of removing nondiscriminating items has been severely criticized by a number of researchers (e.g., Popham & Husek, 1969). First, discrimination indexes are influenced by the range of test scores. Since the discrimination index is a correlation between item and test performance, if the range of test performance is restricted, the correlation is attenuated, and all discrimination indexes are low. Similarly, if a sample representing a wide range of performance is used (Haladyna, 1974), the discrimination index will be maximized. The question of the value of the true discrimination index is difficult to answer when considering who is sampled.

A second criticism of selecting items on the basis of item discrimination is that discrimination indexes are difficult to interpret in CR testing. If a negative or zero correlation were observed, one might attribute this result to a faulty item when, in fact, an instructional deficiency might exist. This problem has been noted in a number of subsequent studies (Haladyna, 1974; Haladyna & Roid, 1976; Haladyna & Roid, 1981).

In conclusion, discrimination tends to be less important in CR testing because the concern is not with how different a group of students are but how they stand with respect to the entire domain of items.

INSTRUCTIONAL SENSITIVITY

The results of a series of studies by the authors suggest that a new item concept, *instructional sensitivity* exists (Kosecoff & Klein, 1974; Haladyna & Roid, 1981). Evidence is building that attests to belief that instructional sensitivity is a very useful and unique test-item concept found only in tests that are used to measure instructionally based achievement.

In systematic instruction, test results should reflect what an instructor believes occurs during instruction relevant to the objectives of instruction. Generally, CR test performance for uninstructed students is low prior to instruction and high following instruction. The difference in preinstruction and postinstruction means is an indicator of instructional effectiveness.

Thorndike (1967) observed, "Each item is in a very real sense a little test all by itself [p. 203]." In other words, what might be true for the test in terms of student responses may also be true for the items that comprise the test. If CR tests of our instructional intent—as operationally defined through the objective or set of objectives on which the test is based—are sensitive to the effects of instruction, then, analogously, items should also be sensitive to the effects of instruction. Items that are instructionally sensitive may be one of the most appropriate indicators of CR item validity.

In summary, instructional sensitivity is the tendency for test items to range in difficulty as a function of instruction. Items that do not detect differences from pretest to posttest should be reviewed to ascertain if (*a*) instruction has been faulty or (*b*) the item is flawed in some way or simply inappropriate.

Research on Instructional Sensitivity

There are four theoretical contexts in which instructional sensitivity has been studied: (*a*) criterion-referenced, (*b*) classical, (*c*) Bayesian, and (*d*) item response. We will discuss each of these briefly and review relevant research that integrates the evidence regarding the existence of instructional sensitivity as a unique CR test item characteristic.

CRITERION-REFERENCED

The movement away from traditional test practices resulted in the creation of many item characteristic indexes that were deemed more appropriate for CR test purposes. The first of many indexes to be used to evaluate CR test items was the *pre-to-post difference index* (PPDI) introduced by Cox and Vargas (1966). This index is the simple difference between the difficulty observed in the post-instruction group and the difficulty observed in the preinstruction group. It therefore ranges from -1.00 to $+1.00$, with indexes of zero or lower quite rare. In most instructional settings, this index, PPDI, typically ranges from .10 to .60.

Similar indexes are the *percentage of possible gain,* or PPG (Brennan & Stolurow, 1971), and the *Brennan index,* or BI (Brennan, 1972). Both these indexes have the advantage of being computationally simple. The percentage of possible gain is based on the notion that with any pretest item difficulty, there can only be a maximum gain, which is 1.00 minus the pretest difficulty. The statistic is computed by the formula

$$PPG = \frac{\text{difficulty (posttest)} - \text{difficulty (pretest)}}{1 - \text{difficulty (pretest)}}$$

The other index defines the two contrast groups as mastery and nonmastery. The dichotomy of mastery–nonmastery is defined by setting a criterion level on the test scale, for example at 75%, and then classifying all examinees above this point in the mastery group and all below in the nonmastery group. The index is determined by the formula

$$BI = \text{difficulty (mastery)} - \text{difficulty (nonmastery)}$$

Another index in this genre was introduced by Popham (1971). A fourfold table is constructed to represent the situation shown in Table 13.1, and a phi coefficient is computed.

Of the four possibilities shown in Table 13.1, only the first represents a desirable state of affairs. Items that follow this response pattern most consistently are sensitive to instruction. The percentage in the cell labeled 01 for a group of examinees who took both pretest and posttest would indicate the instructional sensitivity of the item.

The four instructional sensitivity indexes discussed in this section represent those that have received most attention in research. Recent research suggests that the PPDI is the most consistently related to other instructional sensitivity indexes (Herbig, 1976; Haladyna & Roid, 1981). In Harris, Pearlman, and Wilcox's (1977) study of methods of item analysis, a large number of new statistical methods are described, some of which also fall into this category. Berk (1978) offers other indexes that can be estimated and that seem to represent instructional sensitivity. Traditional discrimination indexes were compared to CR instructional sensitivity indexes by HSU (1971), Popham (1971), Helmstadter (1972), Haladyna (1974), Haladyna and Roid (1976, 1981), Kosecoff and Klein (1974), Wedman (1973), Henrysson and Wedman (1974), and Moyer (1977). The results from these studies revealed a consistently low degree of relatedness between these CR instructional sensitivity indexes and the traditional discrimination index computed with a postinstruction sample. In most of these instances there was a high degree of relatedness among these CR indexes.

Table 13.1
Fourfold Table for Calculating a Phi Coefficient for CR
Test Items[a]

	Posttest	
Pretest	Correct	Incorrect
Incorrect	01	00
Correct	11	10

[a] The table represents typical student responses: 01 represents an incorrect response on a pretest and a correct response on the posttest; 00 represents incorrect responses on both tests; 11 represents correct responses on both tests; 10 represents a correct response on the pretest and an incorrect response on the posttest.

Despite the fact that traditional item discrimination indexes were not highly related to these CR instructional sensitivity indexes, Helmstadter (1972), Haladyna (1974), and Bernkopf and Bashaw (1976) observed high relationships with these CR indexes when the traditional item discrimination (referred to as "COMPBI") was computed using a sample of instructed and uninstructed students. Further, the relationships between this combined sample discrimination index and the more often used posttest-only sample discrimination index (referred to as "POSTPBI") was not high across varying conditions. Therefore, the heterogeneity of the sample appears to be a key factor in determining the usability of the traditional discrimination index as a measure of the instructional sensitivity of a CR test item.

CLASSICAL

The CR test movement appeared to gain momentum in proportion to the expressed dissatisfaction with testing that was not directly keyed to instructional criteria. The classical item discrimination index was rejected, initially due to the suspected lack of variance of CR test scores (Popham & Husek, 1969). More importantly, Millman and Popham (1974) argued that the concepts of item and test variation were unnecessary because the concern in CR testing was for individual responses to a universe of test items and not to relative performances of individuals. The issue of item and test variance has been hotly debated (e.g., Carver, 1974; Haladyna, 1975; Millman & Popham, 1974; Woodson, 1974a, 1974b). The fact remains that item and test variation exists with any sensitive measure that is applied to a sample of examinees who differ with respect to their CR achievement, and these variations can be used to study characteristics of test items. The crux of the issue is the way this knowledge is used.

BAYESIAN

Three discrimination indexes based on the Bayes theorem were introduced by Helmstadter (1974). All three indexes require collateral information in the form of preinstruction test results, or at least a low-performing group. The indexes are (*a*) B1—the probability that a student has knowledge given that he or she gets the item right; (*b*) B2—the probability that the student does not have knowledge given that he or she gets the item wrong; and (*c*) B3—the probability of making a correct classification, that is, mastery or nonmastery. In Helmstadter's study, a moderately high correlation was observed between PPDI and the COMPBI and Bayesian indexes. Haladyna and Roid (1976) detected similar relationships. These Bayesian indexes were the subject of further study (Haladyna & Roid, 1981) as potential instructional sensitivity indexes. The results of that study indicated that these Bayesian indexes were greatly influenced by item difficulty and were unstable across samples.

ITEM RESPONSE

Several item characteristics are derivable from the application of the one-parameter item response (Rasch) model (Wright & Stone, 1979). The item parameter is difficulty, whereas other item statistics include the *mean square fit* (MSF), a measure of the item's conformance to a theoretical item characteristic curve, and *z-difference* (ZDIFF), which is essentially the normalized difference in item difficulty estimates for two samples. ZDIFF appears to function as a type of instructional sensitivity index when applied to instructed and uninstructed samples. Haladyna and Roid (1981) found a high degree of relationship between ZDIFF and instructional sensitivity indexes from other theoretical contexts.

SUMMARY

In the Haladyna and Roid study, item characteristics across these four theoretical perspectives were compared. Indexes representing the item concepts of difficulty, discrimination, and instructional sensitivity were computed for seven data sets ranging in instructional effectiveness from 10% to 56% (the difference in pretest and posttest means). Correlations among all item indexes were studied across all data sets.

The conclusion of this study was that instructional sensitivity is a useful item characteristic, and it is to be distinguished from traditional item concepts of difficulty and discrimination. When working with CR tests, it seems clear that instructional sensitivity is a worthy replacement for discrimination.

Practical Application of Instructional Sensitivity

The theoretical and empirical work presented in this chapter has suggested that instructional sensitivity is a useful and unique CR test item characteristic. Research also suggests that instructional sensitivity can be measured in a number of ways and that the simplest of these techniques, PPDI, is probably the most effective.

PPDI is simply computed as the difference between postinstruction and preinstruction item difficulties. The interpretation of the index is quite direct and does not require the assumptions of a complex mathematical model.

The role of instructional sensitivity indexes in item review is to examine items in the domain to determine if sensible patterns of student response are present.

We do not recommend the use of item review to select items. As Millman (1974) points out, to choose items based on their characteristics destroys the domain-based interpretations we are seeking.

Given that PPDI is one of the most practical of instructional sensitivity indexes, let us look at several hypothetical items and at PPDI's for each as a means of understanding how this statistic can be used to investigate items.

The four items in Table 13.2 and the four PPDI's associated with them represent four possible conditions that we may observe in instruction. Each has a particular interpretation, keeping in mind that item review is intended to examine each item with respect to making one of several decisions: (*a*) retain, (*b*) discard, or (*c*) revise.

ITEM 1

A low PPDI, such as that for item 1 in Table 13.2, would normally suggest either that student learning has failed, because of inadequate instruction or stu-

Table 13.2
Four Examples of the PPDI Index

Item	Posttest	Pretest	PPDI
1	.80	.80	0
2	.25	.25	0
3	.90	.30	.60
4	.30	.50	−.20

dent motivation, or that the item failed to detect what was instructed. No index reviewed in this chapter is designed to identify student versus instructional effects. A low PPDI is only an indication that further investigation is needed to isolate problems due to students, the instruction, or something in the item itself. The development of an index that would isolate these problems would be an important one.

In this particular instance, the high difficulty values on both occasions would indicate that the item was inherently too easy. Also instructional effectiveness was not detected, possibly because of the ceiling effect of high item difficulties. Alternatively, students may have already learned the content represented by item 1 and this performance should not have been changed by instruction. The first alternative would suggest that the item was inappropriate because it was too easy, whereas the last alternative would suggest that the item was inappropriate due to prior learning. In the former instance, the item might be revised and retried. In the latter instance, the curriculum or the test item needs to be revised because there is a lack of articulation between the curriculum, instruction, and testing.

ITEM 2

In this instance, the PPDI is again zero but the item appears to be more difficult on both occasions. Two alternatives again may be proposed: (*a*) instruction was not effective and therefore students failed to show growth; or (*b*) the item was inherently too difficult, and no amount of instruction will change this state. In the first alternative, instruction must be modified to produce a change in difficulty; in the second alternative, the item must be modified.

For both items 1 and 2, once the PPDI is known to be zero or near zero, there is no hard-and-fast method for making these distinctions. The need is for some instructional detective work to ascertain the specific cause of the low PPDI.

ITEM 3

As you might guess, this is a normal pattern for instructionally sensitive test items. We would seldom discard or revise such an item because the pattern of successful responses to this item is very predictable and normal. We might discard such an item on logical gounds, because it tests some trivial aspects of what students are learning, but the empirical review of this item suggests that it be retained in the test item domain.

ITEM 4

A negative PPDI is seldom observed. When it does appear, one can suspect that instruction had a perverse effect on learning. If there are other items with similar PPDIs, this is a possibility, but a rare one. On the other hand, a more common occurrence is that the item was simply miskeyed. Keying errors will result in negative PPDIs; thus item review helps detect these kinds of errors, mistakes that often go undetected in conventional item analysis.

Summary

We have presented a review of traditional item analysis and its attendant problems, the case for instructional sensitivity in the empirical review of CR test items, and the research on these methods for studying instructional sensitivity. Finally, we have presented methods for using a preferred index of instructional sensitivity in reviewing test items.

The goal of empirical item review is to investigate and screen each item to determine if instructional or item deficiencies exist and to revise such troublesome items. This must be done *before* the item domain is finalized so that the final nature of the domain is not constantly being changed by the revision of items. In other words, the goal is to create a domain of high quality items, from which a random sample will be selected to create a test.

The consequence of empirical item review is the accumulation of test items that represent the instructional domain. It is not surprising that this phase of CR test development is often referred to as *item validation*. We prefer *item review* because the validity of any item depends not only on student responses in predictable patterns but a logical analysis of the intent of the instruction and the role that each item plays in representing that intent. Therefore, logical and empirical item reviews are viewed as complementary procedures that lead to the establishment of better item domains. The subsequent effect of such better item domains is that student scores will be more targeted to instruction and there will be fewer errors of student score estimation.

References

Baker, F. B. Advances in item analysis. *Review of Educational Research,* 1977, *47,* 151–178.

Berk, R. A. A consumers' guide to criterion-referenced test item statistics. *NCME Measurement in Education,* 1978, *9*(1), 1–8.

Bernknopf, S., & Bashaw, W. L. *An investigation of criterion-referenced tests under different conditions of sample variability and item homogeneity.* Paper presented at the annual meeting of the American Educational Research Association, San Francisco, April 1976.

Brennan, R. L. A generalized upper-lower item-discrimination index. *Educational and Psychological Measurement,* 1972, *32,* 289–303.

Brennan, R. L., & Stolurow, L. M. An empirical decision process for formative evaluation. *Research Memorandum No. 4.* Cambridge, Massachusetts: Harvard CAI Laboratory, 1971.

Carver, R. P. Two dimensions of tests—Psychometric and edumetric. *American Psychologist,* 1974, *29,* 512–518.

Cox, R. C., & Vargas, J. *A comparison of item selection techniques for norm-referenced and criterion-referenced tests.* Paper presented at the meeting of the American Educational Research Association, 1966.

Gustafsson, J. *Testing and obtaining fit of data to the Rasch model.* Paper presented at the annual meeting of the American Educational Research Association, San Francisco, April 1979.

Haladyna, T. M. Effects of different samples on item and test characteristics of criterion-referenced tests. *Journal of Educational Measurement,* 1974, *11,* 93–100.

Haladyna, T. M. On the edumetric-psychometric dimension of tests. *American Psychologist,* 1975, *30,* 603–604.

Haladyna, T. M., & Roid, G. *The quality of criterion-referenced test items.* Paper presented at the annual meeting of the American Educational Research Association, San Francisco, April 1976.

Haladyna, T. M., & Roid, G. *The stability of Rasch item and student achievement estimates for a criterion-referenced test.* Paper presented at the annual meeting of the National Council on Measurement in Education, San Francisco, April 1979.

Haladyna, T. M., & Roid, G. The role of instructional sensitivity in the empirical review of criterion-referenced test items. *Journal of Educational Measurement,* 1981, *18,* 39–53.

Harris, C. W., Pearlman, A. P., & Wilcox, R. R. *Achievement test items—methods of study.* Los Angeles: Center for the Study of Evaluation, Univ. of California, 1977.

Helmstadter, G. C. *Comparison of traditional item analysis selection procedures with those recommended for tests designed to measure achievement following performance-oriented instruction.* Paper presented at the meeting of the American Psychological Association, Hawaii, 1972.

Helmstadter, G. C. *A comparison of Bayesian and traditional indexes of test item effectiveness.* Paper presented at the meeting of the National Council on Measurement in Education, Chicago, April, 1974.

Henrysson, S., & Wedman, Ingemar. Some problems in construction and evaluation of criterion-referenced tests. *Scandinavian Journal of Educational Research,* 1974, *18,* 1–12.

Herbig, M. Item analysis by use in pretests and post-tests: A comparison of different coefficients. *Programmed Learning and Educational Technology,* 1976, *13,* 49–54.

Hsu, T. *Empirical data on criterion-referenced tests.* Paper presented at the meeting of the American Educational Research Association, New York, February 1971.

Kosecoff, J. B., & Klein, S. P. *Instructional sensitivity statistics appropriate for objective-based test items.* Paper presented at the meeting of the National Council on Measurement in Education, Chicago, April 1974.

Lord, F. M. *Applications of item response theory to practical testing problems.* Hillsdale, New Jersey: Erlbaum, 1980.

Lord, F. M., & Novick, M. R. *Statistical theories of mental test scores.* Reading, Massachusetts: Addison-Wesley, 1968.

Millman, J. Criterion-referenced measurement. In W. J. Popham (Ed.), *Evaluation in education: Current applications.* Berkeley, California: McCutchan Publishing Company, 1974.

Millman, J., & Popham, W. J. The issue of item and test variance for criterion-referenced tests: A clarification. *Journal of Educational Measurement,* 1974, *11,* 137–138.

Moyer, J. E. *Alternative reliability indices.* Paper presented at the annual meeting of the National Council on Measurement in Education, New York, April 1977.

Popham, W. J. Indices of adequacy for criterion-referenced tests. In W. J. Popham (Ed.), *Criterion-referenced measurement.* Englewood Cliffs, New Jersey: Educational Technology Publications, 1971.

Popham, W. J., & Husek, T. R. Implications of criterion-referenced measurement. *Journal of Educational Measurement,* 1969, *6,* 1–9.

Rasch, G. An item analysis which takes individual differences into account. *British Journal of Mathematical and Statistical Psychology,* 1966, *19,* 49–57.

Rasch, G. *Probabilistic models for some intelligence and attainment tests.* Chicago, Illinois: Univ. of Chicago Press, 1980.

Slinde, J. A., & Linn, R. L. An exploration of the adequacy of the Rasch model for the problem of vertical equating. *Journal of Educational Measurement,* 1978, *15,* 23–35.

Slinde, J. A. & Linn, R. L. The Rasch model, objective measurement, equating and robustness. *Applied Psychological Measurement,* 1979, *3,* 437–452.

Thorndike, R. L. *Personnel selection.* New York: Wiley, 1949.

Thorndike, R. L. The analysis and selection of test items. In D. N. Jackson & S. Messick (Eds.), *Problems in human assessment.* New York: McGraw-Hill, 1967.

Wainer, H. & Wright, B. D. Robust estimation of ability in the Rasch model. *Psychometrika,* 1980, *45,* 373–391.

Wedman, I. Reliability, validity and discrimination measures for criterion-referenced tests. *Educational Reports Umea No. 4,* Sweden: Umea Univ., School of Education, 1973.

Woodson, M. I. C. E. The issue of item and test variance for criterion-referenced tests. *Journal of Educational Measurement,* 1974, *11,* 63–64. (a)

Woodson, M. I. C. E. The issue of item and test variance for criterion-referenced tests: A reply. *Journal of Educational Measurement,* 1974, *11,* 139–140. (b)

Wright, B. D. Solving measurement problems with the Rasch model. *Journal of Educational Measurement,* 1977, *14,* 97–116.

Wright, B. D., & Stone, M. H. *Best test design.* Chicago, Illinois: Mesa Press, 1979.

V

SUMMARY AND FUTURE DIRECTIONS

14

The Technology of Item Writing: Summary and Conclusions

One very basic point that could be easily lost in a discussion of item-writing technology is that, directly or indirectly, people will always write test items. Either items will be written individually or people will write the specifications behind the computer programs or clerical procedures that generate items. Thus, the technology of test-item writing as described in this book will help people in two ways: (*a*) by providing guidelines for direct, personal item writing; and (*b*) by providing item forms and methods that generate items indirectly. The inventiveness and imagination of professionals who know their subject matter will contribute more to the improvement of tests than any technology applied unimaginatively. Therefore the quality of items produced by any technology will depend on the purposes and ingenuity of the people behind them.

The purpose of this book has been to provide the test-item writer with tools and concepts that make the task of item writing more efficient and productive.

This concluding chapter will briefly review and summarize each of the steps in the development of criterion-referenced (CR) tests and will comment on each of the item-writing techniques. The final section of this chapter offers a commentary on the future of item-writing technology and speculations on new directions for research and development.

Summary of Steps in Criterion-Referenced Test Development

The steps in CR test development are (*a*) clarification of instructional intent, (*b*) domain specifications, (*c*) item development, (*d*) item review, and (*e*) test development.[1]

STEP 1: CLARIFICATION OF INSTRUCTIONAL INTENT

The first step in CR test development is the clarification of the intent or purpose of instruction. The overall goal of systematic instruction is to assure that the intent of the system, the instructional methods, and the tests used are all precisely coordinated to assure that each student will maximize the opportunity to achieve. This requires the essential first step that the purposes or intent of the training be very clear. Initial job analyses, including needs assessment or task analyses, usually clarify the instructional intent. These analyses are crucially important in that they determine whether instruction or training is really needed. Many behaviors, such as oral hygiene practices, probably do not involve training for an adult but rather motivation. Therefore, the initial analyses must distinguish between motivational and instructional problems. Instructional problems involve knowledge and skill deficiencies that may be task analyzed and defined.

STEP 2: DOMAIN SPECIFICATION

After a general instructional intent has been defined, a more specific definition of the objectives of the instructional system is written. The thesis of this book is that a precise definition, referred to as a *domain specification,* will lead to tests that are optimally interpretable. A domain specification is more complete than a listing of the learning objectives for an instructional system. A domain specification permits the description of all of the possible test items that can be used to assess learning in an area of knowledge or skill. The clearest example of a domain specification is the computer generation of items from an item form.

Practically speaking, not every area of instruction or training will have a precise domain specification. However, the more specific the method by which items are created, the clearer the achieved instructional intent. Domain specifications bring the following advantages:

1. A precise relationship between instructional intent, teaching methods, and the item in tests.

---

[1]It should be noted that test validation normally follows test development and that issues of CR test validity and reliability, including concerns such as test length, cut-off scores, and classification accuracy, go beyond the scope of this book. The reader is referred to excellent reviews by Berk (1980) and Baker, Linn, and Quellmalz (1980).

2. A public record of the item-writing methods employed that permits description or duplication of methods.
3. The control of differences between item writers who are asked to interpret the intent of instruction in order to write items that match that intent.
4. A clarification of the study of reliability by allowing an examination of the generalizability between a test and a domain (Cronbach, Gleser, Nanda, & Rajaratnam, 1972).

In Chapter 3, we reviewed a classification system for different types of learning and the item-writing methods most appropriate for each. The emphasis throughout the book has been on learning in the cognitive domain. Some of the information on rating scales or observations, as described in Chapter 5, could be applied to the affective and psychomotor domains, in which attitudes are assessed, but this is an area beyond the focus of this book.

STEP 3: ITEM DEVELOPMENT

Six unique approaches have been treated in detail in earlier chapters.

Items for Prose Learning

Although recall and comprehension of prose material is frequently maligned as a low level of learning objective, there are essential enabling objectives in which the student must learn basic terminology and facts. Bormuth (1970), Finn (1975), Roid, Haladyna, Shaughnessy, and Finn (1979) and Roid and Finn (1978) have advanced the technology of transforming sentences from prose material into test questions. The purpose of these sentence-based methods, as described in Chapter 6, is to provide a domain specification for tests of reading comprehension. The important sentences occurring in prose materials from instructional systems become the elements in the domain of possible test questions. A random sample or stratified random sample of these important sentences can provide a very objective subtest for assessing some of the learning objectives for an instructional system. At the present time, the technology still remains somewhat rudimentary, in that a great many item-writer adjustments in wording are still required to create sensible items. The techniques are obviously promising, however, and can create large numbers of items if used appropriately on good quality, important sentences.

Item Forms

Hively (1974) was the original developer of the concept of domain specifications, and his method remains as the first example of a technology of item writing. His methodology, as presented in Chapter 7, does not yet have widespread application, partly because of a lack of knowledge of the technique and partly due to the limited number of subject matter areas to which the technique can be applied. Some very sophisticated computer implementations of item forms have been created, however (e.g., Millman & Outlaw, 1978; Millman, 1980; Johnson, 1973). An excellent example of a military application of this method is the development of teaching and testing materials for symbol-recognition by Braby, Parrish, Guitard, and Aagard (1978).

The Mapping-Sentence Method

Facet theory and its method of defining mapping sentences existed for some time as a research tool (Foa, 1968). Recently, however, there have been several applications of facet theory to criterion-referenced test development, as described in Chapter 8 (Berk, 1978; Engel & Martuza, 1976). Facet theory provides a structure and boundaries for domains of testing conditions based on an analysis of the structure of subject matter content. Therefore, it is a method for developing a pool of items representing a domain of instruction. The benefits of facet design and similar procedures have been described by Engel and Martuza (1976) and are listed below:

1. Both item stem and foil can be systematically constructed.
2. Facet design theory is concerned with the structure of subject matter content and its definition. The method of defining mapping sentences clarifies the identification of foils for selected response times. As a consequence, incorrect responses have meaningful interpretations in a diagnostic sense.
3. The procedures provide a logical connection between content and the multiple-choice item.
4. Items produced may be logically compared with respect to content difficulty and appropriateness, thus making the construction of parallel test forms easier and less subject to capriciousness.

Facet theory is a relatively new field of content specification for CR testing. Not a great deal is known about its feasibility for various subject matters or the empirical characteristics of tests constructed using it. The procedures used by Engel and Martuza (1976) in one empirical study led to parallel test forms that functioned equivalently. Also, the results indicated that the method works equally well with both highly structured material like mathematics and more abstract material. It is interesting to note that the facet design can be used with a learning objective like the mapping sentence, thereby capitalizing on existing objectives.

Domain-Based Concept Testing

The work of Tiemann and Markle (1978) is an important addition to the growing technology of item writing at the higher cognitive levels. Tiemann and

Markle, whose work is described in Chapter 9, provide not just a testing technique but a complete system for defining concepts, teaching them, and coordinating teaching with testing. A *concept* is defined as a class of objects or things, and a student's understanding of a concept is tested by the use of examples or nonexamples of class members. A testing domain is defined by listing all the possible examples and nonexamples for a particular concept. Items can then be created by using one or more examples from the list. Tiemann and Markle (1978) have provided a wealth of examples of concept analysis in typical academic areas. It remains for subject matter experts in skill and job-related training areas to complete similar concept analyses of typical work-related concepts. It is clear that an ounce of concept analysis can be worth hundreds of pounds of effort in writing individual test items. One complete concept analysis can generate literally hundreds of excellent concept testing items based on a systematic sample of examples and nonexamples.

Typologies of Higher Level Thinking

Chapters 10 and 11 provide a unique source of information on practical ways to write items for higher level thinking. Based on cognitive typologies similar to the one conceived by Bloom, Engelhart, Furst, Hill, and Krathwohl (1956), Miller *et al.* (1978) and Wulfeck *et al.* (1979) have developed techniques that can be a valuable addition to the tools available to the item writer. Each method provides categories for various types of higher level thinking. In studies by Williams (1977) and the authors of the IQI, the typologies were found to work effectively with inexperienced test-item writers in classifying objectives. There is a need to continue to extend the use of these typologies and the IQI system into a variety of subject matters at various educational levels.

Summary

In critically summarizing most of the major technologies of item writing, such as those discussed in Chapters 6–11 of the present book, the evaluation by Berk (1979, p. 4) is challenging. Berk argued that the rigor and precision of item-writing methods were inversely related to their practicability. The most rigorous domain specifications, such as computerized item forms, are, in Berk's view, not generally practical for all teachers or evaluators in all subject matters. In contrast, methods that rely on typologies, task–content matrices, facet design theory, and methods that allow choice of wordings by the individual item writer may have broad application but do not exactly specify all the items in a domain. Several factors may improve the practicality of rigorous item-writing methods, such as increased knowledge of the methods by educators and the proliferation of inexpensive but powerful computers into schools and training centers. As the authors have said elsewhere (Roid & Haladyna, 1980), one compromise in test development that is currently feasible is to create some items by rigorous domain specifications and others by more subjective methods. If subtests are scored separately, the domain-based observed scores can be strictly interpreted as unbiased estimates of true domain scores.

Durnin and Scandura (1973) have been critical of the method of item forms from a unique perspective.[2] They contend that the development of item forms does not ensure that the rules used by students to solve mathematical problems, for example, will be assessed. Item forms can be developed from the observable properties of sample items, rather than from an analysis of how students learn rules to solve the problems assessed by items. For example, students may use either the rules of borrowing or the rules of equal addition to solve subtraction problems involving columns of numbers. Durnin and Scandura claim that their algorithmic technique assesses rule learning and provides a more complete mapping of the content domain. Their study (Durnin & Scandura, 1973) was based on a rather small and restricted sample of students in the content area of subtraction, and, therefore, more research and development is needed to evaluate the potential of this promising technique.

Other typical criticisms of the technology of item writing can be reduced to two concerns: (*a*) practicability and (*b*) restrictions of applicability. For example, linguistic and sentence-based methods have been occasionally maligned because they require sophisticated knowledge of the structure of language and because of fears that they can produce trivial items. For the student of linguistics, who has a trained team of item writers select important sentences or sets of them, these criticisms are overcome. However, the number of skilled linguists working in test development may currently be limited.

It has always been difficult to write objective test items that challenge the higher level thinking of students. The elegant techniques of Tiemann and Markle (1978), and the typologies of Williams (1977) and of the IQI (Wulfeck *et al.*, 1979) provide conceptual tools for generating items at the higher levels. A challenge for future work would be to apply the same rigor and elaboration found in the concept analysis method (Tiemann & Markle, 1978) to rules, procedures, and principles. Considerable subject matter expertise and inventiveness will be required to develop domains in these areas of complex learning.

STEP 4: ITEM REVIEW

Like any piece of writing, an item must be reviewed for the presence of ambiguities, miskeyings, or other flaws. Two major approaches to item review are logical item analysis and empirical review.

---

[2]The work of Durnin and Scandura requires familiarity with structural learning theory (Scandura, 1973), and it only recently came to the attention of the authors of the present book. Given more time to study the implications of the method, the present book would certainly have devoted more space, perhaps a separate chapter, to the algorithmic method. The reader is encouraged to explore the method in more detail in Durnin and Scandura (1973) and Scandura (1973).

Logical Review

The logical review of CR test items establishes the content representativeness of items. If a complete domain specification is present, the congruence between items and the learning objectives of the program is solved. However, if domain specifications remain somewhat subjective, it will be necessary to have subject matter experts rate the congruence of items with objectives. A statistical method introduced in Chapter 12 provides an index of item–objective congruence. Other sources of logical review may be the initial needs assessment, job analysis, or task specifications. This information may help subject matter experts or a third-party evaluator in assessing the adequacy of observations, checklists and rating systems.

Empirical Review

The simple, yet powerful, technique of empirical item analysis proposed in Chapter 13 involves the concept of instructional sensitivity. Instructional sensitivity is a characteristic of CR test items that reflects the change from pretest to posttest that is a result of highly effective instruction. Students perform poorly prior to instruction, but they perform well after instruction. Clearly, good quality items should follow a similar pattern if they are free from measurement error. This is *not* to say that items are selected on the basis of their instructional sensitivity. Screening out the top few items in terms of an instructional sensitivity index would distort the shape of the domain. Rather, instructional sensitivity is used as a means of item review. A low index indicating that the pretest and posttest item difficulties were very similar is only a sign that something is wrong. There may be a problem in either the instruction or the test item, and the two are sometimes inseparably intertwined. Only good "detective work" can unravel some of the puzzles that occur. Common sense and the collection of further data is frequently needed in order to decide whether an item is defective or instruction is lacking. The inventive work of Sato (1980) on item analysis is a promising new direction for exploration.

The role of field testing of items cannot be overemphasized. The tryout of items on real students or trainees is essential to establish strengths and weaknesses. Many ambiguities or miskeyings cannot be observed by inspection alone, but become obvious only after a field test. Field testing does not have to be an expensive process, because any student data, however limited, is better than no student data at all.

STEP 5: TEST DEVELOPMENT

A key concept in this book is that high quality CR tests are obtained when items are randomly sampled from the domain (or from strata within the domain) of all possible test items. If computerized domain specifications are used, this can be an easy process of computer selection. If domain specification is subjective, one should still assemble a complete item pool and then draw items randomly from that pool. Many CR tests are composed of stratified random samples of items collected from several domains or learning objectives.

The Future of Item-Writing Technologies

The most serious challenge in the future of the emerging technology of item writing is in domain specification. Hambleton (1978, p. 40) for example, has mentioned the importance of domain specification as the crucial next step in the development of CR tests in the assessment of basic skills. Domain specifications will not be a panacea, just as learning objectives have not solved all problems in the area of instructional systems design. However, particularly in the knowledge domains, a great deal of emphasis in the past has been on theories of test scores rather than theories of test domains. What is needed is an integrative theory that encompasses the definition and articulation of instructional intent, instructional methods, and testing. Domain specifications, in the spirit of Tiemann and Markle's (1978) approach, provide the basis for such a total integration.

Shoemaker (1975, pp. 144–145) suggests several anticipated developments in the implementation of item domains in achievement testing. First, Shoemaker projects an increase in the number of commercial firms developing item domains. Large collections of items developed for instructional programs and textbooks have been used for some time. However, domains are different from collections. Domain-based tests allow the precise interpretation of "the proportion of tasks mastered" in a domain. Second, therefore, it seems likely that informed users will demand item domains as part of published instructional packages and tests. Access to the item domain as part of a package would allow teachers to assemble any number of precisely parallel tests. The availability of an inexpensive microcomputer with disc storage may make item domains more accessible.

Shoemaker (1975) also predicted a third development—standardized item domains. As an extension of goal banks and objectives exchanges, the availability of standard item domains for typical content areas (e.g., first-grade reading) would have several advantages. Many instructional packages, texts, or methods associated with a content area could be referenced to a standard item domain. Thus, the effects of teaching a standard content area could be assessed. Since item domains are typically quite large, the problem of "teaching to the test" would not be a factor in such assessments.

Finally, Shoemaker (1975) predicted that the implementation of item domains would lead to more constructive evaluation of instructional programs. Item domains provide a better definition of what is to be taught in an instructional program than a typical list of objectives. Hence, evaluation of instructional intent, the match between teaching and testing, and the effectiveness of a program should proceed with more clarity than is the case when the goals of a program are ambiguous.

COMPUTERIZATION OF ITEM WRITING

The future holds exciting developments in the area of further computerization of item writing and test assembly. The computerized production of training manuals, such as described by Braby, Parrish, Guitard, and Aagard (1978), is an example of a high degree of technical advancement in computer-aided testing. Perhaps such automation will be limited to certain subject matter areas, but clearly it will relieve authors and test-item writers of the tedious burden of writing individual items. The potential contribution of microcomputers is great and they represent an entirely new field for exploring applications of item writing.

Another challenging area for the new technology is in the production of foils for multiple-choice versions of test questions including computer aids for their production. Multiple-choice test questions have demonstrated their wide applicability even to the higher level knowledge domains. Multiple-choice items provide precision in measurement and efficiency in scoring. However, as any experienced item writer knows, the production of good quality, functional wrong answers is one of the most challenging areas of test-item development. Research such as that conducted by Roid and Haladyna (1978) and Roid, Haladyna, Shaughnessy, and Finn (1979) has demonstrated the powerful effect that the choice of foils has on the characteristics of items. Choice of foils dramatically affects the difficulty of the items and, therefore, it can have dramatic effects on the distribution of test scores obtained by a group of students. Perhaps facet theory (Engel & Martuza, 1976) or techniques of computerized keyword identification (Finn, 1978) can provide suggestions to an item writer for the choice of foil wording.

THE MEASUREMENT OF SKILLS

To some extent, a technology of test-item writing has not yet made significant inroads into the evaluation of skills. There are three basic approaches to the assessment of skills: rating scales, observations, and checklists. Rating scales are used when some evaluation by a human observer is necessary to assess variable qualities of a performance or a product. Direct observation is used when only the presence or absence of a behavior or product must be noted. Checklists are useful when a set or sequence of behaviors is being examined in an ongoing performance or in a product. A few item forms have been developed for skills.

For example, Hively (1974) defines an item form for the assessment of target shooting. However, skill assessment and applied performance testing is an area in need of further research and development. Technological gains have been primarily in the development of sophisticated hardware, such as flight simulators and computer-assisted testing systems.

In summary, much greater variety of methods and tools are available to the item writer of today than were available to the item writer of even a decade ago. In times of rapid technological advancement, particularly in relation to computer development and miniaturization of electronic circuitry, predictions for the next decade could only be speculative. Clearly, progress will be made only if individual item writers take it upon themselves to experiment with new methods of item writing. Familiarization with the literature and new developments in this area are encouraged. A rich source of development in any field is frequently a technique or concept developed in a totally unrelated field. For this reason, developments in fields such as linguistics, computer technology, and engineering may be the source of future innovations. In any case, a technology of item writing is clearly emerging, and it promises to provide assistance to the item writer in developing better CR tests for use in instruction and research on teaching and learning.

References

Baker, E. L., Linn, R. L., & Quellmalz, E. S. *Knowledge synthesis: Criterion-referenced measurement*. Los Angeles, California: Center for the Study of Evaluation, University of California, 1980.

Berk, R. A. The application of structural facet theory to achievement test construction. *Educational Research Quarterly,* 1978, *3*(3), 62–72.

Berk, R. A. *A critical review of content domain specification/item generation strategies for criterion-referenced tests*. Paper presented at the annual meeting of the American Educational Research Association, San Francisco, April 1979.

Berk, R. A. (Ed.) *Criterion-referenced measurement*. Baltimore: Johns Hopkins University Press, 1980.

Bloom, B. S., Engelhart, M. D., Furst, E. J., Hill, W. H., & Krathwohl, D. R. *Taxonomy of educational objectives*. New York: Longmans, Green, 1956.

Bormuth, J. R. *On the theory of achievement test items*. Chicago, Illinois: Univ. of Chicago Press, 1970.

Braby, R., Parrish, W. F., Guitard, C. R., & Aagard, J. A. *Computer-aided authoring of programmed instruction for teaching symbol recognition* (TAEG Report No. 58). Orlando, Florida: Training Analysis and Evaluation Group, 1978.

Cronbach, L. J., Gleser, G. C., Nanda, H., & Rajaratnam, N. *The dependability of behavioral measurements*. New York: Wiley, 1972.

Durnin, J. & Scandura, J. M. An algorithmic approach to assessing behavior potential: Comparison with item forms and hierarchical technologies. *Journal of Educational Psychology,* 1973, *65,* 262–272.

Engel, J. D., & Martuza, V. R. *A systematic approach to the construction of domain-referenced multiple-choice test items*. Paper presented at the meeting of the American Psychological Association, Washington, D.C., September 1976.

Finn, P. J. A question writing algorithm. *Journal of Reading Behavior*, 1975, *4*, 341–367.

Finn, P. J. *Generating domain-referenced, multiple-choice test items from prose passages*. Paper presented at the meeting of the American Educational Research Association, Toronto, March 1978.

Foa, U. G. Three kinds of behavioral changes. *Psychological Bulletin*, 1968, *70*, 460–473.

Hambleton, R. K. *Validity of criterion-referenced test score interpretations and standard setting methods*. Paper presented at the First Annual Johns Hopkins University National Symposium on Educational Research, Washington, D.C., October 1978.

Hively, W. Introduction to domain-referenced testing. *Educational Technology*, 1974, *14*, 5–10.

Johnson, K. J. Pitt's computer-generated chemistry exam. *Proceedings of the Conference on Computers in Undergraduate Curricula*, 1973, 199–204.

Miller, H. G., Williams, R. G., & Haladyna, T. M. *Beyond facts: Objective ways to measure thinking*. Englewood Cliffs, New Jersey: Educational Technology, 1978.

Millman, J. Computer-based item generation. In R. A. Berk (Ed.), *Criterion-referenced measurement*. Baltimore: Johns Hopkins University Press, 1980.

Millman, J., & Outlaw, W. S. Testing by computer. *Association for Educational Data Systems (AEDS) Journal*, 1978, *11*, 57–72.

Roid, G. H., & Finn, P. J. *Algorithms for developing test questions from sentences in instructional materials* (NPRDC Tech. Rep. 78-23). San Diego: Navy Personnel Research and Development Center, 1978.

Roid, G. H., & Haladyna, T. The emergence of a technology of test-item writing. *Review of Educational Research*, 1980, *50*, 293–314.

Roid, G., Haladyna, T., Shaughnessy, J., & Finn, P. J. *Item writing for domain-referenced tests of prose learning*. Paper presented at the annual meeting of the American Educational Research Association, San Francisco, 1979.

Sato, T. *The S-P chart and the caution index*. Tokyo, Japan: Computer & Communications Systems Research Laboratories, Nippon Electric Company, 1980.

Scandura, J. M. *Structural learning: I. Theory and research*. New York: Gordon & Breach, 1973.

Shoemaker, D. M. Toward a framework for achievement testing. *Review of Educational Research*, 1975, *45*, 127–148.

Tiemann, P. W., & Markle, S. M. *Domain-referenced testing in conceptual learning*. Paper presented at the meeting of the American Educational Research Association, Toronto, March 1978.

Williams, R. G. A behavioral typology of educational objectives for the cognitive domain. *Educational Technology*, 1977, *17*(6), 39–46.

Wulfeck, II, W. H., Ellis, J. A., Richards, R. E., Wood, N. D., & Merrill, M. D. *The instructional quality inventory: 1. Introduction and overview* (NPRDC Special Report 79-3). Paper presented at the annual meeting of the American Educational Research Association, San Francisco, 1979.

Author Index

Numbers in italics refer to the pages on which the complete references are listed.

A

Aagard, J.A., 121, *125*, 232, 237, *238*
Algina, J., 7, *11*, 28, 29, *36*, 205, *214*
Anastasio, E.J., 121, *125*
Anderson, L.W., 163, *185*
Anderson, R.C., 6, *10*, 91, 92, 93, 97, 101, 111, 112, *113*, 146, 155, 157, 158, *158*, 197, *198*
Andre, T., 145, 154, 158, *159*
Atlas, M., 61, 64, *64*
Ausubel, D., 15, *35*

B

Baker, E.L., 7, *10*, 28, 31, *35*, 133, *143*, 193, *199*, 230, *238*
Baker, F.B., 216, *224*
Baker, M.S., 197, *199*
Bandura, A., 15, *35*,
Bashaw, W.L., 220, *224*
Berk, R.A., 7, *10*, 28, *35*, 132, 133, 136, 137, 143, *144*, 219, *224*, 230, 232, 233, *238*
Berliner, D., 17, 18, *38*
Bernknopf, S., 220, *224*

C

Block, J.H., 4, *10*, 13, 20, *35*
Blood, M.R., 71, *87*
Bloom, B.S., 13, 15, 18, 20, *35*, 42, *47*, 116, *125*, 162, *185*, 194, *199*, 233, *238*
Bormuth, J.R., 4, 6, 7, 9, 11, 31, *36*, 60, *64*, 91, 92, 93, 94, 98, 108, 109, 113, *113*, *114*, 231, *238*
Boutwell, R.C., 197, *199*, 211, *214*
Brady, R., 121, *125*, 232, 237, *238*
Branson, R.K., 23, 25, *36*
Brennan, R.L., 219, *224*
Burton, N.W., 18, 19, *36*, 195, *199*

Caro, P.W., Jr., 78, *87*
Carr, J., 94, 108, *114*,
Carroll, J.B., 95, 97, 102, 107, *114*, 145, *159*
Carver, R.P., 220, *225*
Cocks, P., 60, *64*, 109, *114*
Coffman, W.E., 49, 64, *64*
Cohen, P.A., 4, *11*, 13, 25, *37*
Conoley, J.C., 49, *64*, 110, 112, 113, *114*, 205, *213*

241

Subject Index

A

Amplified objective, 133
Anaphora, 108–109
Application, 110–112

B

Bayesian indexes, 219
Behavioral objectives, *see* Instructional objectives

C

Checklists, 9
Cloze difficulty, 95, 96
Cognitive taxonomy, 42, 162, 194, 198
Cognitive theories, 14–15
Competency-based education, 15, 17–19, 140
Computer-assisted instruction, 7, 120
Computer-based item generation, 120–121, 131, 205, 235–236, 237
Concepts, 7, 10, 97, 111, 123, 210–211, 232–233
    attributes, 148–150
        critical, 148–152

irrelevant, 150
variable, 149–150
close-in nonexample, 151, 211
definition of, 147–148
discrimination, 151, 152
generalization, 150–151, 152
identities, 147–148
Constructed-response items, 45, 47, 49, 58–63, 179
completion, 59, 59–60, 86, 137
extended-answer essay, 59, 60–61, 86
short-answer essay, 59, 62–63, 86
Construct validity, 7–8, 127
Content validity, 46, 47, 204
Criterion level, 27
Criterion-referenced testing, 4, 7, 8, 10, 14, 15, 19, 26, 26–33, 35, 96, 127, 152, 158, 187, 196, 197, 205, 215, 229, 230–236

D

Domains, 115–117, 125, 135, 152, 157, 188–189, 206–207, 234, 236
Domain specification, 30–31, 35, 188, 205, 208, 230–231, 236